TRAVELER

COASTAL ALASKA
PORTS OF CALL & BEYOND

## NATIONAL GEOGRAPHIC
# TRAVELER

# COASTAL ALASKA
## PORTS OF CALL & BEYOND

by Bob Devine
photography by Michael Melford

National Geographic
Washington, D.C.

# CONTENTS

▪ Pages 2–3: Orcas breach in Frederick Sound, a common sight in the waters of coastal Alaska.
▪ Left: Totem pole, Totem Bight State Historical Park, Ketchikan

# TRAVELING WITH EYES OPEN

Alert travelers go with a purpose and leave with a benefit. If you travel responsibly, you can help support wildlife conservation, historic preservation, and cultural enrichment in the places you visit. You can enrich your own travel experience as well.

To be a geo-savvy traveler:

- Recognize that your presence has an impact on the places you visit.

- Spend your time and money in ways that sustain local character. (Besides, it's more interesting that way.)

- Value the destination's natural and cultural heritage.

- Respect the local customs and traditions.

- Express appreciation to local people about things you find interesting and unique to the place: its nature and scenery, music and food, historic villages and buildings.

- Vote with your wallet: Support the people who support the place, patronizing businesses that make an effort to celebrate and protect what's special there. Seek out local shops, restaurants, and inns. Use tour operators who love their home—who love taking care of it and sharing its beauty. Avoid businesses that detract from the character of the place.

- Enrich yourself, taking home memories and stories to tell, knowing that you have contributed to the preservation and enhancement of the destination.

That is the type of travel now called geotourism, defined as "tourism that sustains or enhances the geographical character of a place—its environment, culture, aesthetics, heritage, and the well-being of its residents." To learn more, visit *www.nationalgeographic.com/maps/article/geotourism-principles.*

# COASTAL ALASKA
## PORTS OF CALL & BEYOND

## ABOUT THE AUTHORS & THE PHOTOGRAPHER

**Bob Devine** writes about the environment, natural history, and outdoor travel from his home in Oregon. National Geographic has published several of his works, including *Alien Invasion: America's Battle With Non-Native Animals and Plants* and *National Geographic Traveler Alaska*, plus, most recently, *Alaska: A Visual Tour of America's Great Land.* He first traveled to Alaska on assignment in 1987 and has since returned as often as possible.

**Michael Melford** is a renowned photographer whose assignments include both travel and editorial photography. His award-winning work has appeared in many major U.S. publications, including *National Geographic Traveler, Travel + Leisure, Life, Fortune,* and *Newsweek.* He is a contributing photographer to *National Geographic Traveler* and his work often appears in *National Geographic* magazine. His other books include *Hidden Alaska: Bristol Bay and Beyond* and *Guide to the National Parks: Alaska,* both published by National Geographic. He lives with his family in Mystic, Connecticut.

**Christopher P. Baker**—the Lowell Thomas Award 2008 "Travel Journalist of the Year"—wrote the updates and sidebars for this edition. He is the author of the *National Geographic Traveler* guidebooks to Cuba, Panama, and Dominican Republic, plus Colombia and Costa Rica, both of which he also photographed. He has also been the update editor for Alaska, and six other guidebooks in the *National Geographic Traveler* series, as well as having written and photographed more than 20 other guidebooks to destinations worldwide. He has written widely about cruising coastal Alaska for newspapers and magazines.

# CHARTING YOUR TRIP

Alaska seems to have been created for cruising. Its 6,600 miles (10,622 km) of saltwater coastline offer those on deck an endless array of natural beauty, especially along the southerly shorelines that cruise ships frequent. Cruising is also the only practical way to reach many beauty spots in this huge state, whether they be on islands or in remote mainland places, unreachable by road.

### Where to Visit

Ninety-nine percent of Alaskan cruising takes place in the state's southern waters, along the arc of the Gulf of Alaska's shoreline. That swath can be divided into three regions. The first and most popular for cruising is southeast Alaska, aka the panhandle, home of the fabled Inside Passage. This encompasses the islands and mainland coast from Ketchikan in the south up to Skagway in the north, plus the journey from Vancouver, British Columbia, or Seattle, the two main ports of embarkation. Seattle and Vancouver are wonderful destinations in their own right and well worth a visit before or after a cruise.

The second region is the south-central coast, northwest of the panhandle, at the top of the Gulf of Alaska arc. The south-central coast includes Prince William Sound, the Kenai Peninsula, and up Cook Inlet to Anchorage. This region serves as a gateway to the interior, notably for trips to Denali National Park. Most travelers to this region fly into Anchorage and take a train or bus to Seward or Whittier to begin their voyages.

The third and much less visited region for cruises includes the Alaska Peninsula and Aleutian Islands, sprawling to the southwest of south-central Alaska. This oceanic wilderness includes Kodiak Island, the tiny villages strung along the outer Alaska Peninsula, and the even wilder villages of the Aleutians, plus the island chain's one city, Unalaska. People sometimes fly into Anchorage and make their way to Homer, Seward, or Kodiak to begin these cruises. But aside from the regular state ferry runs, these explorations of the Alaska Peninsula and Aleutians don't follow well-worn patterns. Some itineraries, for example, include the Russian Far East.

### Online Visitor Information

There's a wealth of online visitor information on Alaska available at your fingertips:
General information: *travelalaska.com*, *alaska.org,* and *alaska.gov*
Alaska Public Lands Information Centers: *alaskacenters.gov*
Alaska State Parks: *dnr.alaska.gov/parks*
Bureau of Land Management, Alaska: *blm.gov/alaska*
National Park Service: *nps.gov/akso*
U.S. Fish & Wildlife Service, Alaska region: *fws.gov/alaska*
U.S. Forest Service (Chugach and Tongass NFs): *fs.usda.gov/chugach*

### Ports

Scattered along these southern coastlines are Alaska's port towns, but only Anchorage clearly qualifies as a true city. Juneau—the state capital, boasting a population of a little over 30,000—is a close contender. The rest are port communities of a few thousand people or, in the case of the Alaska Peninsula and Aleutian Islands, villages with only a few hundred residents. So while you can find urban amenities in Anchorage, Juneau, and to some degree in the larger towns, and enjoy plenty of small-town charm in many places, some of the off-the-beaten-track ports are emphatically utilitarian. Their appeal comes from their authenticity. But no matter where you are, even in downtown Anchorage, nature in the raw is never far away. You're always in close proximity to forests, mountains, wildlife, glaciers, and swift rivers. The major port towns of Anchorage, Seattle, and Vancouver are terrific destinations in their own right, and you may enjoy extra days exploring each as your time allows.

## Exploring Beyond a Port of Call

To fully appreciate Alaska, heed the call of the wild and venture out to explore some of that nearby nature in the raw. Large or small, all the cruise ships offer a tempting menu of excursions to watch

■ Brown bear cubs near Brooks River, Katmai National Park and Preserve

# Best Time to Visit

Cruise ships ply the waters of Alaska from mid-May to late September, the months when the weather and long daylight hours create the best conditions for cruising. The shoulder seasons—May and September—offer many advantages, starting with the counter-intuitive fact that May and to some degree September are usually less rainy than July and August. You also will get cheaper fares in these months, encounter fewer biting insects, and avoid the summer crowds that swamp some ports. Note that whatever their stated opening hours, most attractions and tourism-related businesses in Alaskan ports will be open when a ship comes in. Your cruise will no doubt offer many organized tours, but if you are going to set out on your own with a specific destination in mind, always check ahead online or by phone to be sure it is indeed open.

grizzly bears fishing for salmon, take a hike through the lush temperate rain forest, see tidewater glaciers shedding house-size slabs of ice into the ocean, or witness the eating habits of sea otters, as they float on their backs and use their bellies for tables. You can also choose among excursions to see totem poles, gold rush–era buildings, sled-dog kennels, and other cultural and historic sites.

If you prefer to make your own arrangements, you can fashion tailor-made excursions by contacting local visitor information offices and shopping online for reputable tour operators. See also the Need To Know sidebars in this book for details of how to navigate each port of call while ashore. Because Alaska is such a wild place, many visitors seek expert guidance; this has spawned a vast number of guiding businesses, so you'll have ample choices. Of course, you can always travel independently, perhaps by taking a taxi or renting a car. (Aside from the ferries, public transportation is limited in Alaska.) Taxis usually meet the ship at port, and your onboard crew or the local visitor center can be helpful to line up a rental car. But if your independent travel involves even brief excursions into the wilderness, exercise due caution; remember that this is Alaska and not a walk in the park.

## Choosing Your Itinerary

Once you've selected the region you want to visit, you'll have a choice of itineraries, unless your preference is the Alaska Peninsula and Aleutians, where options are limited. Your decision is a matter of taste: If gold rush history enthralls you, make sure your ship docks in Skagway. If glaciers get your pulse pounding, choose a ship that goes into Glacier Bay National Park. In addition, check to see how much time your ship spends at your destinations of choice. The same logic applies if you want plenty of time in ports for long excursions. For a voyage of discovery that takes time to explore the land up close in the company of expert naturalists, National Geographic Expeditions offers six- to 22-day adventure cruises on small ships (*nationalgeographic.com/expeditions*; see also Travelwise p. 165).

## Which Ship?

Often you'll find several ships that go to ports you want to visit. In that case, narrow your choices down using other factors, such as price and onboard amenities. It helps to divide the ships into three categories: large, medium, and small. Most large ships (roughly 800 to 2,500 passengers) provide many onboard activities, such as health spas, Vegas-style shows, pools, casinos, and those huge legendary buffets of finely prepared food. In addition to shipboard activities, most large ships offer a smorgasbord of shore excursions, from shopping and bus tours to kayaking and helicopter landings

■ Sea kayaking is a popular activity in Prince William Sound, where new vistas open around each bend.

on glaciers. But large cruise ships can't slip into narrow passages like a smaller vessel and typically only call on ports with docks that can accommodate ships nearly 1,000 feet long (305 m). Small cruise ships (10 to 100 passengers) provide fewer onboard activities and facilities. That said, many are luxurious and pamper their passengers with fine staterooms, gourmet meals, attentive staff, and typically a strong focus on natural history and cultural education. Passage on most small ships is expensive, but small ships get you closer to the land, figuratively and literally, yielding amazing wildlife- and glacier-viewing. Also, they often go to ports that are ignored or inaccessible to larger ships. Likewise, their shore excursions tend to include less-visited sites. Medium ships (roughly 100 to 800 passengers) possess some large-ship characteristics—a modicum of elaborate entertainment and a fair amount of onboard activities—but to a lesser degree than the behemoths. Medium-size vessels likewise exhibit some traits of small ships—slipping into places huge ships can't go, visiting more off-the-beaten-path ports—but to a lesser degree than the little guys. ■

## Go Local on Alaska's Ferries

The local ferries, run by the Alaska Marine Highway System, give travelers an utterly different experience of Alaska's coastlines. This is how the locals travel. You'll see high school sports teams heading to away games, families going shopping in town, salespeople heading for their next stop, and all sorts of folks going about their daily life. Mainline ferries hold around 500 passengers, while ships that serve smaller communities carry 150 to 250. If you're traveling without a vehicle, you often can board a ferry without a reservation, get off at any port and stay as long as you like, and then board a later ferry; the flexibility is unparalleled. The ferries are less expensive than cruise ships, well run, and reliable. They have only basic amenities, including some simple cabins (reserve these well in advance), restaurants or snack bars, movies, and showers. On overnight trips, passengers without cabins sleep just about anywhere, from their seats to benches to freestanding tents pitched on the deck.

# HISTORY & CULTURE

Above: A young dancer in traditional dress
Opposite: The massive fissured flank of Exit Glacier dwarfs a group of passing hikers.

# ALASKA TODAY

**Alaska. Like Tombouctou, the very name evokes a legendary remoteness. To someone from Peoria or Atlanta or London, Alaska may seem more myth than reality: a wild and, vast place inhabited by grizzly bears, moose, musk-ox, and wolves.**

A dramatic landscape of raw-boned mountains, misty forests, windswept tundra, and glaciers that march into the sea; a realm of snow and ice and perpetual cold; a place peopled by Inuit (Eskimos) and pioneers living off the land—these things are part of Alaska, but the picture they paint is so incomplete that it does indeed teeter on the edge of myth. Alaska also has its lesser-known urbane side, with espresso stands, farms, art galleries, universities, deluxe lodges and spas, four-star restaurants, 80°F (27°C) summer days, and

■ The mural says "Alaska," but the dress of these youths in Juneau would look right at home anywhere in the United States.

even sand dunes. The reality is that Alaska is a fascinating blend of the wild and the civilized, of the traditional and the modern, and of many different landscapes and climates—though it does lean toward the wild.

The basic reason that Alaska has so much wilderness left is straightforward: It is tough country and very few people live there. Though Alaska is by far the largest state in the Union—more than twice the size of number two, Texas—its population barely exceeds 730,000; more people live in metropolitan Albuquerque, New Mexico. This results in a population density almost a thousand times sparser than, say, the state of New Jersey.

Alaska does feature one bona fide urban area: Anchorage. About 300,000 people live in a cityscape familiar to most Americans: It has skyscrapers, traffic jams, hip clubs, suburban sprawl, fine museums, and many of the other amenities and problems of a modern city. But even Anchorage is influenced

> **The basic reason that Alaska has so much wilderness left is straightforward: It is tough country and very few people live there.**

by the proximity of the wilderness. Moose and bears sometimes stroll through backyards. The glacier-streaked Chugach Mountains loom nearby, and from the middle of town residents can drive 20 minutes and be in unspoiled forests and rugged mountains.

**Living off the Land:** Living so close to the land results in many also living *off* the land. Whether an accountant in Fairbanks or a teacher in the state capital of Juneau, it seems that most Alaskans fish or hunt for food. When the salmon are running in summer and fall, outsiders come to Alaska to hook kings and reds and silvers, but the majority of anglers are residents of the state who are looking to pack their freezers with fillets. Likewise, it's common to hear someone in a fine restaurant in Anchorage talk about bagging a moose. A day earlier this person may have been dressed in camouflage, not a business suit, and instead of carving up a rack of lamb, she was carving up the moose she'd just shot.

For some Alaskans those salmon and moose are not just a supplement to food they buy. Thousands of residents in small towns and villages lead subsistence lifestyles, getting the bulk of their food from the land. They not only fish for those prized salmon but for grayling, tomcod, sheefish, eel, and a dozen other species, depending on the region. The list of animals they hunt is equally long, including the obvious, like moose, goose, bear, and caribou, and the surprising, such as porcupine and, for Inuit, beluga whale, seal, porcupine, and walrus. They also trap fox, beaver, marten, and other fur-bearing animals and gather berries, bird eggs, greens, and clams. What others do for sport, these folks do to live. Many of them wouldn't have it any other way, but many also have little choice, especially given the high cost of living in Alaska (which visitors, too, will certainly notice). Those costs are even higher in the remote villages, where food often costs twice as much as it does in the lower 48.

## The People's Land

Fortunately for those who use the land for subsistence, sport-hunting and fishing, and recreation, the vast majority of Alaska lies in public hands, enjoying at least some protection from development. Large chunks are overseen by the state and by native organizations, and more than half of the countryside falls under the steward-ship of the federal government. Unlike many of their counterparts in other states, most Alaska public lands allow subsistence uses and some sport-hunting and fish-ing. This is true even for Alaska's headliner lands, such as Denali National Park and Preserve (the phrase "and Preserve" is found at the end of the names of most of the national parks in the state). But subsistence uses and sport-hunting and fishing may be allowed in designated areas of both park and preserve land; only the wil-derness section—which includes the main tourism area—is usually off-limits. While traveling in the backcountry, you may encounter fishnets, traps, and other tools employed by subsistence users. For your own safety and out of respect for the live-lihoods of locals, it's important to leave these items undisturbed.

## Alaska Natives

Many subsistence hunters and gatherers are Alaska natives, indigenous inhabitants who constitute about 15 percent of the state's population. Contrary to stereotype, not all Alaska natives are Inuit—not even close—though Inuit are the single most populous native group. True, the term "Eskimo" is still widely used for the indige-nous people who live around the circumpo-lar coasts (and is not considered offensive), but most Inuit think of themselves as belonging to smaller cultural divisions.

The vast interior of Alaska and a few bits of the south-central coast are the realm of the Athabaskan, a people related to some of the First Nations of Canada and the lower 48. They generally prefer more specific names that describe the smaller groups to which they belong, such as the Dena'ina, Ahtna, and Tanana.

The Alaska Peninsula and the 1,100 miles (1,770 km) of islands in the Aleutian chain are the domain of the Unangan, often referred to as the Aleut. Closely related and often lumped together with the Unangan are the Alutiiq, who occupy the southeast portion of the Alaska Peninsula, the Kodiak Island Archipelago, and Prince William Sound. Finally, there are the Alaska natives of the southeast: the Tlingit, Haida, and less numerous Tsimshian and Eyak. They share many cultural traits—though not languages—with the Northwest Coast natives of British Columbia and Washington. So plentiful was the bounty of these teeming coastal forests and waters that the tribes enjoyed a life of food abundance. They became the world's most densely populated society of hunters and gatherers.

### Population of Alaska

Recent statistics reflect the fact that the population density of Alaska is slightly more than one person per square mile (2.6 sq km), but this doesn't fully convey how extremely nonurban and unsettled Alaska still is. The fact that it's about five times less densely populated than the second least densely popu-lated state, Wyoming, makes the point a bit more sharply. But to truly grasp the Great Land's lack of cities, consider that only about 33,000 people live in its state capital and second largest city, Juneau, and that only about 9,000 inhabit its fourth largest "city," Sitka.

Grand views of rugged mountain scenery around the port of Juneau open up at the top of the steep Mount Roberts Tramway.

Plenty of time for ritual, recreation, and craft resulted in a profusion of art, which became integrated into virtually all aspects of traditional life. "What must astonish most," wrote French explorer Etienne Marchand in 1791, "is to see painting everywhere, everywhere sculpture, among a nation of hunters."

Nonetheless, in a story line familiar to indigenous peoples around the world, the arrival of outsiders was hard on Alaska natives. Russians invaded the Unangan homeland in the mid-1700s. These acquisitive and well-armed fortune hunters killed most of the Unangan—either directly or via disease and starvation—and enslaved many of the survivors. Unangan numbers plunged from an estimated 20,000 to a tiny fraction of that, and to this day their population remains small. The Tlingit of Southeast Alaska, however, were never conquered; they waged guerrilla warfare against the Russians until the latter departed in 1867. The Russians, as well as American and British whalers in the mid-1800s, also introduced Alaska natives to alcohol, which has done profound harm to native society. Though they have had some success fighting alcoholism, it's still enough of a serious problem that many native communities prohibit the possession or sale of alcohol.

Despite these tribulations, many Alaska natives have improved their lot in recent times, largely thanks to a deal worked out in 1971 and codified by the passage in Congress of the Alaska Native Claims Settlement Act. This legislation secured extensive subsistence-use rights and formed 13 regional native corporations and dozens of village corporations that together own 44 million acres (17.8 million ha) of land. These corporations engage in fishing, logging, mining, oil production and exploration, health care, and tourism and bring in billions of dollars in revenue annually. As this suggests, although many Alaska natives still live close to the land, many now also work regular jobs, earn college degrees, own and manage businesses, and otherwise participate in modern society.

> "Other than holding government jobs, most Alaskans work in resource industries, notably oil, fishing, mining, and logging— and tourism, which also relies on Alaska's rich natural assets."

## European Influence

Despite the impact the Russians had on coastal Alaska, they never settled there in large numbers. However, they left behind a sizeable number of religious converts whose descendants still attend the state's many Russian Orthodox churches. In addition, there are the Russian Old Believers, who split from the Russian Orthodox church centuries ago and roamed the world for many years before a few thousand settled in isolated villages on the Kenai Peninsula and around Kodiak in the 1960s. Travelers may see Old Believers in stores or operating their fishing vessels, the women wearing ankle-length dresses and caps or scarves and the men sporting long beards.

In the years following the 1867 transfer of Alaska from Russia to the United States, almost all newcomers to Alaska were of western European ancestry, particularly German and Irish. Globalization does seem to be bringing some diversity to the state in recent years, even if the 2020 census still showed only small numbers of African, Latino, and Asian Americans in Alaska—roughly 4 percent in total.

## Making a Living

All that salmon and moose meat notwithstanding, most Alaskans still have to earn a paycheck. However, due to transportation costs and the state's remoteness, few large-scale manufacturers other than seafood processors locate in Alaska. The climate and topography also preclude other common industries, such as agriculture, which is very limited in the state. Other than holding government jobs, most Alaskans work in resource industries, notably oil, fishing, mining, and logging—and tourism, which also relies on Alaska's rich natural assets. In one way or another, nearly every Alaskan lives off the land.

Nowadays, oil production is perhaps Alaska's most famous business, and it puts a lot of money into state coffers. It employs thousands of Alaskans, and the oil support industries are some of the state's biggest companies. Oil pumped out of Prudhoe Bay also directly benefits every Alaskan. A 1976 constitutional amendment assures that a percentage of oil profits goes into the Permanent Fund Dividend, which pays an annual sum to every man, woman, and child living in Alaska. In 2020 each qualified resident received $992.

Commercial fishing is a huge industry in coastal Alaska (sportfishing also is a big business). The ports of Unalaska, Dillingham, Kodiak, Cordova, and other towns near rich fishing grounds are home to thousands of fishing vessels and many fish-processing plants. At least half of U.S. commercial fish production occurs here. Not surprisingly, the state has one of the world's best managed fisheries and has mounted a major campaign to promote wild salmon; farming salmon is illegal in Alaska.

Tourism, the state's third largest industry, is for the most part environmentally sustainable, despite the occasional overcrowding at popular parks , and on the islands of the Admiralty Archipelago—the "Inside Passage"—when the cruise ships arrive in droves every summer. But Alaska needs to take care to make sure tourism remains culturally and economically sustainable in the long run. Particularly in the major ports frequented by cruise ships, large national and international firms have been buying significant amounts of the tourist-oriented shops and galleries. Locals,

## Subsistence Living: Getting Your Moose

While you're sitting in a bar in Alaska, maybe slightly disoriented by the midnight sun outside, someone might sidle up and ask you how you're sleeping these nights. However, if you're still there in autumn, the question is much more likely to be, "Did you get your moose?" In a frontier state with a subsistence-living mind-set, it's not surprising that many residents —even coastal denizens—head into the wild, rifle in hand, during the fall moose hunt. After all, *Alces alces giga*—the Alaska-Yukon moose—is the largest of all the moose subspecies ("giga" is derived from the Greek word for giant). A white-tailed deer can weigh up to 130 pounds (60 kg), but a large bull moose can be ten times bigger, with record-setting moose crushing the scales at perhaps 1,800 pounds (815 kg). Each year some 7,000 Alaskan hunters head off to get their moose and stock their freezers with the resulting 400 to 700 pounds (180–315 kg) of meat. The size of an Alaska-Yukon moose has one big drawback, however: Hunters have to pack it out from wherever they shoot it. Hence an old saying: "Never kill a moose more than a mile from a vehicle."

and many travelers, worry that if these outsider-owned stores become too prevalent, the charm and authentic character of these towns will fade.

For now, that local charm and character still prevail. In most ports, passengers coming down the gangplank will find real Alaska soon enough—if not right on the docks, then a block or two beyond. Visitors can explore a wide range of locally owned establishments and an array of tour operators who sell their knowledge and love of the land; instead of stuffed grizzly bears made in China, they provide the opportunity to view actual grizzlies. In a matter of a few hours or even mere minutes, guides can whisk travelers away to island wildlife refuges teeming with seabirds and sea lions, storytelling sessions by Alaska natives, demonstrations by noted sled-dog racers, hikes through the rain forest, spirited presentations of traditional Russian dances, bush-plane flights over mountains and glaciers, whale-watching expeditions, and many other excursions that celebrate the very wild essence of Alaska. ∎

# LAND & LANDSCAPE

Wild, unforgiving, and spectacular, nature's attributes define Alaska. In this
frontier state—stretching from the Arctic Circle to the Gulf of Alaska and
from near Russia to the Coast Mountains of British Columbia—the climate,
the terrain, the ecosystems, and the wildlife make themselves felt at every
turn, even along the coastal margins. They've become the stuff of legends,
humbling even the most cynical of visitors.

## History of the Land

Just as Alaska is a young and dynamic state in terms of its human development, so is it
a young and dynamic land in terms of its geology. Floating on the semisolid mantle of
the Earth, the Pacific plate is drifting northeast into the North American plate. Being
generally denser, the Pacific plate is subducting, or sliding under,
the North American plate. The entire western coastal littoral of
Alaska, including the Aleutian island chain, follow the arc of this
boundary, and Alaska's massive mountains are the result of this
titanic tectonic meeting. Mount Denali, the continent's highest
peak at 20,310 feet (6,190 m), grows yet higher.

This grinding and slow-motion collision of plates also produces
earthquakes and volcanic activity. More
than 50 active volcanoes simmer in the
Aleutian Islands and the Alaska Peninsula, and evidence of past eruptions is
abundant. The cataclysmic explosion
that disintegrated the top of Aniakchak
Mountain some 3,500 years ago, for
example, is apparent in the 6-mile-wide
(9.7 km), 2,000-foot-deep (610 m) cal-
dera that remains. But major eruptions
are not confined to the distant past. In
1912—just minutes ago in geological
terms—Novarupta Volcano blew with
a force that could be heard 1,000 miles
(1,600 km) away. Its eruption cycle lasted for 60 hours, during
which more rock and ash were blasted into the atmosphere than
in any other volcanic event in human history, with the exception of
the 1500 B.C. eruption of Thira in Greece, and that of Tambora, in
Indonesia, in 1815.

An even more recent event left a major impact on modern
Alaska. At 5:36 p.m. on March 27, 1964, a fault line at the bot-
tom of Prince William Sound spasmed and rocked south-central
Alaska for three to five minutes with a magnitude 9.2 earth-
quake—80 times more powerful than the infamous 1906 San
Francisco quake. Terra firma suddenly wasn't firm. An island in

> **More than 50 active volcanoes simmer in the Aleutian Islands and throughout the Alaska Peninsula, and evidence of past eruptions is abundant.**

the sound rose 33 feet (10 m), and streets tilted up like drawbridges. Some coastal flatlands dropped six feet (1.8 m), allowing seawater to flow across them, eventually killing the trees. In downtown Anchorage, the north side of Fourth Street, one of the city's main drags, collapsed, and restaurants and stores dropped out of sight.

Then came the worst part: Tsunamis spawned by the quake swept ashore. A huge wave, some 70 feet (21 m) high, erased the native village of Chenega. In Seward, where the quake ignited fires in dockside fuel tanks, a tsunami pushed that burning fuel eight blocks inland, causing a flood and a fire at the same time. In Valdez, where much of the waterfront slid into the bay and the rest got pounded by a tsunami, the townspeople subsequently abandoned the site and rebuilt in a safer spot 4 miles (6.4 km) away.

Glaciers are another geologic force in Alaska, gouging out fjords and mountain

■ **A cruise ship along the Inside Passage in Glacier Bay National Park and Preserve**

valleys and releasing meltwater to form rivers and creeks. Unlike in the lower 48, where glaciers are an exotic sight in a few high mountains, Alaska's rivers of ice crop up all around, from high elevations to sea level, forming one of the major tourist draws to coastal Alaska. Though the effects of climate change are shrinking many Alaskan glaciers, they still number in the tens of thousands (some are larger than Rhode Island).

Surprisingly, much of Alaska remained free of ice throughout the ice ages, but the worldwide conversion of water into ice lowered sea level a few hundred feet. Several times between 10,000 and 40,000 years ago, the shallow ocean floor of the Bering Sea was exposed for extended periods, creating a broad land bridge linking North America to Asia. The first inhabitants of North America walked across this land bridge from Siberia into what is now the Alaskan mainland.

## Alaska's Extensive Coastline

**Alaska possesses by far the longest coastline of any state in the United States. Measured without following the meandering contours of the shore into every bay and sound, Florida, the state with the second longest coastline, boasts about 1,350 miles (2,170 km) of saltwater shoreline. Measured in the same way, Alaska accounts for about 6,640 miles (10,685 km) of beautiful coastal land-scapes. That's just over half of the total coastal mileage for the entire U.S. Little wonder then that Alaska has proven to be such a paradise for visitors in the age of the cruise ship.**

### Climate

Yes, it gets cold in Alaska. Very cold. Winter temperatures in the interior often sink to about 20°F below zero (-29°C) and occasionally much lower. On the other hand, visitors who make an excursion to Denali National Park and Preserve in the summer may enjoy day-time highs of 65°F (18°C) or 70°F (21°C).

In coastal southeast and south-central Alaska, where most cruise ships and ferries operate, comparatively mild temperatures are typical year-round, and especially during the May through September cruising season. Highs run about 55°F to 65°F (13°C to 18°C), although on rare occasions the temperature can reach 90°F (32°C), which accounts for published advice for summer visitors to these regions to pack shorts and T-shirts as well as jeans and a windbreaker for when the weather gets a bit brisk.

Not that you shouldn't bring the above items—at times shorts and a T-shirt will indeed suffice—but you should also be sure to bring rain gear, warm layers, and a winter jacket even in July or August. Alaska's southern coasts are wet and frequently covered in leaden skies. Even during the summer, chilly winds and drenching downpours can strike. Southeast Alaska receives up to 200 inches (510 cm) of rainfall annually, with summer months in some years receiving as much as in winter, and when your ship is motoring alongside a tidewater glacier and you're being buffeted by the frigid wind coming off that blue ice, you'll want that heavy jacket. Bring it along to Denali, too, because weather surprises lurk throughout Alaska.

When the sun is out, you'll get a good, long look at it; this is the land of the midnight sun, after all. In cruising territory it won't be visible 24 hours a day, as it is north of the Arctic Circle, but even in southeast and south-central Alaska, the midsummer sun will hang around in the sky for 17 or 18 hours daily.

## Landscapes

More than 2,000 miles (3,200 km) separate Attu, at the western end of the Aleutians, from the Arctic National Wildlife Refuge, in the northeastern corner of the state. It's about the same distance from Ketchikan, in the southeast, to Barrow, in the northwest. As you'd expect in a land so vast, Alaska has many distinct habitats, from sand dunes to ice fields. However, the state can be broadly divided into three vegetation zones: rain forest, boreal forest, and tundra.

The coast and coastal mountains of south-central Alaska, and the more than 1,000 islands that compose the 400-mile-long (645 km) Alexander Archipelago of southeast Alaska, are smothered in tens of millions of acres of temperate rain forest, a forest type much less common globally than tropical rain forest. Sitka spruce and hemlock dominate, complemented by some cedars and pines. The southeast forests boast a multitude of massive trees rivaling the 200- to 250-foot (60–75 m) behemoths in the temperate rain forests of British Columbia, Washington, and Oregon. The sodden understory is lush with salmonberry, devil's club, blueberry, columbine, skunk cabbage, ferns, fireweed, huckleberry, and many other plant species that thrive on dampness.

A river laces its way through a valley in Katmai National Park and Preserve.

Boreal forest covers most of Alaska's interior. Visitors to Denali National Park and other inland sites will pass through expanses of birch, aspen, tamarack, willow, and, especially, black spruce. Toward the south these forests grow thick and harbor 80- to 100-foot (25–30 m) trees, but the trees become sparser and smaller as you head north. Eventually the boreal forest turns into a vast bog punctuated by a smattering of stunted, spindly black spruce, as if a Christmas-tree farm had been sprayed with herbicide.

Tundra is the land above the tree line, where the intense cold, short growing season, thin soil, and scouring winds make life impossible for trees. "Above" can mean two things in Alaska: higher elevation or higher latitude. In southern Alaska, tree line occurs at 2,000 to 3,000 feet (610–914 m) and tundra takes over above that elevation. Near the Arctic Ocean, tree line starts at sea level and tundra is all you see at any elevation. Depending on the habitat, tundra may consist mostly of knee-high grasses and sedges, or it may be a riot of blooming lupine, arctic bell heather, mountain saxifrage, wild geranium, tundra rose, and the bright sky blue of the forget-me-not, the Alaska state flower.

Almost anywhere in Alaska, whether rain forest, boreal forest, or tundra, mountains are part of the picture. Even many of the islands in the southeast and in the Aleutians sport jagged peaks—natural enough given that most of those islands are the tops of huge mountains whose bottoms are submerged. The king of Alaska's peaks, and the tallest in North America, is 20,310-foot (6,190 m) Mount Denali, which crowns the Alaska Range and anchors Denali National Park. However, the most impressive peaks are the craggy Wrangell and St. Elias Mountains, neighbors in southern Alaska. In this fastness of lofty summits and mammoth glaciers lie 10 of the 15 highest mountains on the continent. Steepled with snow-capped spires, these glacier-carved peaks form a spectacular backdrop to the impressive majesty of Glacier Bay. The nation's northern-most mountain chain, the Brooks Range forms a great wall 600 miles (965 km) long, stretching across the state from the Canadian border in the east to the Chukchi Sea in the west. Lying just north of the Arctic Circle, the Brooks Range marks the Arctic Divide, sending rivers off its southern slopes to the Bering Sea and off its northern slopes to the Arctic Ocean.

## How Mount Denali Got Its Name

The 20,310-foot (6,190 m) peak we now know as Denali has had many names through the centuries. The Ahtna called it "Dghelaay Ce'e" and the Middle Tanana dubbed it "Diineezi." The Russians labeled it "Bolshaya Gora," but they bore little influence in that part of Alaska, and the name gained no traction. In 1889 a prospector named Frank Densmore named it "Densmore's Mountain," but apparently only Frank was fond of that name, and it soon faded. The peak got the official name of Mount McKinley (in honor of President William McKinley) a few years later—except in Alaska. For years many Alaskans pushed the state and federal governments to call it "Mount Denali," "Denali" being the Koyukon Athabaskan word for "the great one" or "the high one." Finally, in 1980, the Feds agreed to name the national park Denali, but wouldn't change the mountain's name. However, the state did switch the peak's name to Denali on its maps and official records. Turns out the state was prescient: In 2015, President Obama announced that the federal government would officially rename the mountain Denali.

### Wildlife

Any discussion of Alaska's wildlife must begin with bears. Some visitors hardly go outdoors due to a fear of bear attacks, while other people blithely romp through the woods without giving bears a second thought. Both extremes are irrational and underscore the importance of getting accurate information about bears in Alaska. The details of dealing with bears can be learned at public lands throughout the state. (For online information visit the Alaska Public Lands Information Centers' "Bear Safety" web page: *alaskacenters.gov/trip-planning/stewardship/safety/bear-safety*)

Polar bears are a different proposition, but these cream-furred giants are restricted to the coastal zones above the Arctic Circle. They are the world's largest bear species; hunters shot a male polar bear in Alaska that stood 12 feet tall (3.7 m) and weighed about 2,200 pounds (1,000 kg). They are Alaska's only bear species that will routinely hunt humans if they spot or smell us. Alaskans who live in the remote places that polar bears inhabit have always been wary of them, but at least polar bears evolved to spend most of their lives out on the sea ice. However, as climate change continues to melt that sea ice, polar bears are spending more time on land, and people in their range have raised that wariness level a notch or two.

Alaska also hosts grizzlies and black bears, making it the only state inhabited by all three North American bear species. Though polar bears don't live where cruise ships and ferries go, tens of thousands of grizzlies and black bears do. Alert passengers may spot them from the ship, and they will be sure to see bears if they take organized bear-watching tours. Don't be confused if you hear locals refer to "brown bears"—that's just the common name for grizzlies that live around the coast. Due to their salmon-rich diet, coastal grizzlies (brown bears) grow to almost twice the size of their inland brethren, with boars (males) reaching heights of 9 feet (2.7 m) and weights of 1,500 pounds (680 kg). Grizzlies roam various habitats throughout Alaska; you might see them on the beaches, in the forests, in the tundra, up in the mountains, and even on many islands. Black bears also occupy most of the state, but they show a preference for forests.

Most visitors limit their wildlife fears to bears, but they should add moose to the list. It's hard for the uninitiated to be concerned about an herbivore, but many residents of Alaska worry more about moose than bears, and for good reasons—moose are even bigger than brown bears, just as fast, more commonly encountered, and more temperamental. Both Alaskans and visitors get killed and injured each year by these 1,000-pound (454 kg) beasts, even near Anchorage. During the fall rut, bull moose get ornery, but cow moose are even more dangerous if you get near their calves. Exercise common sense and you will not have a problem. Don't walk up to have your photo taken with Bullwinkle. Just keep your distance and enjoy watching them munch on willows or stilt around in ponds on those long legs.

> " More than 400 bird species inhabit or migrate through the state, including some Asiatic species that make serious bird-watchers all atwitter. "

Assuming you don't feed or mistreat them, the rest of Alaska's wildlife generally presents no cause for concern. On the contrary, watching the fascinating and beautiful animals that call Alaska home is a highlight for many visitors. From rain forest to Arctic tundra, listen for the thrilling howls of wolves. On steep slopes look for the brilliant white of Dall sheep, closely related to the bighorns of the lower 48; the males sport curled horns that serve as battering rams during battles over females. On even higher and steeper slopes, scan for mountain goats. In the Alaskan Peninsula and way up north, watch for caribou; the great caribou herds of the Alaskan Peninsula are no more, but hunting is now banned and the Alaska Department of Fish & Game culls wolves to sustain the caribou population.

■ The recognizable horned puffin thrills even veteran bird-watchers.

Not all animals of interest in Alaska wear fur. More than 400 birds species inhabit or migrate through the state, including some Asiatic species that make serious bird-watchers all atwitter. Bald eagles are common in coastal Alaska, and their cousins, the golden eagles, soar above the interior tundra hunting for marmots and hares. Other avian favorites include trumpeter swans, sandhill cranes, and peregrine falcons.

Cruise ship passengers enjoy some of the finest bird-watching in Alaska. The rich coastal waters support huge colonies of seabirds, such as tufted puffins, rhinoceros auklets, cormorants, and pigeon guillemots. Hundreds of thousands will nest on a single small island, where they can lay their eggs and raise their young safe from terrestrial predators, such as foxes. The Alaska Maritime National Wildlife Refuge consists of some 2,500 islands, reefs, spires, islets, and coastal areas scattered throughout the state. These refuge units are especially abundant in the Aleutian Islands, but some are located in the Inside Passage. About 40 million seabirds nest on these rocky havens; that's around 80 percent of all the seabirds of North America.

> **The Alaska Maritime National Wildlife Refuge consists of some 2,500 islands, reefs, spires, islets, and coastal areas scattered throughout the state.**

The same coastal waters beloved by seabirds also sustain an awesome array of marine mammals. Ships may ease past a colony of raucous Steller sea lions. These beefy beasts (males can hit 1,500 pounds/680 kg) endlessly snort, roar, grumble, and growl, but they don't bark—that's left to the seals, often seen lazing on ice floes in Inside Passage fjords. Near the shore passengers might spot dozens of sea otters bobbing on the surface in groups called rafts. Often you'll see them dive and pop up a few seconds later holding a crab or sea urchin, which they will crack open and munch like a hungry human chomping corn on the cob.

Arguably Alaska's most spectacular marine mammals are the whales, and the sight of a cetacean breaching (or cresting) the surface of the water is an Alaskan memory that will last a lifetime. Visitors may see killer, gray, and minke whales, but most commonly spied and most entertaining are humpbacks, which often slap the water with their 15-foot-long (4.5 m) pectoral fins, their powerful tails, or even their enormous heads. Sometimes they propel their 40-ton (36 tonnes) bodies completely out of the water and reenter with a prodigious belly flop. Hundreds of humpbacks migrate to Alaska during the summer cruising season, and most of them frequent the same areas that cruise ships and ferries favor, so your chances of spotting them are excellent.

One last category of wildlife must be mentioned: biting bugs. Led by Alaska's notorious mosquitoes and a variety of biting flies, these pests can spoil outings if you're not prepared—and sometimes even when you are. Learn how to handle them, or find out when their numbers peak in the places you want to visit and time your travels accordingly. Alaska is the Great Land; it's not worth letting a tiny creature like the mosquito spoil your visit.

## Public Lands

Viewing wildlife is made easier by the fact that most of Alaska is public land. Alaska has the United States' biggest national park, its biggest national wildlife refuge, and its biggest state park. Be aware that many of these public lands bear little resemblance to their lower 48 counterparts, where guests often enjoy flush toilets, elaborate visitor centers, extensive trail systems, well-tended campgrounds, and other amenities. Many of Alaska's public lands are raw wildernesses, with perhaps one visitor center or ranger station on the boundary. For information contact the specific site or the excellent Alaska Public Lands Information Centers *(alaskacenters.gov)*. ■

**A humpback whale breaching in Frederick Sound**

# HISTORY OF ALASKA

**Much of Alaska's history has revolved around natural resources. When humans first entered the Western Hemisphere by crossing the Bering land bridge, they probably were on the hunt for mammoths. When Europeans initially sailed into Alaska waters, they came seeking the pelts of sea otters and seals. When Americans first entered Alaska in significant numbers, they searched for gold and later for black gold in the oil fields.**

Yet along with the fortune hunters came people who settled in Alaska, people looking to establish a new home. Whether native peoples who have been around for almost 500 generations or recent arrivals, these resident Alaskans are a major part of the state's history, too. They're the ones who build the clan houses, fly the bush planes, populate villages and towns, and skipper small fishing boats.

## Coming to America

The majority view is that America's first inhabitants arrived between 10,000 and 30,000 years ago, when Ice Age glaciers bound up so much water that sea level dropped about 250 feet (76 m). This exposed the shallow ocean shelf in the Bering Strait, where mainland Russia and mainland Alaska are only some 56 miles (90 km) apart. That shelf constituted the Bering land bridge, though the word "bridge" is misleading because at low water levels, the exposed landmass was hundreds of miles wide. This landmass was probably exposed for thousands of years and perhaps more than once. Over centuries this land would have become a grassy plain inhabited by mammoths, bison, musk oxen, and other Siberian game animals. With this new territory accessible, it's natural that hunters from Siberia would have followed their prey across it and ended up in what is now Alaska.

### Alaska's First Inhabitants

Uncertainty clouds the early years of humans in the Americas (see sidebar left). Authorities debate whether some of these first North Americans stayed in Alaska after migrating from Siberia, or whether all of them moved through Alaska to points south before some later moved back to Alaska. Anthropologists and archaeologists do know that the ancestors of today's Alaska natives lived here for thousands of years. During that time they split into a rich variety of linguistic and cultural groups. Some remained nomadic, while others settled into permanent villages. They developed increasingly sophisticated techniques for making a living from hunting caribou, catching salmon, harpooning bowhead and beluga whales, and gathering plants from the forest and tundra. Many arts flourished, including sculpting ivory and stone, weaving baskets, storytelling, carving totem poles, dancing, and fashioning elaborate masks.

The Tlingit and Haida cultures of southeast Alaska were highly developed—as woodworkers they were unequaled throughout North America. Many clan members earned a living as professional carvers, notable for their totem poles, and for masks used in songs and dance that were proprietary symbols of wealth and gave direct links to the spiritual ancestor world: the keystone of Tlingit and Haida social life and standing.

## The Russians Are Coming

In the early 1700s the European powers were colonizing the world, including North America. Shortly before his death, Tsar Peter the Great of Russia sent Vitus Bering to sail east from Siberia's Kamchatka Peninsula. In 1741 both of the ships in Bering's expedition, separated in foul weather, encountered what is now southern Alaska.

Bering's men brought back animal pelts, including those of sea otters. Many wealthy clients, especially among the Chinese, prized otter pelts for the unmatched density of the warm fur. The expedition's reports of abundant sea otters attracted *promyshlenniki*—trappers and fur traders who typically took local hostages and forced their fellow tribesmen to buy them back with furs. The promyshlenniki inflicted this cruel system on the Unangan, along with European diseases, and wiped out most of the native population. Equally acquisitive but less barbaric Russian fur companies followed and set up operations in southeast and south-central Alaska.

For several decades the Russians kept news of the Alaska sea otters to themselves, but in the 1770s British and Spanish ships explored Alaska and the word spread. Chasing sea otters, the mythical Northwest Passage (an ice-free shipping route between the Pacific and the Atlantic), political advantage, and scientific information, Europeans made some 200 voyages to Alaska waters

This 1981 stamp honors explorer Vitus Bering of the Russian Navy.

by 1805. Still, under the iron hand of Alexander Baranov (1746–1819), manager of Alaska operations for the fur-trading Russian-American Company who came to be called "Lord of Alaska," the Russians consolidated and extended their sway in Alaska.

Overhunting caused a scarcity of sea otters and other furbearers by the 1820s and 1830s. Coupled with wars and political setbacks at home, this decline in furs caused Russia to lose interest in Alaska, where virtually no permanent settlements had been established. Around the same time, Americans expanded their interest in the region as they developed lucrative markets for whales, notably bowhead whales, a species abundant in the Bering Sea and the Arctic Ocean. Bowheads were huge, easy to harpoon, and laden with valuable whale oil and baleen, the comblike structure in the mouth of some whale species through which they filter food out of seawater. In many nations whale oil had become the fuel for lamps, and baleen was crafted into products such as buggy whips and hoopskirts.

During several decades of intensive hunting, commercial whalers killed tens of thousands of whales. This decimated the Alaskan bowhead population, also targeted by Alaska natives. Sailing for months on end in often icy waters, whalers suffered many losses, too, especially during the early decades when wooden ships were used; in 1871 alone, ice crushed 34 wooden whaling vessel hulls. Companies began using steel-plated steamships around 1880, but whaling in the far north remained hazardous until its demise in the early 1900s, due to a scarcity of bowheads.

Back in the mid-19th century, when American whaling was thriving and the Russian fur industry was tanking, there was talk of the Russians selling Alaska to the U.S. This being the colonial era, no one with any power ever questioned the right of the Russians to sell Alaska. Certainly no one asked the Alaska natives. The Russians did not want the region to fall into the hands of the British or any of Russia's other European rivals.

## Seward's Folly

U.S. Secretary of State William H. Seward and his fellow Americans were as eager to acquire Alaska as the Russians were to unload it. Seward was a zealous believer in America's "manifest destiny" to rule over all of North America. Others disagreed, pointing to Alaska's remoteness and brutal climate. These critics panned Alaska as "Seward's icebox," "Walrussia," and "Icebergia." And in 1867, when Seward signed the deal with the Russians and paid them $72 million, they labeled the agreement as "Seward's Folly."

Following the purchase, the Americans wondered just what they'd bought. Neither the Russians nor other Europeans or Asians had explored much beyond the coastline. (The native peoples who lived beyond the coastline knew a little something about what lay in the interior, but no one asked them.) The new owners didn't even know what to call their new property. Seward chose "Alaska," the Unangan word for "great land."

The U.S. government refused to make Alaska a territory, as happened with lands acquired by previous treaties, like the Louisiana Purchase. Territorial status would have conferred citizenship upon all inhabitants and put Alaska on a trajectory toward statehood, and Congress didn't think Alaska rated such treatment. Instead, Alaska's status was left vague. More than anything the arrangement made Alaska resemble a colony.

For the next few decades, the federal government, like the Russians before them, largely ceded day-to-day administration to a fur-trading company: the Alaska Commercial Company, which mainly sought fur seal pelts. With fur seal populations in steep decline, the company and the government agreed upon the taking of 100,000 fur seals a year, while leaving females and pups. Even with these limitations they raked in huge profits.

■ Having rested at The Scales, the last camp on the trail in Alaska, miners bound for Canada's Klondike goldfields labor up the "Golden Stairs" cut into the snow of Chilkoot Pass.

## John Muir & Other Visitors

During those early years of American tenure, Alaska got several interesting visitors, among them naturalist John Muir. Fascinated by glaciers, along with everything else wild, Muir came north to Alaska, which he knew to be heavily glaciated. In 1879 he took a ship to Wrangell, in southeast Alaska, and headed out from there with four Tlingit paddlers and a Presbyterian missionary on what turned into an 800-mile (1,290 km) canoe trip. Among the many places they explored was Glacier Bay, where today visitors will find what is now known as Muir Glacier. Muir's glowing stories about his visit to Glacier Bay and an 1880 return trip are said to have launched Alaska tourism. Within a decade thousands of people had cruised up the Inside Passage to witness the grandeur of Glacier Bay and southeast Alaska.

Numerous others, including missionaries and military men, also were exploring Alaska during the 1870s and 1880s, slowly figuring out whether Seward's purchase of this vast land had been folly or not. They found a diversity of intriguing Alaska natives, prolific fisheries, ample wildlife, and spectacular landscapes—but all of that was overshadowed by the discovery of gold.

## Gold Rush

When Alaskans talk about the gold rush, they're referring to the stampede of miners to the Klondike that started in 1898. However, there were many other significant discoveries of gold, too. Joe Juneau and Richard Harris hit it big at Gold Creek in 1880, at the site of the city that now bears Joe's name. But independent miners in Juneau faced a problem: Those gold deposits required hard-rock mining, which in turn required big companies with expensive equipment to drill tunnels into mountainsides and money to build stamp mills to extract the gold from the ore. Classic gold rushes, in which thousands upon thousands of people converge on an area, occurred in places where gold had filtered out into streams and could be found by individual miners panning for the yellow metal. In Nome three prospectors struck gold in 1898, and in 1899 people found gold flakes amid the beach sands on the Bering Sea near town. By the summer of 1900, some 20,000 fortune hunters were camped out on that beach. One prospector found a gold nugget that weighed an incredible 6.7 pounds (3 kg)—the largest ever recorded in Alaska.

Perhaps the strangest thing about the Klondike gold rush is that the Klondike isn't actually in Alaska. The Klondike River and its tributary creeks where the gold was discovered lay fully 60 miles (97 km) to the east, in Canada's Yukon Territory. This rush became an Alaska legend because the most popular routes to the Klondike passed through

### The Storied Gold Rush

The gold may have given out long ago, but gold rush drama and characters have continued to make money year after year for storytellers. Twenty-year-old Klondike stampeder Jack London turned his youthful adventures into such tales as *The Call of the Wild* and *To Build a Fire*. Jules Verne wrote *The Golden Volcano* about the Klondike. Filmmaker Charlie Chaplin struck it lucky with his 1925 movie *The Gold Rush*. In 1936 Mae West made the motion picture *Klondike Annie*. A 1955 Jimmy Stewart movie called *The Far Country* is set in Skagway and Dawson City during the gold rush. James Michener's epic historical novel *Alaska* devotes a chapter to the era. Gold has fired up the imaginations of more than just prospectors.

Alaska, and because this influx was huge. Ships carrying news of the Klondike strike—and carrying a ton (0.9 tonne) of gold—arrived in Seattle in July 1897. Because the Klondike was hard to reach, July was too late to start out, so most people waited until 1898. In spring some 50,000 gold seekers headed north, with another 50,000 leaving later that year or in 1899. Of those 100,000, only about 30,000 to 50,000 made it to the goldfields. Most of the rest managed to straggle back to civilization, but a terrible number died trying.

One party of 18 New Yorkers decided to cross the Malaspina Glacier, in southeast Alaska, unaware that it is the largest piedmont glacier in the world. For three agonizing months they struggled. One man fell into a crevasse and died. Three died in an avalanche. The rest got off the glacier but were utterly lost when winter caught them, so they threw together a rickety shelter to wait for spring. Some went insane with cabin fever and struck out into the teeth of winter to reach the Klondike; they were never heard from again. The seven who survived until spring recrossed the glacier back to where they had started, in Yakutat Bay. Only four were alive when a ship found them, and two had suffered snow blindness. When the four broken men were dropped in Seattle, *The Seattle Times* incorrectly reported that the men had returned with half a million dollars worth of gold.

Most stampeders sailed to Skagway or Dyea, neighboring southeast Alaska towns that vied to be the gateway to the Klondike. From there they made for the goldfields via Chilkoot Pass, a route the Tlingit had been using for centuries to trade with interior peoples. It took 33 miles (53 km) of steep, difficult hiking to reach Lake Lindeman or Lake Bennett, where the gold seekers had to build crude boats and float 550 miles (885 km) to the goldfields.

> **Ships carrying news of the Klondike strike—and carrying a ton (0.9 tonne) of gold—arrived in Seattle in July 1897.**

Although the Klondike fields yielded about $300 million in gold, the vast majority of stampeders didn't strike it rich. Some moved on to Nome or some other gold strike. Most went back to where they came from. But some stayed and made Alaska home; from 1890 to 1900 the state's year-round population doubled from 30,000 to 60,000. This migration jump-started the 20th century in Alaska, boosting the building of the railroads, the founding of cities and towns, and the growth of industries like fishing and logging. Alaska grew steadily, but its next great leap forward was World War II.

## World War II

Few people know that the Japanese invaded Alaska during World War II: The flag of the Rising Sun flew over American soil for nearly a year in the Aleutians. The invasion was not a total surprise. U.S. military planners knew that the westernmost Aleutian Islands lay closer to Japan than to Anchorage, and that San Francisco was 1,000 miles (1,600 km) closer to Tokyo via the Aleutians than Hawaii. In early June of 1942, the Battle of Midway was about to begin 1,500 miles (2,414 km) to the south, and the Japanese hoped an attack in Alaska would draw American forces away. So on June 3 they bombed Unalaska/Dutch Harbor, killing 25 servicemen and creating confusion in the Aleutians. The tactic didn't work: The Japanese suffered a stunning defeat at Midway.

Partly to save face, the Japanese forces at Alaska's door then invaded two far-western Aleutian Islands, Attu and Kiska, which were undefended and nearly unpopulated. The Japanese built an airfield and bunkers and brought in several thousand soldiers. In response, the Allies island-hopped westward through the Aleutians, setting up bases ever closer to Attu and Kiska. American planes repeatedly bombed the two islands and the supply ships coming from Japan, and American ships fought a major engagement with a Japanese supply convoy in March 1943. But the main battle occurred in May of that year.

On May 11, 1943, some 12,500 Allied troops landed on Attu, which was defended by about 2,400 Japanese soldiers. For the next 18 days, one of the war's most brutal battles raged. In the end, all but 28 Japanese were dead, and Allied casualties reached nearly 4,000. An equally bloody battle seemed inevitable on Kiska, but the Japanese evacuated under cover of fog. When the Allies stormed ashore, they didn't find anyone to fight.

No more combat occurred in Alaska, but war-related development continued apace, notably the construction of airfields and the Alaska Highway, which connected Alaska to the lower 48. The war also brought tens of thousands of American troops to Alaska, many of whom fell in love with the Great Land and returned later to live and work and raise families there. World War II rapidly transformed Alaska from a frontier backwater into part of modern America, albeit a part that remained a frontier in many ways.

## Modern Times

The end of World War II was soon followed by the beginning of the Cold War. With the Soviet Union looming just miles from Alaska, the military presence in Alaska expanded in the decades following. Mostly due to the influx of military personnel and their families, the population of Anchorage jumped from 3,000 in 1940 to about 47,000 only 11 years later. By 1950 one in six Alaska residents served in the military. All the new residents, plus massive military construction and spending, caused the Alaskan economy to surge. As a rapidly modernizing region and a vital link in America's national defense, Alaska was declared the 49th state in 1959.

Statehood notwithstanding, Alaska had one more frontierlike boom up its sleeve. In 1968, oil company geologists found a huge oil field on the North Slope—the vast Arctic Ocean coastal plain north of the Brooks Range. Environmental concerns and native land rights raised serious questions about its development particularly the construction of the 800-mile (1,285 km) pipeline to Valdez and the shipping of oil through pristine waters, but the Arab oil embargo in 1973 gave oil advocates a boost. Buoyed by the resulting oil shortages, Congress authorized the pipeline in a 50-to-49 vote in the Senate. Oil money soon poured into Alaska—and oil poured into the waters of Prince William Sound when the *Exxon Valdez* tanker ran aground in 1989, in the world's worst such ecological disaster to date. This episode epitomizes the issues that Alaska still faces in the 21st century as it continues to try to balance the use and the conservation of its bountiful natural resources. ■

### Disaster Strikes

You can get a feeling for both the immense resources and fragile ecology of Alaska by learning about the 1989 *Exxon Valdez* oil spill at the **Valdez Museum** *(tel 907-835-2764, valdezmuseum.org, closed a.m. & Mon. mid-Sept.–mid-May, $$).* The exhibition profiles the environmental damage caused when the tanker ran aground, and 11 million gallons (42 million L) of crude oil fouled 1,500 miles (2,414 km) of shoreline in Prince William Sound.

# THE ARTS

**For a state populated by slightly more than 700,000 people, Alaska enjoys a varied and vibrant arts scene. The visual arts are especially robust, but lovers of music, theater, dance, and literature also will find much to enjoy.**

Not surprisingly, given the powerful presence of the surrounding landscape, many Alaska artists pursue themes related to wilderness, wildlife, and the relationship between human beings and the land. Some express these themes through traditional methods; others use cutting-edge styles.

## Visual Arts

The earliest visual artists were the Alaska natives from past centuries whose names have long been lost to time. While most of their work also is gone, happily a few pieces survive in museum collections. The University of Alaska Museum of the North, for example, displays several walrus-ivory toys unearthed in an archaeological dig on St. Lawrence Island. Coastal Eskimos have been carving ivory figures since at least 500 B.C.

Museums through Alaska and the rest of North America teem with pieces of argillite, totem poles, and ferociously expressive carved masks of the Tlingit, Haida, Tsimshian, and Kwakitutl of southeast Alaska—an artistic heritage described by the famous French anthropologist Claude Levi-Straus as "on a par with that of Greece and Egypt." Up and down the coastline of the Inside Passage, Native American communities had integrated art into virtually every aspect of their lives: Even utilitarian objects, such as fish hooks, paddles, and spoons were elaborately carved and decorated with representations of human and animal spirits. Each kin group held hereditary rights to specific masks, songs, and dances that linked the people to their land and traditions. The display of such wealth was expressed through the potlatch—a massive gift-giving festival that reasserted social ranking and wealth.

A new wave of art washed into Alaska when European explorers arrived. Typically an expedition would bring along an artist the way today's travelers bring along a camera. One expedition artist was John Webber, who sailed with Capt. James Cook, the renowned British seafarer, on his third and last voyage, from 1776 to 1780. Webber drew and painted landscapes, wildlife, and some of the Alaska natives he encountered.

The first prominent, professionally trained artist to live in Alaska was Sydney Laurence (1865–1940), who would become the state's most famous and influential painter. Born in Brooklyn, New York, he roamed the world as a young man, studying painting in Paris and London. In 1904

Laurence headed north to Alaska, where for several years he eschewed painting in favor of prospecting—even artists can catch gold fever. Necessity rather than artistic passion forced him back to his brushes; Laurence generally painted traditional, even iconic Alaska subjects, such as Mount Denali and trappers. His specialty was large canvases that glorified Alaska's wild landscapes. Today his major works sell for sums well into six figures. Most of his paintings hang in private collections, but the Anchorage Museum and the Alaska Heritage Museum (also in Anchorage) have good selections; the former devotes an entire gallery to him.

A contemporary of Laurence's who became nearly as famous was Eustace Ziegler (1881–1969), born in Detroit, Michigan. He began painting at age 7, and by the time he turned 20, he was selling his work professionally. He had plenty to sell, producing paintings from age 20 until just a few months before his death, at age 87, and averaging about 40 paintings a year. Like Laurence, Ziegler was fascinated by the Alaska outdoors, but he was equally fascinated by the people of Alaska. He traveled all over via packhorse, canoe, riverboat, and dogsled, meeting folks from all walks of life. In an honest, sympathetic style he painted fishermen, prospectors, native mothers, gamblers, priests, and prostitutes.

**World-renowned Tlingit master carver Nathan Jackson adds his own creative flair to traditional totem pole motifs.**

Unfortunately, the arrival of Europeans had a devastating effect on indigenous culture. Not least, the potlatch was outlawed. Incentives for producing artwork—the currency of the potlatch—were eroded. Coherent tribal life and culture diminished, along with the population. Although such aging artists as Willie Seaweed (1873-1967) and Mungo Martin (1879-1962) kept Kwakiutl art alive, the few natives of other tribes still carving departed from traditional design to appeal to the tourist market. An Alaska Steamship Company brochure for 1912 promised tourists they would see "crude gropings toward art by a primitive people." When, in 1958, Haida artist Bill Reid was commissioned to reconstruct a Haida village on the University of British Columbia campus, he had to study books to learn his ancestors' "expressive language."

**Native Artists Today:** Anolic Unneengnuzinna Aalughuk, also known as Ted Mayac, Sr., is an Inupiat Eskimo from King Island, a pinpoint of land about 30 miles (48 km) off the coast of the remote Seward Peninsula. The Inupiat have been carving walrus ivory for thousands of years, and Mayac carried on this tradition; today his son, Ted Mayac, Jr., keeps his father's tradition alive. Inspired by the migrating birds that pass through the island, he shapes incredibly intricate and lifelike figures of some 70 different species, often shown engaged in behaviors that reveal his intimate knowledge of these birds.

## Master Artist

Widely heralded as the father of modern Alaskan art, Ron Senungetuk (1933–2020) was renowned for his unique wood paintings. Using vibrant colored oils, he brought to life such Alaska icons as whales, seabirds, seals, reindeer, and the aurora borealis, in intriguing forms that combined abstract, minimalist, and Alaskan Native sensibilities. An Inupiat born in a tiny village on the Seward Peninsula, Senungetuk sold his ivory carvings to tourists when he was still just a boy. He later earned advanced art degrees, launched the University of Alaska, Fairbanks's Native Arts Center, and headed the university's art department, all the while producing his award-winning works.

Meanwhile, Reid's role proved pivotal in a renaissance of Haida and Tlingit art in the past half-century. Using his uncle (and supreme Haida artist) Chief Charlie Edenshaw's work as a "Rosetta stone" to break the code of the Northwest Coast Indian style, Reid's exploration of the ancestral art forms helped stimulate the memory of dormant rituals and, eventually, to spark a revitalized pride in traditional culture. Today, art galleries from Seattle to Skagway (and well beyond) are filled with "objects of bright pride," to use Bill Reid's own words—works that have moved away from the tourist curio market and are authentic to age-old tradition. Carved masks intended for use in dance ceremonies by such contemporary artists as Robert Davidson, Richard Hunt, and Tommy Joseph can fetch $10,000 or more, while their totem poles may cost the same price per foot (30 cm).

The new Sealaska Heritage Arts Campus (*sealaskaheritage.org*) in downtown Juneau, is a multidisciplinary venue to foster the Tlingit, Haida, and Tsimshian artistic cultures of southeast Alaska, with classes from basketry and printing to totem pole carving and dance performance.

■ The architectural setting of the Sheldon Jackson Museum in Sitka complements the collections.

**Totem Poles:** One of the most celebrated and unusual media that has long been used by Alaska native artists is the totem pole. This consists of a carved log, usually cedar, that often stands 20 to 30 feet (6–9 m) high. (The tallest totem pole in Alaska towers 132 feet/40.2 meters above the village of Kake, on Kupreanof Island in southeast Alaska.) Totem poles are an integral part of Northwest Coast native culture, which includes the peoples of southeast Alaska: the Tlingit, Haida, Eyak, and Tsimshian. These traditional works of art generally include at least one carved figure representing the totem of a clan or other social group, usually an animal such as a raven, wolf, or orca.

Though often quite artistic, totem poles traditionally are not simply works of art. Some are memorial poles, created as a tribute to an important member of the clan upon his or her death. Others commemorate major events and are a visual means of telling stories and preserving clan histories.

> " Though often quite artistic, totem poles traditionally are not simply works of art. Some are memorial poles, created as a tribute to an important member of the clan upon his or her death. "

Perhaps the most famous carver of totem poles today is Nathan Jackson (1938– ), a Tlingit who for several decades has deftly used his adze to shape beautiful poles that are firmly rooted in tradition yet show a creative flair. These stand outside in public places, in Alaska's major museums, and in museums in the lower 48, England, and Japan. He has represented Alaska at the Smithsonian Folklife Festival.

## Performing Arts

Alaska has little of the urban critical mass that is typically needed to support high-level performing arts programs, but Anchorage and certain individual groups based elsewhere do provide fine music, theater, and dance experiences.

It comes as no surprise that Anchorage occupies center stage in Alaska's performing arts scene—it's the only big city in the state. Anchorage also has an advantage over other communities: oil money. Through taxes and direct contributions, the oil companies that loom so large in the Alaska economy have put millions into the state's performing arts, particularly in Anchorage. The city's Alaska Center for the Performing Arts, an outstanding facility, hosts major traveling shows as well as the highly regarded Anchorage Symphony Orchestra (which almost always sells out its 2,000-plus-seat auditorium) and the Anchorage Opera.

The poet Robert W. Service (1874–1958), known as "the Bard of the Yukon"

Independent performing artists and groups also thrive in Anchorage, epitomized by the group Pamyua (pronounced BUM-yo-ah). This high-energy foursome of Yup'ik and Inuit performers got together in 1996 and has blossomed into one of Alaska's most beloved groups. They're enjoying success beyond the state, too, appearing at world music festivals and winning record-of-the-year honors at the Native American Music Awards—the first Alaska artists to win them. But labeling their work as "world music" or "Alaska native music" doesn't fully capture their diversity and creativity. Their eclectic blend of traditional song, drumming, and dancing has hints of jazz, gospel, rhythm and blues, funk, hip-hop, and doo-wop. They even throw in some comedy and storytelling.

For proof that Anchorage doesn't have a monopoly on performing arts in Alaska, one need look no further than the Perseverance Theatre in Juneau. Considered one of the finest regional theaters in the nation, PT, as locals call it, likes to mix challenging classics with innovative and often edgy lesser known works. Even the classics range widely, from *Death of a Salesman* to *Hair* to a rendition of *Macbeth* set in Tlingit culture and featuring an all-Alaska native cast. Plus, most venues on the cruise ship itineraries host Northwest Coast Indian dance companies that offer traditional performances.

## Literature

More than most places, Alaska provides the kind of setting that inspires people to write, to grope for words to capture what they see and to express what they feel. Many Alaska authors have used fiction and poetry to examine life in the Great Land. Certainly this is true for Seth Kantner, whose work reflects the untamed landscape surrounding his home in remote northwest Alaska. Kantner was born and raised in a sod house on the tundra, where fishing, trapping, and hunting were part of his family's subsistence life. Today he still engages in those traditional pursuits but he has added "famous author" and "wildlife photographer" to his resume. In 2005, Kantner's debut novel, *Ordinary Wolves,* was published to rave reviews. Kantner followed up in 2009 with a well-received nonfiction title, *Shopping for Porcupine,* richly illustrated with his own photographs. Its essay topics range from hunting to odd Alaska characters to the vanishing wilderness.

These themes also are explored in the fascinating chronicles of recent and contemporary life found in the excellent collection of writings in *Authentic Alaska: Voices of Its Native Writers* (1998), edited by Susan B. Andrews and John Creed. Also of note, award-winning author Sherry Simpson gazes deeply at issues facing America's last frontier in *The Way Winter Comes* (1998). *The Accidental Explorer: Wayfinding in Alaska* (2008) recounts her experiences exploring the Great Land.

> **Alaska provides the kind of setting that inspires people to write, to grope for words to capture what they see and to express what they feel.**

Other standout Alaska writers include Richard Nelson, a former Alaska State Writer Laureate and the author of many books on Alaska life, most famously *Make Prayers to the Raven: A Koyukon View of the Northern Forest,* which was made into an award-winning public television series; and Jo-Ann Mapson, who has written numerous novels, several of them national best sellers.

Linda McCarriston and Robert Service, both poets, deserve attention for their compositions. McCarriston, a National Book Award finalist and university professor, pursues complex truths about family life, friendship, and children. Service, on the other hand, came to the Yukon around the time of the Klondike gold rush era. Writing poems for the people and not the critics, Service was immensely popular in his time. Some of his works, such as "The Cremation of Sam McGee" and "The Shooting of Dan McGrew" (both first published in his 1907 book of verse *Songs of a Sourdough*), are still memorized by Alaskan schoolchildren to this day. ∎

## Go Trolling for Art

Enter Ray Troll's little shop in Ketchikan (see p. 70; *trollart.com*) and you'll see a smorgasbord of locally themed items for sale. These might include an illustrated "Fish Worship" cap and a T-shirt bearing the image of a salmon and the words, "If You Must Smoke, Smoke Salmon."

You might conclude this store is just another souvenir shop, albeit one with a strikingly off-center sense of humor, but a close look at the artwork on the merchandise will reveal unusual imagination and skill. Look further and you'll see Troll's art posters and other work that trend toward fine art, though he self-deprecatingly labels his efforts as "fin art." You'll notice Troll largely hews to fishy themes, sometimes including marine life from past epochs, as in his poster "Dream of Didymoceras," which depicts these ancient ammonite cephalopods hovering dreamlike above a slumbering couple in their bedroom. This scientific bent is understandable—Troll has lectured at Yale and Harvard and exhibited at the Smithsonian and many other major scientific institutions. A resident of Alaska since 1983, Ray Troll has even had a ratfish named after him, a New Zealand species called *Hydrolagus trolli*.

Seattle, with its futuristic architecture, edgy culture, and scenic sound setting; Vancouver, with its fine parks and multicultural mix

# SEATTLE & VANCOUVER

◾ The steam clock in Gastown, Vancouver
Opposite: Seattle's Space Needle offers 360-degree views of the sound and beyond.

# SEATTLE & VANCOUVER

**If your voyage to Alaska starts from either of the main embarkation ports of Seattle and Vancouver, you are sailing with the winds of history behind you. Back in 1897–1898, these two cities were also the jumping-off points for tens of thousands of prospectors heading for Alaska in an attempt to reach the Klondike goldfields and strike it rich.**

These two budding ports did much of the outfitting for those bygone fortune seekers; consider a typical gold rush–era ad from a Vancouver store hawking "Heavy Klondike Clothing that you cannot do without if you intend to skim the icy waters of the Yukon." In Seattle the ties to the gold rush are explored at a unit of Klondike Gold Rush National Historical Park, whose main facility in Skagway attracts Inside Passage cruisers.

Unlike the 19th-century stampeders, you shouldn't be in any hurry to leave either of these towns. Similar in many ways, Seattle and Vancouver are young, energetic, and prosperous hubs of the dynamic Pacific Rim. Their cultural institutions, restaurants, fine shops, art and music scenes, and stunning natural settings will all vie for your attention, should you have a few days to roam either city before boarding a ship bound for Alaska. The urban cores of Seattle and Vancouver are very walkable, enabling visitors to comfortably get around without having to rent a car, pay for a cab, or search for parking.

The similarities between Seattle and Vancouver extend to their environs; both are bordered by mountains, temperate rain forests, and beautiful bodies of water. In keeping with the gifts nature has bestowed on them, Seattle and Vancouver rank among the most sustainable cities in North America. This green ethic is evidenced in ways large and small, from the municipalities' progress in using clean energy to such small details as the rooftop garden of Vancouver's Fairmont Waterfront, which has its own apiary—the hotel even employs a "bee butler" to care for their buzzing little pollinators.

## Culture & Identity

Both Seattle and Vancouver have long been major ports. Their location on the Pacific Rim has led to strong ties to Asia, made manifest in numerous ways, from the sizeable number of citizens of Asian heritage to the influence of Asian cooking on the local food scenes. The Main Vancouver Royal Centre bank, for example, includes on its list of languages in which it is prepared to do business Mandarin Chinese, Tagalog (the main language of the Philippines), Hindi, and Yue Chinese (Cantonese). The bank lists no European or Latin American languages.

Though Seattle and Vancouver began as ports and remain ports at heart, over the decades they have expanded well beyond their waterfronts. Some of these outlying areas harbor distinctive neighborhoods that are as much fun for out-of-towners as they are for residents such as Seattle's historically countercultural Fremont neighborhood; many hip boutiques and bistros have gentrified

### NOT TO BE MISSED:

**Commune with local marine life at the Seattle Aquarium** 46

**Watch the fish fly at Seattle's Pike Place Market** 50–51

**Admire the view and walk the glass floor atop the Seattle Space Needle** 52

**Walk through Vancouver's trendy historic Gastown** 58–59

**Cycle or stroll through Stanley Park** 61–63

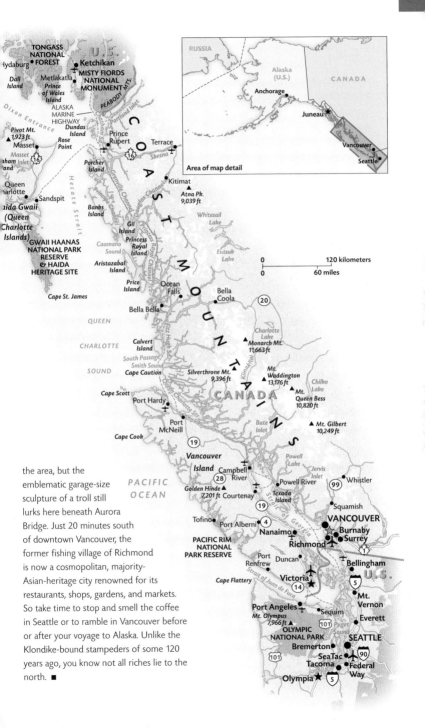

RUSSIA

Alaska
(U.S.)

CANADA

Anchorage

Juneau

Vancouver

Area of map detail

Seattle

TONGASS
NATIONAL
Hydaburg • FOREST • Ketchikan
Metlakatla • MISTY FIORDS
NATIONAL
MONUMENT

Dall
Island    Prince
of Wales
Island

ALASKA
MARINE
HIGHWAY    Dundas
Island    Prince
Rupert    Terrace

Pivot Mt.
▲ 1,923 ft    Rose
Masset •    Point
aham    16
land

Porcher
Island

16

Sheena

Queen
harlotte
•Sandspit

aida Gwaii
(Queen
Charlotte
Islands)
GWAII HAANAS
NATIONAL PARK
RESERVE
& HAIDA
HERITAGE SITE

Banks
Island

Gil
Island
Princess
Royal
Island

Caamaño
Sound

Aristazabal
Island

Kitimat

Atna Pk.
9,039 ft

Whitesail
Lake

Eutsuk
Lake

120 kilometers

0

60 miles

Cape St. James

Price
Island

Ocean
Falls

Bella
Coola

20

Bella Bella

QUEEN

CHARLOTTE

SOUND

Calvert
Island

South Passage
Smith Sound
Cape Caution

Cape Scott

Silverthrone Mt.
9,396 ft

Charlotte
Lake
Monarch Mt.
11,663 ft

Mt.
Waddington
13,176 ft    Chilko
Lake
▲ Mt.
Queen Bess
10,820 ft

CANADA

Port Hardy

Cape Cook

Port
McNeill

Bute
Inlet

▲ Mt. Gilbert
10,249 ft

19

the area, but the
emblematic garage-size
sculpture of a troll still
lurks here beneath Aurora
Bridge. Just 20 minutes south
of downtown Vancouver, the
former fishing village of Richmond
is now a cosmopolitan, majority-
Asian-heritage city renowned for its
restaurants, shops, gardens, and markets.
So take time to stop and smell the coffee
in Seattle or to ramble in Vancouver before
or after your voyage to Alaska. Unlike the
Klondike-bound stampeders of some 120
years ago, you know not all riches lie to the
north. ■

PACIFIC

OCEAN

Vancouver
Island    Campbell
River
28    Powell River
Golden Hinde ▲
7,201 ft  Courtenay
19

Powell
Lake    Jervis
Inlet    • Whistler

Texada
Island    99

Tofino•    Port Alberni    4
Nanaimo•
PACIFIC RIM
NATIONAL
PARK RESERVE

Squamish

VANCOUVER
Burnaby
Richmond • Surrey

1

Port
Renfrew    Duncan•

Cape Flattery    Victoria ★    14

Bellingham

U.S.

5

Mt.
Vernon
Everett

Port Angeles
Mt. Olympus
7,966 ft ▲    Sequim    101
OLYMPIC
NATIONAL PARK
Bremerton•
101    SeaTac ★    90
Tacoma•
Olympia ★    5

SEATTLE

Federal
Way

Strait of Juan de Fuca

Puget
Sound

Strait of Georgia

# SEATTLE

High tech. Craft beer. Aerospace. Coffee. Rain. Seattle is known for many things, but before it acquired any of these traits—except the rain—the city was first and foremost a port. Born on the beautiful shore of Elliott Bay, Seattle's focus was largely directed to the island-dotted waters of Puget Sound and the ships coming in from the Pacific. Though today this city of 776,000 (3.5 million in the metro area) has expanded inland and become economically diverse, the port and waterfront remain integral to Seattle's identity.

Seattle's waterfront

Of Seattle's visitors, about 1.2 million a year are passengers either boarding or disembarking from one of the 180 to 200 cruise ships that dock here each summer. Some cruise lines use Pier 66, on the downtown waterfront, home to the **Bell Street Pier Cruise Terminal**—an excellent starting point for an exploration of the city. Others use Pier 91, about 3 miles (4.8 km) up the shore from downtown, home to the **Smith Cove Cruise Terminal.** Still others use the new **Terminal 46,** near Pioneer Square, completed in 2022.

## Seattle

🗺 Map p. 45

**Visitor Information**

✉ Visit Seattle Center, Washington State Convention Center, 7th Ave. & Pike St.

☎ 206-461-5840 or 866-732-2695

🕐 Open daily in summer

**visitseattle.org**

## Olympic Sculpture Park

🗺 Map p. 45

✉ 2901 Western Blvd.

☎ 206-654-3100

**seattleartmuseum.org**

Your first impression of Seattle will probably be its commercial seaport, one of the busiest in the U.S. But beyond the hulking cargo ships, constantly loading and unloading in the busy harbor at the sound end of downtown, you'll find a diversity of sights worth seeking out. Numerous marinas packed with pleasure craft notch the shoreline, giving an air of romance, adventure, and leisure. The sprawling Fisherman's Terminal shelters the North Pacific Fishing Fleet and other work boats. Happily for walkers, many of the main attractions are located on or near the waterfront.

## The Waterfront & Downtown

At the north end of the recently re-landscaped downtown waterfront, six or so blocks up from Pier 66, you may come face-to-face with a 19-foot, 4-inch (5.9 m) typewriter eraser. This mutant fiberglass-and-steel imagining of an archaic office tool stands in the **Olympic Sculpture Park,** a unit of the Seattle Art Museum. The park scatters some 20 pieces over 9 acres (3.6 ha) that occupy a grassy rise above the waterfront (great views of the bay) and a sunken area. Many of the works are monumental objects that come from

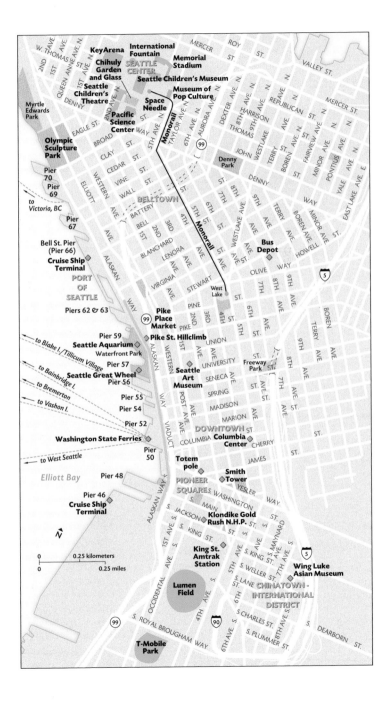

KeyArena
International Fountain
Chihuly Garden and Glass
SEATTLE CENTER
Memorial Stadium
Seattle Children's Museum
Seattle Children's Theatre
Museum of Pop Culture
Space Needle
Pacific Science Center
Myrtle Edwards Park
Olympic Sculpture Park
Monorail
MERCER ST.
ROY ST.
VALLEY ST.
MERCER ST.
W. THOMAS ST.
2nd AVE. W.
1st AVE. W.
QUEEN ANNE AVE. N.
1st AVE. N.
2nd AVE. N.
DENNY WAY
EAGLE ST.
BROAD ST.
CLAY ST.
CEDAR ST.
VINE ST.
WALL ST.
ELLIOTT AVE.
WESTERN AVE.
3rd AVE.
TAYLOR AVE. N.
AURORA AVE.
6th AVE. N.
5th AVE. N.
DEXTER AVE. N.
REAVE N.
REPUBLICAN ST.
HARRISON ST.
THOMAS ST.
JOHN ST.
WESTLAKE AVE. N.
TERRY AVE. N.
BOREN AVE. N.
FAIRVIEW AVE. N.
MINOR AVE. N.
PONTIUS AVE. N.
YALE AVE. N.
EAST LAKE AVE. E.
99
Denny Park
DENNY WAY
BELLTOWN
BATTERY ST.
BELL ST.
1st AVE.
2nd AVE.
3rd AVE.
4th AVE.
5th AVE.
6th AVE.
7th AVE.
8th AVE.
9th AVE.
WESTLAKE AVE.
TERRY AVE.
BOREN AVE.
MINOR AVE.
Monorail
BLANCHARD ST.
LENORA ST.
VIRGINIA ST.
STEWART ST.
Bus Depot
HOWELL ST.
OLIVE WAY
5
Pier 70
Pier 69
to Victoria, BC
Pier 67
Bell St. Pier (Pier 66)
Cruise Ship Terminal
PORT OF SEATTLE
Piers 62 & 63
ALASKAN WAY
WEST LAKE
PINE ST.
99
Pike Place Market
PIKE ST.
UNION ST.
UNIVERSITY ST.
SENECA ST.
SPRING ST.
MADISON ST.
Freeway Park
ST.
7th AVE.
8th AVE.
9th AVE.
TERRY AVE.
BOREN AVE.
Pier 59
Seattle Aquarium
Waterfront Park
Pier 57
Seattle Great Wheel
Pier 56
Pier 55
Pier 54
Pier 52
WESTERN AVE.
1st AVE.
POST AVE.
2nd AVE.
3rd AVE.
4th AVE.
5th AVE.
6th AVE.
Seattle Art Museum
to Blake I./Tillicum Village
to Bainbridge I.
to Bremerton
to Vashon I.
Washington State Ferries
Pier 50
to West Seattle
Pier 48
Elliott Bay
Pier 46
Cruise Ship Terminal
N
Totem pole
DOWNTOWN
MARION ST.
COLUMBIA ST.
Columbia Center
CHERRY ST.
JAMES ST.
Smith Tower
YESLER WAY
PIONEER SQUARES
WASHINGTON ST.
S. MAIN ST.
S. JACKSON ST.
Klondike Gold Rush N.H.P.
ALASKAN WAY VIADUCT
OCCIDENTAL AVE.
1st AVE. S.
0   0.25 kilometers
0   0.25 miles
King St. Amtrak Station
Lumen Field
T-Mobile Park
S. KING ST.
S. WELLER ST.
S. LANE ST.
S. CHARLES ST.
S. PLUMMER ST.
S. ROYAL BROUGHAM WAY
4th AVE. S.
5th AVE. S.
6th AVE. S.
7th AVE. S.
8th AVE. S.
MAYNARD AVE. S.
Wing Luke Asian Museum
CHINATOWN - INTERNATIONAL DISTRICT
DEARBORN ST.
5
90
99

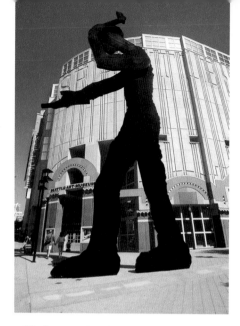

■ **"The Hammering Man" by Jonathan Borofsky looms outside the Seattle Art Museum.**

### Seattle Aquarium

- ⛰ Map p. 45
- ✉ 1483 Alaskan Way, Pier 59
- ☎ 206-386-4300
- 💲 $$$$$

seattleaquarium.org

### Pike Place Market

- ⛰ Map p. 45
- ✉ Pike Place Market Information Center, 1st Ave. & Pike St.
- ☎ 206-228-7291

pikeplacemarket.org

the hands of renowned artists, such as **"Eagle,"** a 39-foot-high (12 m) abstract by Alexander Calder. Other smaller, more fanciful works include three pairs of **"Eye Benches,"** by Louise Bourgeois—functional benches carved from black granite that look like surrealistic open eyes. Seriously unique, **"Neukom Vivarium,"** by Mark Dion, combines art and science in an installation set in a custom-built greenhouse, with a 60-foot-long (18.3 m) nurse log. This decaying tree trunk hosts all manner of lichen and plants. The museum regularly rotates a major artwork.

From the sculpture park, head back south on **Alaskan Way,** the street that runs along the waterfront. The bay side of the street was recently landscaped into a pedestrian parkway and bike path between Pioneer Square and

the Seattle Aquarium; it is busy with pedestrians, joggers, cyclists, and people lounging on benches savoring the view. The piers alongside are packed with souvenir shops, seafood cafés, and arcades.

**Seattle Aquarium & Pike Place Market:** Pier 59 is home to the Seattle Aquarium. The aquarium's strength is its in-depth presentation of its home waters. Start at **"Window on Washington Waters":** The 20- x 40-foot (6.1 x 12.2 m) window of this huge tank greets you just inside the aquarium's entrance. More than 800 native fish and invertebrates inhabit this exhibit. Even more immersing is the **"Underwater Dome,"** whose glass walls and ceiling provide wraparound views of the 400,000-gallon (1,514,165 L) tank filled with salmon, sturgeon, sharks, and other Puget Sound creatures. Next head outdoors to some of the open-air exhibits, such as **"Birds and Shores,"** aflutter with oystercatchers, rhinoceros auklets, and tufted puffins. **"Marine Mammals"** offers aboveground and underwater areas so you can view the sea otters, river otters, fur seals, and harbor seals from all angles. A new state-of-the-art **Ocean Pavilion,** due to open in 2023, will feature a 325,000-gallon tank with sharks, stingrays, and other marine critters native to the South Pacific.

From the aquarium head up the series of steps and elevators known as the **Pike Street Hillclimb,** which leads to Pike Place Market (see pp. 50–51) and downtown. Other than its two hot spots—Pike Place Market and Pioneer Park—downtown is mainly a commercial district of office towers. Still, it's an architecturally handsome area with fine restaurants, shops, pleasant parks, and, at the corner of University and First, a few blocks southeast of the Hillclimb, the main unit of the Seattle Art Museum.

## Seattle Art Museum & Environs:

SAM, as locals know it, is easy to spot. The marble, limestone, and granite exterior, designed by celebrated architect Robert Venturi, stands out. So does the sculpture towering over the entrance: **"Hammering Man,"** a 48-foot-high (14.6 m) black steel silhouette—and the hammer actually swings. The mechanical arm brings down the hammer four times every minute except on Labor Day, when the worker gets

### Sunless in Seattle?

Despite its soggy reputation, Seattle does not endure constant rain. Sure, it rains about half the time, but usually it's more of a drizzle or even just a mist. On average, the city gets only 37 inches (94 cm) of rain a year, less than New York City, Boston, or Atlanta. Best of all, it seldom rains during the summer—maybe 3 or 4 inches (7.6–10.2 cm) during the entire season. Most summer days are sunny, with highs of 70° to 75°F (21°–24°C).

a rest. Inside this superb museum you'll find extensive permanent collections and prime traveling exhibits. These include not only Northwest and Native American art, but surprises such as Australian Aboriginal and Islamic art.

Back at the bottom of the Hillclimb, **Waterfront Park** stretches along the shore from Pier 59 to Pier 57. Sprawling wooden decks extending over the water tempt passersby with benches, picnic tables, a fountain, statues, and two viewing platforms from which you can gaze up at the downtown skyline, out to Puget Sound, or south to the bustling port. At the south end of the park, Pier 57 is chockablock with restaurants, a carousel, an arcade, and shops—and, of course, that 175-foot-tall (53.3 m) Ferris wheel, the **Seattle Great Wheel,** with its 42 fully enclosed gondolas, plus **Wings over Washington** ($$$$) the realistic "flying theater" that uses state-of-the-art dynamic wraparound laser 42 fully enclosed gondolas, plus **Wings Over Washington** ($$$$), the realistic "flying theater" that uses state-of-the-art dynamic wraparound laser images to take you on a tour of the state.

Amble south a few blocks to Pier 52, which serves as a dock for the busy **Washington State ferry system.** These hardworking ferries haul millions of passengers every year, many of them commuters from islands in Puget Sound. For about the price of a pizza, you can hop on a ferry for the 35-minute trip to Bainbridge Island, spend 15 to 20 minutes in Bainbridge harbor, and then return.

### Seattle Art Museum
- Map p. 45
- 1300 1st Ave.
- 206-654-3100
- Open Thurs.–Sun. 10 a.m.–5 p.m. Closed Mon.–Wed.
- $$$$

seattleartmuseum.org

### Seattle Great Wheel
- Map p. 45
- 1301 Alaskan Way, Pier 57
- 206-623-8607
- Mon.–Thurs. noon–8 p.m.; Fri.–Sat. 11 a.m.–10 p.m.; Sun.: 11 a.m.–8 p.m.
- $$$

seattlegreatwheel.com

### Washington State Ferries
- 206-464-6400 or 888-808-7977

wsdot.wa.gov/ferries

**Pioneer Square**

🗺 Map p. 45

**Visitor Information**

☎ 206-667-0687

pioneersquare.org

**Smith Tower**

🗺 Map p. 45

✉ 506 2nd Ave.

☎ 206-624-041

💲 $$

smithtower.com

**Columbia Center Sky View Observatory**

🗺 Map p. 45

✉ 700 4th Ave.

☎ 206-386-5564

💲 $$$$–$$$$$

skyviewobservatory.com

**Klondike Gold Rush National Historical Park**

🗺 Map p. 45

✉ 319 2nd Ave. S.

☎ 206-220-4240

🕑 Closed Mon.–Tue.

nps.gov/klse

**Gallery4Culture**

✉ 101 Prefontaine Pl. S.

☎ 206-263-1589

🕑 Closed Sat.–Sun.

4culture.org

**Greg Kucera Gallery**

✉ 212 3rd Ave. S.

☎ 206-264-0770

🕑 Closed Sun.–Mon.

gregkucera.com

## Pioneer Square District

Head inland from the south end of Pier 52 and you enter the Pioneer Square District, the historic 20-square-block area where Seattle was settled in the early 1850s. Pretty much the whole town burned to the ground in 1889, but the citizens soon rebuilt, mostly using less-flammable brick, stone, and steel. Many of these grand, elaborate buildings are still standing, home to galleries, restaurants, bookstores, coffee shops, and apartments. The area also has many bars and clubs, and can get a little wild after dark.

The heart of the district is **Pioneer Square,** at the intersection of Yesler Way, James Street, and First Avenue. It is graced by a towering **Tlingit totem pole** and the sumptuous **Pioneer Building,** an 1891 Victorian beauty. For a 360-degree view of the district and far beyond, stroll a block up Yesler to Second Avenue and **Smith Tower,** a 1914-vintage skyscraper whose 42 stories made it the tallest building on the West Coast for decades. Still an active office building, Smith Tower invites you to take its old-fashioned, copper and brass elevator (still run by a human operator) up to the 35th floor observation deck. For the ultimate high, however, walk two blocks north and two east to the 76-story **Columbia Center**—fourth tallest building west of the Mississippi—for the view from the top-floor **Sky View Observatory.** In barely more than one minute you're whisked from ground level to 902 feet (275

m) elevation, where you can even look down on the Space Needle, which is 300 feet (184 m) shorter. You'll probably want to linger at the café and bar and savor the mesmerizing view over a glass of wine. Reserve online (*$$$$*), and consider paying a

---

**INSIDER TIP:**

**Baseball fans can buy a 1940-vintage San Francisco Seals replica cap with golden seal embroidered in felt at Ebbets Field Flannels.**

—LARRY PORGES
*National Geographic Travel Books editor*

---

little more to access the priority line to avoid the queue.

To reach back further in Seattle's history, go one block east down Second Avenue to Washington Street, where Second Avenue South bisects; take Second Avenue South obliquely to the right. After two blocks, at the intersection with South Jackson Street, is the **Klondike Gold Rush National Historical Park.** Contained in a single brick building, this is the Seattle unit of the larger park in Skagway, Alaska. Inside, movies, journal entries of stampeders, and ranger demonstrations tell the tale of the gold fever that sent thousands of fortune seekers from Seattle to Skagway and on to the Klondike diggings in the late 1890s.

In addition to its rich history, the Pioneer Square District is known for its eye-catching local stores. But above all, the district brims with art galleries. To see work by some rising talents, try the public **Gallery4Culture,** several blocks inland from Pioneer Square on Yesler and just a few steps down Prefontaine Place South. A couple of blocks south, on Third Avenue South just past South Washington, you can find the esteemed **Greg Kucera Gallery,** which for decades has carried a heady mix of top regional, national, and international artists, including household names like Roy Lichtenstein and David Hockney. Meanwhile, just two blocks southwest on South Jackson Street, **Seattle's National Park Store** is a great resource for finding just the right travel books, hiking guides, maps, etc. for your Alaskan adventure.

A few hundred yards down Occidental Avenue South from the Pioneer Square District you'll see **Lumen Field,** the stadium of the NFL's Seattle Seahawks and Major League Soccer's Seattle

Sounders FC. On Fridays and Saturdays, except on game days, you can take an hour-and-a-half tour ($$$) of this beautiful facility. From the skyboxes you can see a wide swath of Puget Sound and the distant Olympic Mountains. Immediately next to Lumen Field lies its baseball cousin, **T-Mobile Park,** home to Major League Baseball's Seattle Mariners. One-hour tours run two or three times daily.

## Seattle Center

The city's other hot spot within easy ambling distance of the cruise ship terminal at Pier 66 is Seattle Center, a cluster of major public attractions built on the 74-acre (30 ha) site of the 1962 World's Fair. The center houses museums, sports arenas, theater companies, gardens, the concert hall used by the Seattle Opera and Northwest Ballet, a famed fountain, a science center, IMAX theaters, a skate park, an amphitheater, and lots of open space. And, above it all, is the icon of Seattle: the Space Needle.

(continued on p. 52)

### Seattle's National Park Store

- ⊠ 164 S. Jackson St.
- ☎ 206-220-4286
- 🕑 Closed Sat.-Sun.

### Lumen Field

- 🅰 Map p. 45
- ⊠ 800 Occidental Ave. S.
- ☎ 206-381-7555
- 🕑 Call for tour times
- 💲 $$$

**lumenfield.com**

### T-Mobile Park

- 🅰 Map p. 45
- ⊠ 1250 1st Ave. S.
- ☎ 206-346-4001
- 🕑 Check website for tour times

**mlb.com/mariners/ballpark**

### Seattle Center

- 🅰 Map p. 45
- ⊠ 305 Harrison St.
- ☎ 206-684-7200

**seattlecenter.com**

## Space-Age Space Needle

It's no accident that the Space Needle has the word "space" in its name. (Originally it was called the "Space Cage," but that didn't take.) It was built at the dawn of the Space Age, from 1961 to 1962, when the first human was launched into space and the first astronaut orbited the Earth. How could the architects not make the structure's "halo" look like a flying saucer? How could the Space Needle's female attendants not dress in skintight golden "space suits" during the 1962 World's Fair? How could there not be a shadowy (and perhaps craft beer–inspired) organization called the Committee Hoping for Extra-Terrestrial Encounters to Save the Earth (C.H.E.E.S.E.), which claims to have discovered plans from the World's Fair showing that the Space Needle was built as a transmission tower to send signals to aliens in other solar systems?

# PIKE PLACE MARKET

**From its modest beginnings in 1907 as a street corner where a few farmers sold their produce, Pike Place Market has ballooned into a 9-acre (3.6 ha) alternative universe visited by more than 10 million people annually—a blend of tourists and locals coming to eat and shop and listen to musicians and chat with craftspeople and relish the view and watch the busker with his trained cats and then maybe eat again.**

The salty-mouthed fishmongers of Pike Place Fish Market have fun with flying fish.

Pike Place Market is part farmers market, part live-in community, part crafts fair, part quirky shopping center, and part eatery extravaganza, plus a hearty dash of carnival. Located just inland from Pier 59, this multilevel rabbit's warren is bounded by Virginia Street, First Avenue, Pike Street, and Western Avenue.

The classic spot from which to begin a ramble through Pike Place Market is at **Rachel the Pig.** Rachel is a full-size bronze statue that lives where Pike Street intersects Pike Place, near the big landmark clock and sign reading "Public Market Center." The slot on Rachel's back reveals that she is in fact a 550-pound (249 kg) piggy bank; every year marketgoers put thousands of dollars into Rachel, money

that helps support the hundreds of low-income seniors who live in the market, many in apartments above the retail businesses.

About 100 feet (30 m) up Pike Street from Rachel is a **Visit Seattle kiosk,** where you can get information and a map of the market. Even with a map it would take days to explore every nook and cranny, so instead channel the unruly spirit of Pike Place Market and simply start wandering. But be careful and don't get hit in the head by a flying fish; near this main entrance are the big fish stores, including **Pike Place Fish Market,** where fishmongers famously fling fish to and fro (see sidebar p. 51). If you fancy one of those flung fish, you can arrange to ship it home.

## Highstalls & Crafts

From the clock, head up the cobblestones of Pike Place, the heart of the market. Along the street and in the adjacent arcades you'll encounter the so-called highstalls: permanent stands overflowing year-round with both local and imported produce. The offerings include staples such as apples, lettuce, and cherries, as well as more exotic items like wild truffles and bee pollen. Down Pike Place around Pine and Stewart Streets, a stretch of white tents houses about 80 independent growers; this is the traditional, seasonal **farmers market,** where you can enjoy summer's bounty of tomatoes, corn, blueberries, and other fresh fruit and veggies.

## Shops & Other Attractions

Pike Place also harbors many of the more than 200 craftspeople who sell their wares in the market. By market rules, everything must be handmade. Here is a very short list of items you may come across: quilts, dog toys, Hmong needlework, silk scarves, rubbings of Northwest Coast petroglyphs, sheepskin slippers, candles, cigar-box guitars, goat-milk soap, teepees for kids, Chinese calligraphy, and cribbage boards made from naturally shed antlers.

The mind-boggling variety continues in the noncraft shops that pepper the market. You'll stumble upon businesses that sell ordinary goods (books, clothing, toys, etc.) but with an idiosyncratic twist. And you'll come upon businesses that are pretty much pure idiosyncratic twist, like the gift shop **Ugly Baby and La Ru** or **Orange Dracula 5 & 10.** The market is particularly well stocked with food shops. At **The Tasting Room Seattle** you can sample vintages from several small Washington wineries. **Mick's Peppourri** offers pepper jellies at eight different levels of heat and with all sorts of unusual flavors, like pomegranate or horseradish. Artisanal chocolate tempts visitors at **The Chocolate Market** and **indi chocolate; Totem Smokehouse** produces mouthwatering smoked fish; and **Beecher's Handmade Cheese** sells local and exotic cheeses, while

**DeLaurenti Specialty Food & Wine** has more than 200 cheeses, all sorts of cured meats, and at least 1,800 wines.

The market has delis, burger joints, clam chowder outlets, doughnut shops, and a hot dog stand. If you're in the mood for something more exotic, you can go global with Bolivian, Greek, Japanese, Tibetan, Thai, Korean, Nepalese, or other international cuisines.

Finally, there are the sights in the market that don't fit neatly into any category. The **Giant Shoe Museum** would be one. Owned and operated by the folks at the adjacent Seattle institution **Old Seattle Paperworks,** the museum is an old-school-carnival-style attrac-

## Flying Fish

**Fresh salmon, Alaskan spot prawns, Dungeness crab—Pike Place Fish Market has been selling great seafood since 1930. But in recent decades customers also come to watch the high-spirited antics of the staff, who toss fish around while bantering with customers. We're talking a 15-pound (6.8 kg) fish being hurled 30 feet (9.1 m). Not to mention the fishmongers occasionally chasing kids around with a giant octopus. The shop even has live webcams so distant fans can check and see if the fish are flying.**

tion in which you sit in front of a garish facade and look through little brass portals at, well, giant shoes. The **Gum Wall** is another thing you don't see every day—thankfully. For reasons unknown, in the early 1990s people began sticking used chewing gum on the Post Alley wall of the Market Theater. Employees scraped it off a couple of times, but each time fresh wads of gum reappeared. Now the multihued mass of gum covers an area about 15 feet (4.6 m) high and 50 feet (15.2 m) wide, although city officials have scraped it clean several times (most recently in 2017) as a health hazard.

## Seattle Monorail

🅰 Map p. 45

☎ 206-905-2620

🕐 Check website for summer hours

💲 $

**seattlemonorail.com**

## Space Needle

🅰 Map p. 45

✉ 400 Broad St.

☎ 206-905-2100

🕐 Open Mon.–Wed. noon–7 p.m., Thurs.–Fri. noon–9 p.m., Sat. 10 a.m.–10 p.m., Sun. 10 a.m.–8:30 p.m.

💲 $$$$–$$$$$

**spaceneedle.com**

## Pacific Science Center

🅰 Map p. 45

🅰 200 2nd Ave. N.

☎ 206-443-2001

💲 $$$$

**pacificsciencecenter .org**

## Chihuly Garden and Glass

🅰 Map p. 45

✉ 305 Harrison St.

☎ 206-753-4940

🕐 Open Mon.–Thurs. noon–5 p.m., Fri.–Sun. 11 a.m.– 6 p.m. (closes occasionally for events)

💲 $$$$

**chihulygarden andglass.com**

If you want to stroll the half-mile (0.8 km) from Pier 66 to Seattle Center, simply look north, lock in on the 605-foot (184 m) Space Needle, and start walking. If you prefer to travel in a style appropriate to the destination, work your way east a little over a quarter mile (0.4 km) from Pier 66 to Westlake Center, a big shopping complex at Fifth Avenue and Pine Street. Here you can board the famed **Monorail,** a remnant of the World's Fair that still carries thousands of people a day between Westlake and the station near the Space Needle.

However you reach the **Space Needle** (see sidebar p. 49), your journey there will not be complete until you get to the Observation Deck, with its all-new wall of glass at the 520-foot (158 m) level, just above the revolving Loupe lounge bar. Following a dramatic $100 million make-over in 2018, The Loupe got a glass floor. It's best (and slightly cheaper) to go online and reserve Observation Deck tickets for a particular time. From the deck you can see for miles across the city, over Puget Sound, out to the Olympic Mountains, and even southeast 60 miles (96.6 km) to Mount Rainier.

Back on terra firma the rest of Seattle Center awaits beginning, perhaps, with the **Pacific Science Center.** This six-acre (2.4 ha) complex tempts visitors with all sorts of activities, including a light show in the Laser Dome, a planetarium show, live science shows, and educational and Hollywood movies in two IMAX theaters. Insect Village has both live little six-legged

critters and giant insect robots. In Adventures in 3Dimensions, you'll see how 3-D movies are made. The Tropical Butterfly House lets you sit back in 80°F (26.7°C) warmth and watch these creatures of incandescent colors flutter about. The center even makes health fun in Professor Wellbody's Academy of Health & Wellness. At the Sneeze Wall, for example, large projected images of people sneezing are coupled with hidden water misters.

**INSIDER TIP:**

Go to the top floor of Seattle's spectacular Central Library [1000 Fourth Ave., spl.org] or take a self-guided tour via the website.

—JUSTIN KAVANAGH
*National Geographic
Travel Books editor*

**Chihuly Garden and Glass & Beyond:** Continue clockwise about 200 yards (183 m) and you will come to the dazzling, radiant, resplendent Chihuly Garden and Glass. Preeminent avant-garde glass artist Dale Chihuly turned more than an acre (0.4 ha) of Seattle Center into a garden wonderland dotted with his glass works, which appear in surprising installations amid the living plants. The centerpiece is the huge Glasshouse, a 40-foot-high (12.2 m) structure housing a 100-foot-long (30.5 m) piece of Chihuly's art that is a riot of orange, red, yellow, and amber. A theater has videos of the artist and his team at work.

About 50 feet (15 m) north sits the Seattle Center Armory. Instead of tanks and artillery, it now contains about a dozen local eateries, a performance venue with free public programs, and the **Seattle Children's Museum.** Cog City, Construction Zone, Global Village, Imagination Studio, and all the other areas are aimed at kids 10 months to 10 years. Note: Your party must have at least one child 10 or younger to gain admission.

Catercorner from the armory is the **International Fountain** (305 Harrison St., seattlecenter.com). In the middle of a 220-foot-diameter (67 m), low-slung bowl rises a 10-foot-high (3 m), 27-foot-wide (8.2 m), silvery half dome bristling with 137 water jets that shoot water up to 120 feet (36.6 m) high. The fountain is a delight for kids as it blasts water over those who dare come close.

About a quarter mile (0.4 km) southeast of the fountain sits the **Museum of Pop Culture.** Frank Gehry's scintillating design is fashioned from about 21,000 stainless steel and painted aluminum shingles, and is alive with a riot of curves and colors and folds, exuding the exuberant energy of rock 'n' roll. Inside you can peruse the Guitar Gallery's 20 vintage guitars that once belonged to iconic musical legens, ranging from Hank Williams and Muddy Waters to Eric Clapton and Howlin' Wolf's 1965 Epiphone Casino. The sci-fi part of the museum thrills fans with items such as original manuscript pages from The Hobbit. Opened in 2015, the Infinite World of Science Fiction transforms a vast gallery into the interior of an alien space ark, with goodies for sci-fi film buffs. Other galleries span tattoo culture to the indie games revolution. ∎

**Seattle Children's Museum**

🅰 Map p. 45

✉ 305 Harrison St.

☎ 206-441-1768

💲 $$ (Adults must be accompanied by a child under 11.)

**thechildrensmuseum .org**

**Museum of Pop Culture**

🅰 Map p. 45

✉ 325 5th Ave. N.

☎ 206-770-2700

🕐 Open Thurs.– Sun. 10 a.m.– 6 p.m.

**mopop.org**

## NEED TO KNOW

Ships dock at either the **Bell Street Pier Cruise Terminal**, the **Smith Cove** Cruise Terminal or the new **Terminal 46**. The first is near the north end of the downtown waterfront, the second is about 3 miles (4.8 km) farther north, and the third is at the southern end of the waterfront. All the places mentioned here are within about a mile (1.6 km) of the Bell Street Pier, and two miles (3.2 km) of Terminal 46 so for most visitors arriving there it's best to simply walk everywhere. People arriving at the Smith Cove terminal should take a taxi (about ten minutes). Taxis should be available at the dock. If not, or if you would like to rent a car, your cruise ship crew or the visitor center will be helpful.

### Seattle Highlights

You could spend half a day or longer at any of these attractions, but listed below are suggested times to help you make the most of your time in Seattle:

• Pike Place Market: 3 hours
• Museum of Pop Culture: 2 hours
• Pioneer Square District: 3 hours

Be aware that until about 2024, the Seattle downtown waterfront will be undergoing extensive upgrades. The end result should be extremely appealing, but in the meantime, check with visitor information about possible attraction closures, transportation issues, and other changes caused by the construction.

# VANCOUVER

A kind of twin-sister to Seattle, cosmopolitan Vancouver is likewise surrounded by water and framed by a dramatic backdrop of mountains glistening with snow in the winter sunshine. The downtown waterfront, where cruise ships dock, is a *Venus de Milo* compared to the gritty freighter port across the harbor. This seaport is defined by its natural and architectural beauty.

■ **The spectacular sails of the roof of Canada Place welcome cruise ship passengers to Vancouver.**

**Vancouver**

⛰ Map p. 55

**Visitor Information**

✉ Visitor Centre,
   200 Burrard St.

☎ 604-683-2000

**tourismvancouver
.com**

**TransLink
(Public Transit)**

☎ 604-953-3333

**translink.ca**

**Canada Place**

⛰ Map p. 55

✉ 999 Canada
   Place

☎ 604-665-9000

**canadaplace.ca**

The beauty begins when you enter the cruise ship terminal, a complex called **Canada Place.** Designed to resemble a sailing ship, it is topped by five towering white sails and narrows to a point jutting into the sea like a ship's prow. Canada Place also hosts a convention center, the luxurious Pan Pacific Hotel, and a perimeter promenade. Along with fine views of the harbor and the city, the promenade holds surprises such as an artwork called **"Canadian Trail"**—scores of colored, recycled-glass tiles that are right under your feet. Each tile bears the name of a Canadian community, from Toronto and Calgary to obscure towns such as Cupids and Tuktoyaktuk.

The most exciting venue at Canada Place is **FlyOver Canada,** which takes you into a dome for a simulated cross-country flight, projected on a spherical screen. Flyover will definitely get your heart racing. After attendants ensure you are strapped into your seat, the ride begins and you take off, the seat leaning and banking in sync with the simulated flight path over the Canadian countryside. Images of forests and mountains and farms and cities unreel before your eyes in a way that at times makes you feel as if you're streaking low across the landscape like a falcon chasing its prey, and other times as if you're a hawk soaring high above. At various points the realism is heightened by air blowing in your face, scents wafting past, and mist tickling your cheeks. By the end of the eight-minute ride, most people are a little weak in the knees but leave sporting a huge grin. The whole experience takes 30 minutes and opens with an audiovisual tour of Canada and a preflight briefing.

From Canada Place you have three basic choices: go southeast to Gastown and Chinatown; go southwest to downtown and Granville Island; or go northwest to enjoy the waterfront promenade and Stanley Park. All these places, except for parts of Stanley

Park, are within 1.5 miles (2.4 km) of the cruise ship terminal and make for easy walking.

## Gastown

One might suppose that the city of Vancouver was founded on the downtown waterfront, but it actually planted its roots in Gastown, the compact neighborhood of just 15 or 20 square blocks that borders the downtown waterfront to the east. To get a nice sampling

of Gastown, take Howe Street one block inland from Canada Place and then walk east two blocks on West Cordova Street to where **Water Street** angles off to the left. Only three blocks long, Water Street leads through the historic area of cobblestone streets, old-fashioned lampposts, and venerable buildings. "Eclectic" hardly begins to describe the odd assortment of businesses you'll encounter, including high-toned

### FlyOver Canada
✉ 201–999
Canada Place
☎ 855-463-4822
💲 $$$$$
**flyovercanada.com**

### Gastown
✉ Gastown Business
Improvement
Society,
318 Homer St.,
Suite 210
☎ 604-683-5650
**gastown.org**

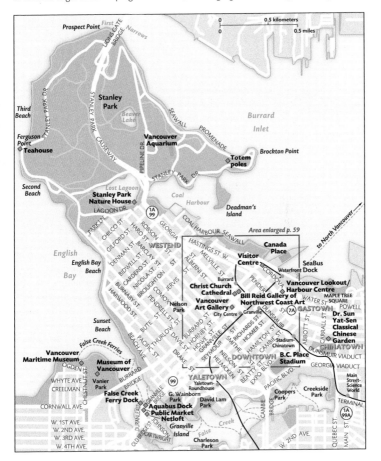

**Dr. Sun Yat-Sen Classical Chinese Garden**

🗺 Map p. 55

✉ 578 Carrall St.

☎ 604-662-3207

🕐 Open April–May, Sat.–Sun. 11 a.m.–4 p.m.; June–Aug., Fri.–Sun. 11 a.m.-4 p.m.

💲 $$$$

**vancouverchinese garden.com**

restaurants, souvenir shops, a hipster take on an old-fashioned general store, chichi clothing shops, dive bars, an ultramodern home furnishings store, sketchy clubs, a designer sneaker shop, and a nonprofit manufacturer of fine chocolate. The neighborhood fell on hard times during the Great Depression and remained downtrodden until the 1960s. But for decades Gastown has been on the upswing, and is today a gourmet ghetto and one of Vancouver's trendiest enclaves.

Begin at the Victorian-style **Steam Clock** at Water Street and Cambie Street. Erected in 1977, it whistles and blows out steam, as it's connected to pipes from a nearby generating plant. At the end of Water Street, where it intersects with Carrall Street, you'll come to **Maple Street Square.** This is where Vancouver was founded in 1867, when "Gassy Jack" Deighton opened a saloon next to the lumber mill that was

the only outpost of development in a forested wilderness. There's a bronze statue of Gassy Jack atop a whiskey barrel in the square. First named "Gastown," then "Granville," the town was renamed "Vancouver" in April 1886. Two months later Vancouver burned to the ground, with only two of some 400 buildings surviving. But the locals soon rebuilt—using less-flammable materials—and a fair number of those buildings remain today, leading to Gastown's being declared a National Historic Site in 2009. You'll see many of them near Maple Street Square and if you walk south on **Carrall Street,** the city's oldest thoroughfare.

## Chinatown

If you keep going south on Carrall a few blocks, you'll be in Chinatown, as evidenced by dragon figures on the street lamps, signs written in Chinese characters, and the traditional Chinese architecture of some of the buildings. Four blocks up Carrall from Maple Street Square puts you on the doorstep of a tranquil oasis in the big city: the **Dr. Sun Yat-Sen Classical Chinese Garden.** Opened in 1986, this was the first authentic classical Chinese garden built outside of China. The gardens of the city of Suzhou during the Ming Dynasty (1368–1644) served as the model. Scores of experts from Suzhou came to Vancouver during construction to ensure the design, materials, techniques, and even the tools used conformed to classical standards. You can look at the displays in the interior halls or sit in the

## The Colorful 'Ksan Mural

A surprise awaits you in the lobby of the Royal Bank of Canada on the corner of West Georgia and Burrard Streets (see map p. 59; 1025 W. Georgia St., tel 604-665-6991). Go up the steps to the mezzanine level and behold the 'Ksan Mural, a 120-foot-long (36.6 m), 8-foot-high (2.4 m) frieze carved from western red cedar and painted by hand. Created in 1972 by five master carvers of Northwest Coast First Nations heritage, this boldly colored work depicts the exploits of Weget, the Man-Raven. Before you walk along the mural get the brochure explaining the figures and events shown on the panels.

■ Dr. Sun Yat-Sen Classical Chinese Garden: Suzhou recreated in Vancouver

**Pendulum
Gallery**

🅰 Map p. 59

✉ 885 W. Georgia
St. (HSBC Bank
Building)

☎ 604-250-9682

🕐 Closed Sun.

**pendulumgallery
.bc.ca**

garden and enjoy the purposeful blend of trees, pond, koi, swooping tiled roofs, and manicured landscape. Or you can pick up the brochure and take the self-guided walk. Better yet, join one of the six or seven 45-minute guided tours given daily (included with the price of admission) and learn the meaning of the bamboo, limestone rocks (imported from near Suzhou), and jade-colored water of the pond.

## Downtown

Downtown starts immediately inland from Canada Place, occupying about one square mile (2.6 sq km). It's full of office towers and government buildings, but also offers plenty of fine eating, shopping, and sightseeing for travelers. Amid the utilitarian glass skyscrapers you'll discover many attractive and historic edifices, such as the **Marine Building,** just a couple of blocks up Burrard Street from Canada Place. This 321-foot (97.8 m) art deco beauty was the tallest building in the British Empire when it opened in 1930. The exterior, especially around the elaborate entrance, is a tidal wave of fanciful decoration populated by lobsters, sea stars, sea horses, crabs, and other creatures, in keeping with the building's marine theme—not to mention the train, biplanes, and a zeppelin. This wondrous excess continues in the lobby with extravagant elevators (check out the 12 kinds of hardwood inlaid in the elevators' interior walls), a huge clock with marine animals instead of numbers, and many other elaborations.

Downtown also harbors several cultural gems, such as the **Pendulum Gallery,** four blocks up Burrard from the Marine Building and a block and a half southeast on West Georgia Street. This public gallery in the HSBC Bank building features ever changing exhibits of challenging works shown in a resplendent seven-story atrium whose glass walls bathe the space in natural light. Overhead swings the colossal kinetic sculpture aptly titled *(continued on p. 60)*

# WALK: DOWNTOWN VANCOUVER

**Downtown Vancouver is a bustling commercial hub, its skyscraping office towers packed with banks, investment firms, government offices, and trading companies. But amid all that enterprise are many sites of interest to travelers, starting with the architectural beauty of some of those buildings, both new and historic.**

The downtown mix also includes inviting pocket parks, grand hotels, restaurants by the score, shops by the hundreds, and several major attractions.

Start on the waterfront at Canada Place (site of the cruise ship terminal) and head up Burrard Street. At that first corner you can duck into the **Tourism Vancouver Visitor Centre** ❶ for some information about the city. Walk another couple of blocks and you'll come to the corner of West Pender Street, where you'll find **"Public Service/Private Step"** ❷, one of the multitude of public artworks that graces Vancouver. This is sited in front of the 19-story Environment Canada and Oceans & Fisheries Building (hence the "public service" in the title). Artist Alan Storey created a 60-foot-tall (18.3 m) representation of the building's elevator core. Electronically interfacing with the actual building's actual elevators, the artwork features five little elevator cars that go up and down the towering steel columns at the same time and for the same proportional distance as the real elevators operating in the government building.

Continue on Burrard Street another block and a half to a lovely park where you can sit on a bench next to the waterfall wall. Just past the park rise the dark stone walls of **Christ Church Cathedral** ❸ *(690 Burrard St., tel 604-682-3848, cathedral.vancouver.bc.ca)*. Built in the Gothic style in 1895, this Canadian Anglican Church welcomes visitors at appropriate times, usually 10 a.m. to 4 p.m. When it's open to the public, the church puts a sign outside near the entrance at the corner of Burrard and West Georgia Streets. The soaring interior features a stunning ceiling of cedar planking and beams, and the floor is made of old-growth Douglas fir—a true Northwest edifice. The cathedral

**NOT TO BE MISSED:**

Christ Church Cathedral • Vancouver Art Gallery • Bill Reid Gallery of Northwest Coast Art • Vancouver Lookout

is famed for its stained-glass windows, many of them impressively intricate, some of them more than 100 years old. A brochure maps out their locations and explains some of the symbolism and meaning in these works of art. On the corner of West Georgia and Burrard Streets, in the Royal Bank of Canada, you'll find the **'Ksan Mural** ❹ (see sidebar p. 56; *1025 W. Georgia St., tel 604-665-6991*).

Continue two blocks on Burrard Street to Robson Street and turn left—that is, if you can resist turning right and wallowing in the storied Robson Street shopping district. Proceed one block on Robson to Hornby Street and you'll come to the **Vancouver Art Gallery** ❺ *(750 Hornby St., tel 604-662-4700, $$$$, vanartgallery. bc.ca)*—despite the "gallery" in its name, this is actually the city's public art museum. Housed for now in a historic courthouse, the gallery is slated to move to new quarters a few blocks away by 2024. This excellent museum displays internationally renowned artists and traveling shows, as well as showcasing local and regional artists, such as Emily Carr, a British Columbia painter known for her wavy watercolors.

From the art gallery head back toward the waterfront along Hornby Street, which borders the northwest side of the gallery. On the next block you'll come to the **Bill Reid Gallery of Northwest Coast Art** ❻ *(639 Hornby St., tel*

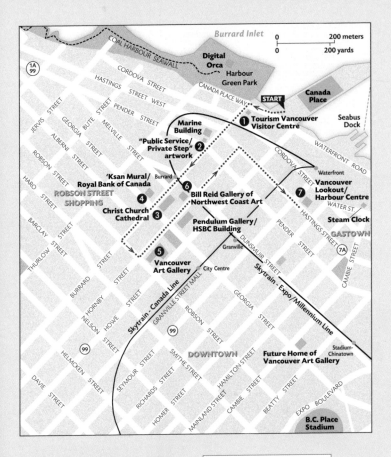

604-682-3455, $$, billreidgallery.ca), another "gallery" that is more of a museum. Of Haida ancestry, Reid (1920–1998) was not only one of Canada's most acclaimed artists but a writer and spokesman who led the revival of Northwest Coast First Nations art. A master goldsmith, carver, sculptor, and jeweler, Reid created hundreds of works, many on display here alongside works of other Northwest Coast First Nations artists.

Proceed two blocks down Hornby to West Hastings and go right three blocks to the **Harbour Centre** 7, a massive complex that includes a shopping mall, offices, and a university campus. Atop the building in a

| 🅰 | Also see area map p. 55 |
| ▶ | Canada Place |
| 🕐 | 2 hours with stops |
| ↔ | 1 mile (1.6 km) |
| ▶ | Vancouver Lookout |

flying saucer–shaped structure perches the **Vancouver Lookout** (555 W. Hastings St., tel 604-689-0421, open daily 9 a.m.–9 p.m., $$$$, vancouverlookout.com), a 553-foot-high (168.6 m) observation deck with 360-degree views that you can reach via a dizzying exterior glass-paneled elevator. Above the deck, a revolving restaurant is a perfect venue to end your day.

## Granville Island

🗺 Map p. 55

☎ 604-666-6655

**granvilleisland.com**

## Aquabus

☎ 604-689-5858

🕓 See website for schedules

💲 $–$$

**theaquabus.com**

## False Creek Ferries

☎ 604-684-7781

🕓 See website for schedules

💲 $–$$

**granvilleisland ferries.bc.ca**

"Pendulum." (For more sites down-town, see pp. 58–59.)

To reach Granville Island, con-tinue another mile or so (1.6 km) southwest from downtown until you dead-end on **False Creek,** a narrow inlet of English Bay that stretches about 4 miles (6.4 km) east through the heart of Vancouver. Once a polluted eyesore, False Creek has been transformed over the last few decades into a sparkling waterway alive with sailboats, cabin cruisers, kayaks, and yachts—and the busy little ferries that will get you to the island.

### Granville Island

Two competing local outfits, **Aqua-bus** and **False Creek Ferries,** operate

Granville Island: An industrial wasteland reimagined

small ferries that connect points along the length of three-mile (4.8 km) False Creek. The rainbow-hued Aquabus boats depart from a small dock at the foot of Hornby Street, and the blue and white False Creek Ferries boats leave from a dock at the foot of Thurlow Street. No need

to consult a schedule; boats show up every 5 to 15 minutes. Both companies also offer 25-minute tours of False Creek that motor past the inlet's wealth of pretty creekside communities, marinas, and parks. You can buy an all-day hop-on/hop-off pass that lets you explore the many sights, including the shops and cafés of Yaletown, Science World, the Edgewater Casino, and a number of popular shoreside pubs.

Granville Island is a peninsula; a narrow strip of land on the south side connects to the main-land. But everyone calls it an island, perhaps because it feels like a place apart. In the mid-20th century Granville Island was an industrial wasteland, littered with decrepit factories and burnt-out warehouses—earlier its official name had been Industrial Island. But in the 1970s the Canadian government initiated an urban renewal project that made a silk purse out of this sow's ear. Today Granville Island's 37 acres (15 ha) of shops, theaters, parks, restaurants, brewpubs, and galler-ies attract more than 10 million visitors a year.

The **Public Market** anchors the island and food anchors the public market. Scores of vendors tempt the throngs of shoppers with mouthwatering displays of cherries, fresh salmon fillets, corn, apples, exotic herbs and spices, racks of lamb, blueberries, aromatic fresh breads, and a cornucopia of provisions. If you are hungry and looking for prepared food, there are dozens of options, including gelato, wine, fish and chips, fudge, homemade cheeses, sausages, smoked salmon, and some long cases stacked with alluring pastries. Elsewhere in this sprawling indoor maze you'll come across local craftspeople selling jewelry, stained glass, hats, and homemade soaps.

Beyond the Public Market you'll find even more shopping opportunities. More than 100 shops occupy the island, all of them local and unique—no chain stores are allowed. Most are clustered in two areas: the **Netloft** and the four buildings of the **Maritime Market,** immediately southwest of the Public Market, and the **Railspur District,** a couple of blocks southeast of the Public Market. When you're done shopping, maybe take a brewery tour at **Granville Island Brewing** (*tel 604-687-2739, gib.ca/en-CA*) and check out the **"The Chain & Forge" murals,** under the Granville Street Bridge, and the six **"Giants,"** concrete silos by Brazilian graffiti artists OSGEMEOS.

## Stanley Park

Having gone southeast and southwest from Canada Place, it's time to go northwest, strolling along the waterfront promenade to Stanley Park. But don't think of the promenade as merely a path to the park; it's an inviting destination all its own. Most of the broad promenade is divided into two lanes, one for cyclists and in-line skaters and one for pedestrians and runners.

Officially known as the **Coal Harbour Seawall,** this 1.4-mile (2.3 km) paved pathway provides one of the prettiest urban walks anywhere. You can look across the waters of Coal Harbour and Burrard Inlet at Vancouver's commercial port (the busiest seaport in Canada), North Vancouver, and the snowy mountains beyond. Freighters, fishing boats, oil tankers, tugboats, and sailboats crisscross the water, along with the odd yacht. On shore you'll pass restaurants, galleries, waterfront condos, fountains, marinas, public art, and a floatplane dock from which you can take off on a flightseeing tour. Next to the seaplane center,

### SeaBus: A Ride With a View

Riding public transportation just for the fun of it ranks pretty low on most travelers' wish lists, but for Vancouver's SeaBus, make an exception. A five-minute stroll east from Canada Place lands you at the SeaBus dock, from which double-ended catamarans run every 15 minutes and every 30 minutes at nonpeak times and on Sundays. These busy ferries carry up to 400 passengers back and forth between downtown and Vancouver's North Shore. The scenic cruise across Burrard Inlet takes only 12 minutes, and you can catch the same ferry back minutes after arriving at the North Shore, all for just a few dollars.

**SeaBus**

- Map p. 55
- 601 W. Cordova St.
- 604-953-3333
- $–$$

**translink.ca**

A fall run along the Stanley Park Seawall offers fiery flora, marina views, and spectacular cityscapes.

## Vancouver Aquarium

Map p. 55

845 Avison Way

604-659-3474

$$$$$

**vanaqua.org**

Douglas Coupland's breaching **"Digital Orca"** looks like it's leaping out of a video game.

When you've walked to the end of the Coal Harbour Seawall, you'll be at the West Georgia Street entrance to Stanley Park, at 1,000 acres (405 ha) the largest city park in Canada. Set on a peninsula reaching into Burrard Inlet, the park encompasses the wild and the civilized. Nearer the central city are a swimming pool, playgrounds, a cricket pavilion, a rose garden, tennis courts, a short golf course, a miniature railway, and an aquarium. The bulk of the park, stretching to the north, is forest. It includes sizeable tracts of old growth, largely undeveloped except for some hiking and mountain-biking trails.

A great way to explore is by bicycle: You can rent bikes near the park entrance, close to Canada Place. Clinging tightly to the shore, the one-way (counterclockwise) perimeter path is also open to pedestrians and runs 5.5 miles (8.9 km) along the seawall plus 1.1 miles (1.8 km) on another path to return to the West Georgia starting point. You'll start out along the north shore of Coal Harbour, passing sites like the historic Tudor-style clubhouse of the Vancouver Rowing Club and the small naval station on Deadman's Island, named for its role as a First Nations burial ground and later as a pioneer cemetery. After about 1.3 miles (2.1 km) you reach **Brockton Point,** where there's a lighthouse, a locally famous bronze statue titled "Girl in a Wetsuit" perched on an offshore rock, and spectacular views of Burrard Inlet and the city. A few hundred yards farther, just inland from the path, a number of handsome totem poles rise in a forest clearing, replicas of some 1920s poles carved by a First Nations band on Vancouver Island.

### Vancouver Aquarium:

Just another few hundred yards takes you to the turnoff for the hugely popular Vancouver Aquarium. The main building has galleries devoted to native British Columbia marine life as well as halls displaying tropical denizens. Outside tanks are home to popular attractions, including dolphins, penguins, and beluga whales.

## Prospect Point & Around:

Back on the seawall, pedal a mile (1.6 km) to Prospect Point, the northernmost tip of the park and peninsula, where the Lions Gate Bridge arches overhead, spanning Burrard Inlet to North Vancouver. From there the path angles southwest along a largely rugged coastline for a mile (1.6 km) to **Third Beach,** where the rocky shore softens into a sandy beach. Just inland from the southern end of Third Beach, at **Ferguson Point,** you can revive your weary legs and enjoy grand views at the **Teahouse** restaurant.

From Ferguson Point, a half-mile (0.8 km) ride will take you back to civilization at **Second Beach,** with its pool, playground, and tennis courts. But you can enjoy one final oasis of wildness when you turn off the seawall and cut east back to the loop's starting point. Immediately beyond the Second Beach pool there's a

concession stand where you can find refreshments; here, the seawall path branches right toward the bay. Instead, keep straight, due east, to cross Stanley Park Drive; follow the creek on your right, which after 100 yards (96 m) opens alongside a 40-acre (16.2 ha) body of water—Lost Lagoon. The path continues clockwise around the lake.

**Lost Lagoon:** Lost Lagoon used to be part of Coal Harbour, but it got cut off from the sea when the Stanley Park road was built. Over time it transformed from saltwater to freshwater, and now it supports a freshwater wetland ecosystem. Willows and bulrushes line the shore and yellow lilies brighten the shallows. The lagoon is a noted bird sanctuary, with geese, ducks, great blue herons, and many songbirds. At the southeast end of the lagoon you can learn about the local ecology at the **Stanley Park Nature House.** Just past the Nature House is the West Georgia Street entrance, where the loop began. ∎

### Teahouse
- Map p. 55
- 7501 Stanley Park Dr.
- 604-669-3281

**vancouverdine.com /teahouse**

### Stanley Park Nature House
- Map p. 55
- 604-257-8544 or 604-257-8544 (ext. 102)
- Sept.–June: weekends only 10 a.m.–4 p.m. July–Aug.: Tues.–Sun. 10 a.m.–5 p.m.

**stanleyparkecology .ca/education /nature-house**

## NEED TO KNOW

The cruise ship terminal is part of Canada Place, the complex on the downtown waterfront. All the sites mentioned in this section are within 1.5 miles (2.4 km) of the terminal and easy to walk to, with the exception of the farther reaches of Stanley Park. Vancouver has excellent public transit; look on the Translink website to find out about bus schedules, Sea-Bus fares, bicycle routes, etc. The website also shows mobile phone apps you can use for transit information. And of course you can always hail a cab.

### Vancouver Highlights

You could spend half a day or longer at these attractions, but here are suggested times:
- Stanley Park: 4 hours
- Granville Island: 2 hours
- Vancouver Art Gallery: 2 hours

Vancouver is one of the most bicycle-friendly cities in North America, with many bike paths, including some on major streets separated from vehicle traffic by barriers. Many hotels provide bikes for guests' use. Several city center outfits rent bikes, including some near Canada Place.

A remote realm of islands, forests, fjords, mountains, and wildlife,
but also of appealing towns and a rich human history

# SOUTHEAST ALASKA

■ Above: The bald eagle, ubiquitous
along Alaska's southern coastlines
Opposite: Glacier Bay National Park

# SOUTHEAST ALASKA

**Alaska's panhandle, Southeast Alaska, consists of a narrow strip of mainland and hundreds of islands bounded by British Columbia and the Coast Mountains to the east and the Pacific Ocean to the west. Only three towns—Skagway, Haines, and Hyder—connect to the rest of Alaska by road, and to reach them motorists must drive hundreds of miles through remote regions of Canada. Coastal cruisers, on the other hand, have easy access to these ports of call.**

WRANGELL-ST. ELIAS
NATIONAL PARK
AND PRESERVE    RUSSELL
FIORD
WILDERNESS
Yakutat
Bay    Russell
Fiord
Yakutat

ALASKA MARINE HIGHWAY
BABAZON RANGE
ALASKA RANGE
Dry
Bay
Mount
Fairweather
15,299 ft
Tarr
Inlet
FAIRWEATHER RA.
Tatshenshi
Tatshen
Masel

Gulf of Alaska

The rest of the southeast is only accessible by air or water, but the plane service is decent and the opportunities to travel by ship are legendary. This is the home of the fabled Inside Passage: the route through protected waters that slaloms among islands almost the whole length of the southeast. Every year hundreds of thousands of visitors and locals board cruise ships and ferries to traverse all or part of this wildly scenic waterway.

Mountains, some rising thousands of feet out of the sea, seem to tower everywhere. Ship passengers may be able to sneak a quick hike partway up one of these peaks, but the easiest way to sample the subalpine meadows and alpine tundra of the high country is to take the tramway from the waterfront in Juneau up the flank of Mount Roberts. Helicopter and bush plane tours out of southeastern towns, such as Ketchikan, Haines, Juneau, Skagway, and Sitka, present another way to reach the pinnacles.

This cool, wet region is covered by temperate rain forest, designated as Tongass National Forest (the nation's largest at 17 million acres/ 6.9 million ha). Many areas receive more than 100 inches (2.5 m) of precipitation a year, some receive more than 150 inches (3.8 m), and at least one place—Little Port Walter—receives approximately 225 inches (5.7 m) annually, making it the wettest place in the U.S. outside Hawaii. Needless to say, bring rain gear; it rains fairly often even during the cruising season.

Shrouded in mist, the lush forest of spruce and hemlock teems with life—grizzly bears, black bears, mountain goats, wolves, deer, and eagles all thrive here. The Inside Passage waters also harbor abundant wildlife, including humpback whales, sea lions, porpoises, orcas, and sea otters. Passengers can sometimes spot these and other critters from the ship; often a crew member will announce sightings over the loudspeaker. Excursions from almost all the ports will take you to view both marine and terrestrial animals, especially bears and whales. Several adventure cruise operators specialize in nature experiences using small vessels and expert guides.

Though it is home to only about 70,000 residents, the southeast offers many civilized

---

**NOT TO BE MISSED:**

**The boat/plane tour of Misty Fjords National Monument**  72–73

**Viewing humpback whales feeding in Frederick Sound**  77

**Exploring Southeast Alaska's indigenous cultures at Sealaska Heritage Institute**  86

**Watching the glaciers calve at Glacier Bay National Park**  96–97

**Riding the historic White Pass & Yukon train through the mountains above Skagway**  100–101

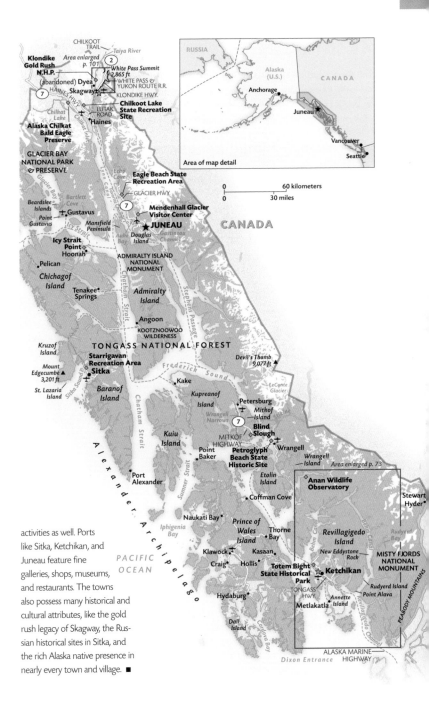

CHILKOOT TRAIL
*Taiya River*
Klondike Gold Rush N.H.P.
Area enlarged p. 101
White Pass Summit 2,865 ft
WHITE PASS & YUKON ROUTE R.R.
(abandoned) Dyea
Skagway
KLONDIKE HWY.
HAINES HWY
Chilkoot Lake State Recreation Site
*Chilkat Lake*
Haines
LUTAK ROAD
Alaska Chilkat Bald Eagle Preserve
GLACIER BAY NATIONAL PARK & PRESERVE
*Glacier Bay*
*Echo Cove*
Eagle Beach State Recreation Area
GLACIER HWY.
Beardslee Islands
*Bartlett Cove*
Gustavus
Point Gustavus
Mansfield Peninsula
Mendenhall Glacier Visitor Center
JUNEAU
*Icy Strait*
Icy Strait Point
Hoonah
Douglas Island
*Auke Bay*
*Gastineau Channel*
Pelican
Chichagof Island
Tenakee Springs
ADMIRALTY ISLAND NATIONAL MONUMENT
Admiralty Island
*Chatham Strait*
Angoon
KOOTZNOOWOO WILDERNESS
*Stephens Passage*
Kruzof Island
Mount Edgecumbe ▲ 3,201 ft
St. Lazaria Island
Starrigavan Recreation Area
Sitka
TONGASS NATIONAL FOREST
*Sitka Sound*
Devil's Thumb 9,077 ft ▲
*Frederick Sound*
LeConte Glacier
Baranof Island
Kake
Kupreanof Island
Petersburg
Mithof Island
*Wrangell Narrows*
*Stikine R.*
Blind Slough
MITKOF HIGHWAY
Wrangell
Kuiu Island
Point Baker
Petroglyph Beach State Historic Site
Wrangell Island
Area enlarged p. 73
Port Alexander
*Summer Strait*
Etolin Island
Anan Wildlife Observatory
Stewart
Hyder
Coffman Cove
*Behm Canal*
Naukati Bay
Prince of Wales Island
Thorne Bay
Revillagigedo Island
*Rudyerd Bay*
*Iphigenia Bay*
Klawock
Kasaan
New Eddystone Rock
MISTY FJORDS NATIONAL MONUMENT
Craig
Hollis
Totem Bight State Historical Park
Ketchikan
Rudyerd Island
Point Alava
Hydaburg
TONGASS HWY.
Annette Island
Metlakatla
PEABODY MOUNTAINS
Dall Island
*Cordova Bay*
ALASKA MARINE HIGHWAY
*Dixon Entrance*
A l e x a n d e r   A r c h i p e l a g o
PACIFIC OCEAN
CANADA

**Inset map:**
RUSSIA
Alaska (U.S.)
CANADA
Anchorage
Juneau ★
Vancouver
Seattle
Area of map detail

0   60 kilometers
0   30 miles

activities as well. Ports like Sitka, Ketchikan, and Juneau feature fine galleries, shops, museums, and restaurants. The towns also possess many historical and cultural attributes, like the gold rush legacy of Skagway, the Russian historical sites in Sitka, and the rich Alaska native presence in nearly every town and village. ∎

# KETCHIKAN

This town of just over 8,000 is the first stop for most northbound cruise ships heading up the Inside Passage. Drizzle often greets you on arrival at this famously soggy place, where an average of about 160 inches (406 cm) of rain falls every year. But fear not: Ketchikan offers many natural and civilized attractions that more than compensate for the weather.

■ Waterfront diners relish a sunny day in Ketchikan.

**Ketchikan**

⌖ Map p. 67

**Visitor Information**

✉ Ketchikan
Visitors Bureau,
131 Front St.

☎ 907-225-6166
or
800-770-3300

**visit-ketchikan.com**

Many people come here to chase salmon and halibut—Ketchikan bills itself as the "Salmon Capital of the World." The abundance of salmon and timber led to the founding of the town in the 1880s. By the 1930s more than a dozen canneries produced 1.5 million cases of salmon annually. While those numbers have declined, the industry remains a mainstay, as seen by the multitude of fishing boats in the harbor. Even as commercial fishing and canning have decreased, sportfishing has grown into a big business.

## The Waterfront

Start your visit at the **Welcome Arch,** where Mission Street deadends against the **waterfront promenade.** Beyond the arch lies the compact downtown, which can be explored in two or three hours. Or turn south on the promenade and sample the shops and eateries lining Front Street.

For a small town, Ketchikan has a large number of galleries, most of which feature local Alaska native art. Many Tlingit, Haida, and Tsimshian artists, both traditional and contemporary, work in Ketchikan. Keep an eye open for totem poles fashioned by world-renowned master carver Nathan Jackson and other local carvers.

---

INSIDER TIP:

Cruisers can take a short charter fishing trip and ship their catch home.

—TOM O'NEILL
National Geographic
magazine writer

---

After a few blocks the promenade makes an abrupt turn when it bumps into the mouth of the **Thomas Basin Boat Harbor.** Packed with commercial fishing boats, sportfishing boats, and pleasure craft, this is the hub for those heading out to fish, kayak, or sightsee. Just a block or so after making the turn, the promenade passes the site of the **Great Alaskan Lumberjack Show.** Part show, part contest, these programs feature highly skilled individuals competing against each other in such events as sawing, chopping, logrolling, and the astounding speed climb, when contestants ascend very tall poles with monkey-like quickness.

A few steps inland from the lumberjack show is the **Southeast Alaska Discovery Center,** a facility that wears several hats; it's part Alaska Public Lands Information Center, part center for the Tongass National Forest, and part museum. Here you'll find plenty of fine Alaska native art on display. The lobby features three sumptuous totem poles: one Tlingit style, one Haida, and one Tsimshian. The center presents other aspects of native life, too; one exhibit re-creates a traditional fish camp, and another lets you listen to recordings of native elders discussing traditional ways of life. Much of the center delves into the natural world and the use of natural resources. Interactive exhibits detail the seven major ecosystems in southeast Alaska, from tide pools to alpine tundra.

## Along Ketchikan Creek

Continue on the promenade beside the boat harbor and you'll run into Stedman Street, where the pathway takes a 90-degree turn. In about a minute you'll be crossing the mouth of **Ketchikan Creek** on the **Stedman Street Bridge.** Look down. At various times during spring, summer, and fall, salmon head up the creek to spawn, and the bridge provides an excellent vantage point from which to watch them gathering to funnel into the creek.

Cross the bridge and take a quick left up **Creek Street,** which is both the name of the street and the name for this former red-light district. As the locals like to say, Creek Street was where "both fish

---

**Great Alaskan Lumberjack Show**

✉ 420 Spruce Mill Way
☎ 907-225-9050 or 888-320-9049
🕐 Closed Oct.–April
💲 $$$$$

**alaskanlumberjack show.com**

**Southeast Alaska Discovery Center**

✉ 50 Main St.
☎ 907-228-6220
🕐 Closed Sat.–Thurs., Oct.–April
💲 $ May–Sept. Free rest of year

**alaskacenters.gov /visitors-centers/ ketchikan**

Lush vegetation along the trail to Punchbowl Cove in Misty Fjords bears testament to the area's rainfall.

### Totem Heritage Center

- 601 Deermount St.
- 907-225-5900
- Closed Mon.; Sat.–Sun. Oct.–April
- $ May–Sept. Free rest of year

**ktn-ak.us/totem-heritage-center**

### Saxman Totem Park

- Killer Whale Ave. & Totem Way
- $ for unguided entry May–Sept. Free rest of year. Tickets available at village store.

and fishermen went upstream to spawn." Dozens of bordellos lined the creek during the half century from 1903, when the city council forced all houses of ill repute to relocate from downtown to the far side of the creek, until 1953, when prostitution was outlawed.

Today Creek Street is a boardwalk lined by galleries, cafés, shops, and residences that mostly occupy the district's original buildings, many of which are built on pilings and hang over the creek. Near the start of the winding boardwalk sits the historic **Star Building,** once a dance hall and now home to two notable galleries: **Alaska Eagle Arts** (*www.alaskaeaglearts.com*) and Soho Coho, owned by the internationally renowned artist Ray Troll (see sidebar p. 39).

Just past the Star Building you can glimpse the district's bawdy history near the start of Creek

Street at **Dolly's House** (*24 Creek St., tel 907-225-6329*), formerly the bordello run by Ketchikan's most famous madam, Dolly Arthur. Visitors can tour the garishly decorated house, which has been kept much as Dolly left it, complete with antique furnishings. Another five minutes of strolling brings you to a footbridge. Beyond and just to the right lies the **Tongass Historical Museum** (*60 Dock St., tel 907-225-5900*) and public library. Exhibits take visitors from the town's early incarnation as a Tlingit fish camp to the present.

Back across the footbridge and a few minutes up the Creek Street boardwalk is the **Salmon Ladder.** Salmon fighting to reach spawning grounds farther upstream get a human assist here in the form of water flowing down concrete steps. Just past the ladder Creek Street dead-ends at Park Avenue, where you can turn left to cross a bridge into downtown. Or turn right and walk about ten minutes to the **Totem Heritage Center,** recognizable by the beautiful contemporary totem poles outside, a Nathan Jackson creation called "Raven-Fog Woman," and a second pole called "Honoring Those Who Give," commemorating those who make the center possible.

Is Ketchikan the Totem Pole Capital of the World? It's certainly a legitimate claim, given that more than 80 poles grace the town and surrounds. Inside the heritage center are more than 30 poles, about half on permanent display. These are original, unrestored works that were rescued from abandoned

## Shame Totem Poles

Visitors to Saxman Totem Park may notice a plain-shafted pole topped by the figure of former Secretary of State William H. Seward—the man who acquired Alaska for the U.S. This is a replica of a "ridicule" pole, thought to have been carved after Seward visited a Tlingit village in 1869 and didn't reciprocate the villagers' gifts and hospitality. Also known as "shame" poles, they were considered a thing of the past, until a new one made news a few years ago. Created by Tlingit artist Stephen Jackson, this third iteration of the "Seward Pole" was dedicated in April 2017 after a second pole, erected in the 1930s as a Works Progress Administration project, succumbed to weather and termites. Jackson followed a long tradition of caricature in Northwest Coast depictions by carving Seward with bulging eyes, avaricious for the goods he was given (represented by a box upon which he sits), while his red ears depict his shame at not reciprocating the 1869 potlach—a failure to honor Chief Ebbits of the Taant'a kwáan, as tradition demanded. Although Seward was unaware of the tradition at the time of his visit, once informed he never fulfilled his obligation. The insult cannot be forgiven until a reciprocal potlatch for tribal elders is held.

Tlingit and Haida villages. The center also exhibits other historic and modern carvings, beadwork, and basketweaving. Sometimes visitors can watch Alaska native artists at work on new pieces.

### Tongass Highway

A short taxi ride about 2.5 miles (4 km) south on the shore-hugging South Tongass Highway and one block left on Totem Row lands you in **Saxman Totem Park,** the site of one of the world's largest collections of standing poles. You can wander on your own or take a guided **Saxman Native Village** tour (*Cape Fox Tours, 2711 Killer Whale Ave., tel 907-225-4421, $$$$$, capefoxtours.com*), which offers a visit to a tribal house and a traditional dance performance. About 10 miles (16 km) north of Ketchikan on the North Tongass Highway, at **Totem Bight State Historical Park,** a short trail through a seaside forest takes you

to 14 totem poles and a replica clan house.

Visitors wishing to explore the forest that embraces Ketchikan can go 8 miles (13 km) down the South Tongass Highway and left on Wood Road to the **Alaska Rainforest Sanctuary.** Here guided tours include lush rain forest, a salmon spawning stream, an historic sawmill, the working studio of master carvers, a Raptor Center where you can see eye-to-eye with bald eagles, and zip lines to whisk you through the treetops. ■

### Totem Bight State Historical Park

- ✉ 9883 N. Tongass Hwy.
- ☎ 907-247-8574
- 💲 $ May–Sept. Free rest of year

dnr.alaska.gov/parks

### Alaska Rainforest Sanctuary

- ✉ 116 Wood Rd.
- ☎ 907-225-8400
- 🕐 Closed Oct.–April
- 💲 $$$$$

alaskarainforest.com

### NEED TO KNOW

**Port Logistics: Ketchikan**
Most cruise ships dock on the downtown waterfront, so you can walk to the center and nearby attractions in half a day. The Tongass Highway is minutes away by taxi; a boat or plane tour of Misty Fjords will take 3–5 hours (see pp. 72–73).

# BOAT RIDE: CRUISING THROUGH MISTY FJORDS

**Misty Fjords National Monument is as striking and mysterious as its name suggests. A vista of waterfalls, eagles, volcanic plugs, rugged mountains, and lush rain forest unfolds as your boat delves deep into the monument's 2.3 million acres (0.9 million ha). You'll likely see bears and salmon and perhaps humpback whales, deer, and otters. Some travelers take round-trip boat excursions, while others cruise one way and fly back on a floatplane.**

Many outfits offer trips to Misty Fjords, and they take a number of somewhat different routes; the one presented here is representative. After weighing anchor in Ketchikan, your boat heads east down Tongass Narrows and out into Revillagigedo Channel. For about 6 miles (9.7 km) you'll pass by the forested northern coast of **Annette Island ❶**, home to Alaska's lone Native American reservation, on the starboard side (your right, as you face the front of the boat). About 1,300 Tsimshian and a smattering of non-Tsimshian people live on the island. Led by a Church of England missionary, a group of Tsimshian left their British Columbian homeland in the late 1800s and settled on this remote island.

Just past Annette Island the boat turns north into the monument via **Behm Canal ❷**. The canal is a nearly straight, 100-mile-long (160 km) natural waterway, framed at this end by low mountains and curtains of hemlock, spruce, and cedar. Scan the tall trees along the shore for bald eagles and their nests and survey the water for Dall porpoises, sea lions, and killer whales.

After about another 8 miles (13 km), the boat steers for the western shore and squeezes through the narrows between Revillagigedo and little **Rudyerd Island ❸**. Back in the 1920s, someone established a fox farm here—a common enterprise in Alaska at that time, when fox furs were popular. Abundant fish made feeding the foxes easy. The Great Depression brought these enterprises to an end. However, their remote locations appealed to bootleggers, who

**NOT TO BE MISSED:**

New Eddystone Rock • Punchbowl Cove • Rudyerd Bay waterfalls • Nooya Creek wildlife

during Prohibition smuggled liquor into the U.S. from Canada via some of these former fox farms. About 15 miles (24 km) up Behm Canal from Rudyerd Island, **New Eddystone Rock ❹** juts 237 feet (72 m) over the water. A six-million-year-old volcanic plug, it is the remains of an eroded volcano. The rock was named in 1793 by Capt. George Vancouver—on his four-year-plus voyage of exploration—for its resemblance to the lighthouse on Eddystone Rock in the English Channel.

## Into Rudyerd Bay

A couple of miles north, the tour turns east into **Rudyerd Bay ❺**. Waterfalls pour off burly granite cliffs, which shoulder in close around this half-mile-wide (0.8 km) waterway. A few miles farther, the boat stops in **Punchbowl Cove ❻**, facing a sheer, 3,000-foot (914 m) cliff. Nearby is a pictograph (rock carving) thought to mark the grave of a Tlingit shaman. Several miles deeper into the fjord, **Nooya Creek ❼** tumbles into the bay. Look for bears, seals, and eagles—and salmon from mid-July through September. From here in Rudyerd Bay, many boat passengers opt to catch a 30-minute floatplane flight back to Ketchikan, which provides a whole new perspective of Misty Fjords.

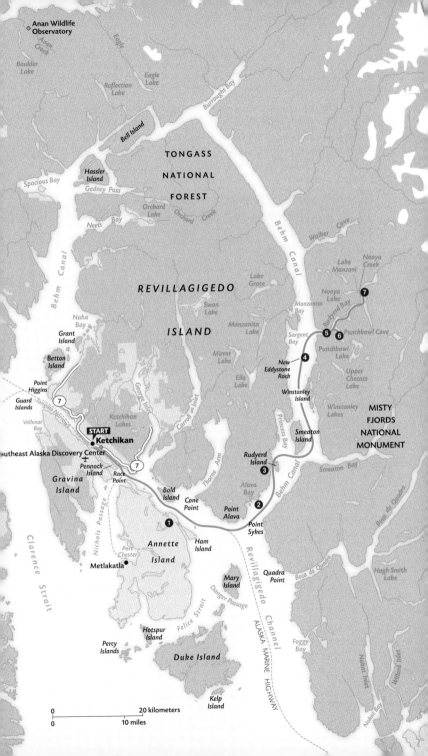

# WRANGELL

Travelers seeking a low-key southeast Alaska experience will relish Wrangell, a friendly town of about 2,400 folks perched on the northern tip of Wrangell Island. Its docks host ferries, as well as some small and medium cruise ships, keeping its modest waterfront and commercial area laid-back. Wrangell also serves as a jumping-off point for day trips to the Stikine River, Anan Wildlife Observatory, and the LeConte Glacier.

The ferry from Petersburg to Wrangell offers travelers scenic vistas of the Inside Passage.

**Wrangell**

⚏ Map p. 67

**Visitor Information**

✉ Wrangell Visitor Center, 293 Campbell Dr. (in Nolan Center)

☎ 907-874-2829 or 800-367-9745

**wrangellalaska.org**

Start at the **Wrangell Museum,** found along the waterfront on Campbell Drive where the shore-hugging street turns inland, just a few blocks from the cruise ship and ferry docks. This fine museum covers the town's unique history; Wrangell is the only Alaskan municipality that has been governed at various times by four different sovereigns—the Tlingit, Russians, British, and Americans. Just inside the entrance stand four of Alaska's oldest carved house posts, fine Tlingit work dating from the late 1700s. The museum

also displays photos from the rowdy decades following the 19th-century gold rushes. One exhibit tells how Wyatt Earp filled in as marshal in Wrangell, when he disarmed a man he'd arrested 20 years earlier in Dodge City.

From the museum, walk inland a block and you'll enter the little downtown. Geared toward residents, not tourists, Wrangell's commercial heart leans toward hardware stores, churches, and grocery stores, and offers only a few souvenir shops or art galleries. You will encounter public art in the form of totem poles, about a dozen of which are scattered around town, including several fine examples at **Kiksadi Totem Park,** near the southern end of Front Street, a downtown drag.

---

**INSIDER TIP:**

If you golf at Muskeg Meadows, don't forget the "Raven Rule": If a raven steals your ball, you may replace it without penalty.

—JUSTIN KAVANAGH
*National Geographic
Travel Books editor*

---

To see the greatest concentration of totem poles, continue south on Front Street one block until it turns into Shakes Street, and then follow Shakes one block down to the harbor. Here a narrow footbridge leads out to **Chief Shakes Island.** In the harbor, alive with the comings and goings of the commercial fishing fleet and sportfishers, this diminutive islet is an oasis of calm and reflection. Several totem poles ring the **Chief Shakes Tribal House** *(tel 907-874-4304),* a replica of a 19th-century tribal house that has stood on this grassy island for more than 70 years. This artful historic structure and the nearby poles underwent a major refurbishing in 2013.

To view relics of an earlier native culture, perhaps of ancestors of the Tlingit, follow Evergreen Avenue for about a mile

(1.6 km) north along the shore of Zimovia Strait to **Petroglyph Beach State Historic Site.** Even the native elders don't know the origins of the 50 or so rock carvings on the beach, but experts think they're at least 1,000 years old. Wander the boulders nearby and you will see some of the mysterious etchings.

## Nearby Attractions

Local outfits, many clustered near the cruise ship dock, offer boat and floatplane excursions to some of the wild places that envelop Wrangell, notably **Anan Wildlife Observatory, LeConte Glacier,** and the **Stikine River.** Located on the mainland some 30 miles (48 km) southeast of Wrangell, Anan Creek enjoys huge pink salmon runs. This fishy largesse attracts both black and brown bears, eagles, harbor seals, and other hungry critters, all of which can be watched from the observatory. The very active LeConte Glacier lies about 25 miles (40 km) north of Wrangell, calving huge chunks of ice into the sea. The mouth of the Stikine gapes a few miles north of town. ∎

**Wrangell
Museum**

- ✉ 296 Campbell Dr.
- ☎ 907-874-3770
- 🕐 Closed Sun. May–Sept. & Sun.–Mon. Oct.–April
- 💲 $$

**nolancenter.org/museum.html**

**Anan Wildlife
Observatory**

- ✉ Wrangell Ranger Station
- ☎ 907-874-2323
- 🕐 Reservations required July–Aug.
- 💲 $$

**fs.usda.gov/tongass**

---

**NEED TO KNOW**

**Port Logistics: Wrangell**
Most cruise ships dock on the downtown waterfront; to thoroughly explore Wrangell on foot, allow 2–3 hours. Stikine River boat excursions will take 3–6 hours, offering you the chance to see bears, moose, a glacier, and a hot spring.

# PETERSBURG

Proud of its Norwegian ties, Petersburg bills itself as Alaska's "Little Norway." This heritage shows in many ways, such as the use of the word *Velkommen* (welcome) by local businesses, the annual Little Norway Festival, and the house and building exteriors that feature *rosemaling*—the colorful, flowing floral painting that developed as a folk art in 18th-century Norway.

Petersburg's Norwegian roots and fishing heritage are evident throughout town.

## Petersburg

Map p. 67

**Visitor Information**

Petersburg Visitor Information Center, 1st & Fram Sts.

907-772-4636

**petersburg.org**

The town's 3,000 residents enjoy a splendid setting on the northern tip of Mitkof Island, circled by forest and mountains and bounded on two sides by the Wrangell Narrows and Frederick Sound. Small cruise ships and the ferry call on Petersburg, but those narrow waterways and a shallow harbor preclude larger vessels, so this is generally a quiet little town.

The **Sons of Norway Hall** is the cultural heart of Petersburg. Modeled on midwestern barns of the early 20th century, the handsome building erected in 1912 is decorated by some of the finest examples of rosemaling in town. Adjacent **Bojer Wikan**

**Fishermen's Memorial Park** hosts a memorial monument to local fishers who have lost their lives at sea, plus an ersatz replica of a Viking ship that is hauled through town for the Little Norway parade each May.

The Sons of Norway Hall and the park rest on pilings at the mouth of **Hammer Slough**, on the waterfront at the south end of downtown. They face the middle of the three adjacent harbors that shelter the hundreds of seiners, gillnetters, longliners, and other fishing boats in this top fishing port. Gaze up Hammer Slough and you'll see many homes also built on

INSIDER TIP:

For Norwegian sweaters and outdoor gear, stop by Lee's Clothing Store [212 N. Nordic Dr., tel 907-772-4229].

—PETER GWIN
National Geographic
magazine writer

pilings hanging over the narrow waterway.

Head north up quaint **Sing Lee Alley** to browse local businesses, including a bookstore, a café, a toy store, and a craft shop. In just a few blocks the alley dead-ends on Gjoa Street; go east just a few steps and you'll run into the town's main commercial street, **North Nordic Drive,** where grocery stores, banks, and other businesses mix with shops.

If you crave some of that seafood being hauled ashore at the harbor, go two and a half blocks north to **Coastal Cold Storage,** which sells shrimp burgers, halibut beer bits, fish tacos, and the like at its restaurant, and smoked salmon and black cod, spot prawns, scallops, and such at its retail store.

Two blocks inland from North Nordic Drive on Fram Street is the **Clausen Memorial Museum.** It houses Tlingit artifacts, a massive lighthouse lens, and a monumental salmon thought to be the largest salmon ever caught.

## Around Petersburg

If you are taking an excursion or renting a car, you can savor the scenery by heading south from Petersburg on the Mitkof

Highway along the Wrangell Narrows. Near Mile 14 the road intersects the **Blind River Rapids Boardwalk,** a quarter-mile (0.4 km) trail that crosses muskeg bogs to a favorite local fishing spot. At Mile 16 you can peer out from the **Blind Slough Swan Observatory;** the slough hosts migrating trumpeter swans in the fall and salmon and bears just downriver in summer. For its last few lovely miles, the highway hugs the island's eastern shore and provides views across Frederick Sound to the Stikine River Delta.

North of town, **Frederick Sound** is one of North America's top venues for whale-watching. Its glacier-fed waters abound with herring and krill, drawing hundreds of humpback whales from Hawaii in summer. Orcas and Dall's porpoise are also frequently seen. Tour operators in Petersburg offer boat excursions.

You can also arrange a tour to the Stikine River from Petersburg, or boat trips to the LeConte Glacier. Petersburg operators also offer flights to the glacier and to **Devils Thumb,** a 9,077-foot (2,767 m) peak on the Canada border. ∎

**Clausen Memorial Museum**

✉ 203 Fram St.
☎ 907-772-3598
🕐 Closed Sun.
💲 $

clausenmuseum.com

## NEED TO KNOW

### Port Logistics: Petersburg

Most cruise ships dock on the downtown waterfront; to thoroughly explore Petersburg on foot, allow 2–3 hours. LeConte Glacier boat excursions (see Travelwise p. 181) take half a day and offer you the opportunity to see the glacier calving ice into the sea.

# SITKA

Even by Inside Passage standards, Sitka is remote—and technically speaking, it's not in the Inside Passage. Of all the southeastern Alaska ports served by the Alaska Marine Highway and visited by cruise ships, only Sitka lies on the outside, facing the open Pacific. This means the town is more exposed to storms, but the summer weather is generally mild, and the area receives far less rain than, say, Ketchikan.

The Russian Orthodox St. Michael's Cathedral sits at the head of Sitka's main drag, Lincoln Street.

**Sitka**

🗺 Map p. 67

**Visitor Information**

✉ Sitka
Convention &
Visitors Bureau,
104 Lake St.

☎ 907-747-8604

**visitsitka.org**

Sitka was a busy port during the first half of the 19th century, when Novo Arkhangelsk ("New Archangel," the early Russian name for what is now Sitka) was the capital of Russian America. The ships coming for sea otter pelts brought merchandise from around the globe, and Sitka became, for a New World outpost, a large and sophisticated town by the mid-1830s. One overheated but not entirely irrational visitor dubbed it "the Paris of the Pacific."

The spice of Tlingit and Russian culture continues to season this town of 9,000 (the fourth most-populous city in Alaska). Sitka's port still bustles with influx from a large commercial fishing fleet, hundreds of charter fishing boats, and cruise ships that frequently anchor here throughout the summer.

Note the verb "anchor." Because Sitka lacks a downtown dock that can accommodate large cruise ships, during the summer a fleet of tenders busily ferries passengers to and fro between their berths anchored just offshore in Sitka Sound and the O'Connell Bridge Lightering Facility at the foot of downtown. (Some tenders also take people back and forth to another landing, and some ships dock several miles away and bus passengers into downtown.) For years a bumper sticker battle has waged between locals who support building a pier that can handle large cruise ships and those who oppose the project.

Begin your visit to Sitka at **Baranof Castle State Historic Site,** on the knoll right above the O'Connell Bridge Lightering Facility. Though not even 100 feet (30 m) high, Castle Hill provides a fabulous 360-degree view. It lies between the terrestrial attractions and the marine activities and served as the starting point of American Alaska. On October 18, 1867, the Russians lowered their flag here and the Americans raised the Stars and Stripes, signaling the change in government.

As you stroll around Castle Hill, take time to appreciate the striking scenery: mountains and forest to the north and east, and islands and ocean to the south and west. Not to mention the picture-perfect volcanic cone (with the tip snipped off) of **Mount Edgecumbe** pointing skyward from Kruzof Island, 10 miles (16 km) to the west, on the other side of Sitka Sound. Now set your sights a little lower to survey the layout of the town, from its several harbors to downtown to residential areas that stretch east and north for miles along the shore.

## Lincoln Street & Downtown

Descend from Castle Hill to Lincoln Street, Sitka's main artery. As you head northeast up Lincoln, the first street on your left is Katlian. Look down Katlian about a block and you'll see the boldly carved and painted entryway of the **Sheet'ka Kwaan Naa Kahidi Tribal Community House.** This is a modern version of a traditional clan house, as indicated by a rough translation of its Tlingit name, "the clan house for all the people of Sitka." During the summer, it hosts the renowned Sheet'ka Kwaan Naa Kahidi Native Dancers, in a song-and-dance performance that the local Tlingit say has changed little in thousands of years. The elaborately costumed dancers stage performances daily when large cruise ships are in port. Private shows can also be arranged.

Along Lincoln Street and down some of the side streets, you'll encounter a wide variety

**Baranof Castle State Historic Site**

✉ Harbor Road

☎ 907-747-6249

dnr.alaska.gov/parks

**Sheet'ka Kwaan Naa Kahidi Tribal Community House**

✉ 200 Katlian St.

☎ 907-747-7137

🕐 No tours/ performances Oct.–April

💲 $$

sitkatours.com

## Fooling Around

Mount Edgecumbe is erupting! That was the message being shouted on the streets of Sitka one spring morning in 1974, as residents hurried out of their houses and saw black smoke rising from the volcano just a few miles out of town. But those townspeople could have saved themselves a lot of grief if they'd checked their calendars; it was April 1 and they were on the receiving end of an elaborate April Fools' prank set up by a local named Porky Bickar. He had secretly taken hundreds of tires up to the crater and set them on fire.

## Old Money

These days, bank notes printed on walrus skin would get flagged as an absurdly inept attempt at counterfeiting. But in the early 1800s the tsar of Russia authorized the Russian-American Company to issue currency printed on walrus- and sealskin for use in Alaska. It was also an early example of recycling; sea otter pelts were shipped in (waterproof) walrus- and sealskin bags, and then the empty bags were cut up and the material was repurposed as a substitute for paper, which was expensive and hard to come by. Today collectors pay thousands of dollars for one of these extremely rare bills.

### St. Michael's Cathedral

- ⊠ 240 Lincoln St.
- ☎ 907-747-8120
- ⏱ Open for tours, days vary
- 💲 Donation

oca.org/parishes/ oca-ak-sitsmk

### New Archangel Dancers

- ⊠ Harrigan Centennial Hall, 330 Harbor Dr.
- ☎ 907-747-5516
- ⏱ Shows May– Sept., call for times

newarchangel dancers.com

### Sitka Historical Museum

- ⊠ Harrigan Centennial Hall, 330 Harbor Dr.
- ☎ 907-338-3766
- ⏱ Closed Sun. May–Sept., Sun.–Mon. Oct.–April
- 💲 $

sitkahistory.com

of restaurants and shops. At the corner of Lincoln and Barracks, just a block up from Katlian, bibliophiles can poke around in **Old Harbor Books** (201 Lincoln St., tel 907-747-8808, oldharborbooks .net), a classic local independent. About a block and a half beyond the bookstore, Lincoln runs into **St. Michael's Cathedral** and splits like a river meeting a rock, flowing around the church on both sides, but with the main fork continuing northeast. A national historic landmark that offers tours, this elaborate Russian Orthodox edifice is home to a congregation dating from the 1840s. The original building burned down in 1966, but residents managed to save most of the artifacts from the flames, and soon a near replica of the original was erected on the site and filled with the rescued treasures. These include one of the finest collections of Russian icons in Alaska, some of which are on display. The cathedral also has a gift shop right across the street (on the cathedral's northwest side). The nearby **Russian-America Company** (134 Lincoln St., tel 907-747-6228) sells colorful nested dolls

and other quintessentially Russian crafts, while the **Island Artists Gallery** (205 Lincoln St., tel 907-747-6536, islandartistsgallery. com) carries fine art and crafts by local artists.

### Crescent Harbor Area

A couple of blocks farther east on Lincoln lies Crescent Harbor, one of numerous ports that grace this seafaring city. Several attractions border the harbor, including **Harrigan Centennial Hall** on the southwest corner, best known as the home of the **New Archangel Dancers.** This group of local women has been performing dances and folk songs from Russia and nearby areas since 1969. The hall also is home to the modest **Sitka Historical Museum** and its centerpiece, a sprawling, intricately detailed model of 1867 Sitka. Its collection of old photos also merits.

Lincoln Street bends eastward as it traces the curve of Crescent Harbor. Just a few hundred feet from that northwest edge, at Lincoln's intersection with Monastery Street, you can visit the **Russian Bishop's House** (501 Lincoln St., tel 907-747-0110), an outlying unit of Sitka National Historical Park. (The main unit awaits about half a mile/0.8 km down the road.) The Bishop's House dates from 1842, making it one of only four original Russian structures remaining in the entire Western Hemisphere. Constructed from Sitka spruce, this handsomely restored building housed bishops from its completion until 1969. These bishops oversaw an enormous Russian Orthodox diocese that encompassed part of Alaska and Siberia, and reached all the way down the Pacific Coast into California. Displays include fancy clerical garments and a large brass samovar.

Walk another quarter of a mile (0.4 km) along the harbor on Lincoln, turn left on College Drive, and after about 100 yards (91 m) you'll be at the doorstep of one of the finest collections of Alaska native art in southeast Alaska, housed in the airy confines of the **Sheldon Jackson Museum.** The architecturally striking interior, with its vaulting domed ceiling, provides a fitting atmosphere in which to appreciate the native artifacts that missionary Rev. Sheldon Jackson accumulated from all over Alaska during the late 1800s. Scary shaman masks, armor made from walrus ivory, mukluks (boots) fashioned from fish skins—the quality and diversity of the objects is remarkable. The Eskimo whaling outfit, for example, a bearded-sealskin creation that looks like a space suit, is waterproof and airtight. It was worn while butchering whales, which required wading in icy water because the dead whales were floated to the shallows.

To dip into the area's natural history, a two-minute walk down Lincoln brings you to the **Sitka**

**Sheldon Jackson Museum**

- ⊠ 104 College Dr.
- ☎ 907-747-8981
- 🕐 Closed Sun.–Tue.
- 💲 $$

**museums.alaska .gov/sheldon _jackson/sjhome .html**

Snowcapped Mount Edgecumbe looms majestically above Sitka's harbor.

## Sitka Sound Science Center

✉ 834 Lincoln St.

☎ 907-747-8878

🕓 Closed Sun. mid-May–mid-Sept.; closed Sun.–Mon., Wed., & Fri. rest of year

💲 $

**sitkasoundscience center.org**

## Sitka National Historical Park

✉ Main unit, 103 Metlakatla St.; Russian Bishop's House, 106 Monastery St.

☎ 907-747-0110

🕓 Main unit visitor center closed Sun.–Mon. Oct.–April; Russian Bishop's House closed Oct.–April except by appt.

💲 $ (guided tour of house)

**nps.gov/sitk**

## Alaska Raptor Center

✉ 1000 Raptor Way

☎ 907-747-8662

🕓 Call ahead for opening times Oct.–April

💲 $$$

**alaskaraptor.org**

**Sound Science Center.** Here you may be surprised to learn that the chilly waters of the sound harbor one of the most productive marine ecosystems in the world. Sea cucumbers, wolf eels, rock crabs, and other underwater denizens of the sound are on view. Visitors also can tour the adjacent hatchery, in which millions of coho, pink, and chum salmon are raised.

Keep going down Lincoln for a quarter of a mile (0.4 km) until it becomes Metlakatla Street. There you will find the main unit of **Sitka National Historical Park,** established to commemorate the Battle of Sitka, an 1804 conflict between the Tlingit and the Russians. Artifacts on display at the **Visitor Center** and **Southeast Alaska Indian Cultural Center** tell the stories of both cultures before and after the battle. Though few in number, the objects are of high quality; note the ceremonial bone dagger inlaid with abalone and the bib made from red, yellow, white, black, blue, and turquoise beads. Native artists work at the center. Outside, miles of easy walking trails cut through the park's lovely forests along the shores of Sitka Sound and the estuary of the Indian River. Southwest of the estuary stand totem poles and the actual site of the 1804 battle; the eastern area contains picnic facilities and the Russian Memorial.

Along the park's northern boundary perches the **Alaska Raptor Center,** where raptors and other birds are rehabilitated and, when possible, released. To educate people about the area's birds of prey, the center gives presentations using its residents—those eagles, hawks, falcons, and owls nursed back to health but unable to return to the wild.

**INSIDER TIP:**

Don't miss the chance to see injured bald eagles being retrained for the wild in an aerobic flight area at the Alaska Raptor Center.

—NEIL SHEA
National Geographic
*magazine writer*

## Beyond City Center

If you rent a car, take a taxi, or go on organized excursions, you'll have several outstanding options of just-out-of-town destinations. Located about 5 miles (8 km) east of downtown, **Fortress of the Bear** takes in orphaned brown and black bears and provides them with a home. (This nonprofit hopes to return bears to the wild one day.) Visitors watch the bears from a covered viewing platform while a naturalist educates them about these feared and admired animals.

For an accessible introduction to the landscape surrounding Sitka, head 7 miles (11 km) north on Halibut Point Road to the **Starrigavan Recreation Area** around **Old Sitka State Historic Park,** site of the Battle of 1802 between Russians and Tlingit at the mouth of Starrigavan Creek. Here, three trails provide a glimpse into most of the region's main ecosystems. The **Forest and Muskeg Trail,** an easy, 0.75-mile (1.2 km) jaunt, winds through spruce-hemlock forest and along a boardwalk through muskeg. Look for the tiny but voracious sundews—carnivorous plants smaller than a dime. At the trail's east end you can cross the bridge over Starrigavan Creek and start right into the **Estuary Life Trail,** a quarter-mile (0.4 km) boardwalk through the marshes of the creek's estuary. Early morning visitors might spot a variety of birds and maybe a brown bear or Sitka black-tailed deer. Continue to the far end, beyond the end of the estuary, and you'll arrive at the best of the three hikes: the **Mosquito Cove Trail.** This 1.25-mile (2 km) loop hugs the comely shores of Starrigavan Bay and Mosquito Cove and then circles back through the amazingly lush coastal rain forest.

To explore **Sitka Sound,** you can ship out with a variety of local operators, many based at Crescent Harbor. Tours are varied, ranging from one-hour trips to all-day ventures. Whichever you choose, you're quite likely to spot sea otters. Perhaps you will cruise through the immense shadow of **Mount Edgecumbe,** the 3,201-foot (976 m) volcano on Kruzof Island. During the summer you'll probably see humpback whales; the boat captain may cut the engines so you can hear the humpbacks' blows.

If the seas aren't too rough, the boat may head to the mouth of the sound and St. Lazaria Island (landing not allowed), part of the **Alaska Maritime National Wildlife Refuge,** a conglomerate of 2,500 coastal islands, spires, rocks, and headlands. In summer St. Lazaria's 65 acres (26 ha) teem with hundreds of thousands of nesting seabirds. You'll see (and hear!) kittiwakes wheeling boisterously around the steep cliffs, cormorants spreading their wings to dry, and lovable puffins diving for food. ∎

**Fortress of the Bear**

- ✉ 4639 Sawmill Creek Rd.
- ☎ 907-747-3550
- 🕐 Closed Mon.–Fri. Oct.–April
- 💲 $$$

**fortressofthebear .org**

**Starrigavan Recreation Area**

- ✉ Tongass National Forest, Sitka Ranger District, 204 Siginaka Way
- ☎ 907-747-6671

**www.fs.fed.us/ wildflowers/regions/ alaska/Starrigavan**

## NEED TO KNOW

### Port Logistics: Sitka

Sitka's docks can't accommodate large cruise ships, so most anchor offshore and use tenders to take passengers to one of two lightering facilities on the downtown waterfront (10 min.).

Occasionally ships dock 5 miles (8 km) out of town and bus passengers to downtown (15 min.).

### Sitka Highlights: Sitka is larger than Wrangell and Petersburg, but you can still take in the central city and most of the attractions that lie within walking distance of the docks in half a day. If you wish to see the outlying attractions in Sitka—or any of the southeast Alaska towns mentioned in this chapter—and you're not signed up for an excursion organized by your ship, go to the town's visitor information centers, located either right at or within a few blocks from the docks. The friendly folks at the centers can tell you about taxis, shuttles, rental cars, tour operators, etc.

- Sheldon Jackson Museum: 1–2 hours
- Alaska Raptor Center: 2–3 hours
- Boat trip into Sitka Sound: 1–8 hours

# JUNEAU

Juneau is not your ordinary state capital: No roads connect it to the outside world, bears sometimes roam the edges of town, and its setting is drop-dead gorgeous. Built along the shore of Gastineau Channel, the city backs up against heavily forested mountains that elevate abruptly to heights of several thousand feet—more like the backdrop for a Swiss resort than a state capital.

Aerial view of Juneau

**Juneau**

Map p. 67

**Visitor Information**

Juneau Convention & Visitors Bureau, 800 Glacier Ave., Suite 201 (kiosk at cruise ship terminal May–Sept.)

907-586-2201 or 888-586-2201

**traveljuneau.com**

In the second largest city in Alaska, Juneau's 33,000 residents enjoy a town of fine restaurants, art galleries, lively pubs, plentiful cultural activities, and a wealth of historic buildings.

On the waterfront at the cruise ship docks you'll find the bottom of the **Goldbelt Tram,** which hauls passengers steeply up to the 1,800-foot (549 m) level of the 3,819-foot-high (1,164 m) eponymous mountain that looms over downtown Juneau. As the

tram rises, the views grow from fine to jaw-dropping, reaching far beyond the city to encompass hundreds of square miles of forest, mountains, and sea. Many of the tram operators are Alaska natives (an Alaska native corporation owns the tram) who will talk about their peoples' history and culture as they take visitors up and down the mountain.

The native influence continues up top at the tram's terminus: A **theater** presents films and live shows, often about Tlingit culture; **Raven Eagle Gifts & Gallery** carries many Alaska native arts and crafts and serves as something of a museum; and native artists sometimes work where visitors can watch them. In addition, the terminus complex includes **Timberline Bar & Grill,** which affords sweeping views; a **nature center;** and an outpost of the **Juneau Raptor Center,** which houses eagles and other raptors. But the best thing about Mount Roberts is the mountain itself.

Beyond the nature center sprawls a network of easy-to-moderate, well-marked trails that lead up the mountainside through increasingly sparse forest to a stunning expanse of subalpine and alpine habitat. It only takes 10 to 15 minutes to reach the tree line, above which marvelous vistas open up, revealing mountains, waterfalls, and shimmering bodies of water far to the west and south of Juneau. During summer wildflowers blaze from the meadows, where hoary marmots graze. Porcupines lumber through the undergrowth, bears pass through, and mountain goats occupy the highest slopes. If you feel energetic, have lots of time, and bring proper gear, you can roam for miles—even choosing to return to the city via the 4.5-mile (7.2 km) **Mount Roberts Trail,** which has its trailhead on the northeast edge of downtown, a mile (1.6 km) or so north of the cruise ship docks.

## South Franklin & Around

Near the downtown waterfront, especially along South Franklin Street, a bevy of shops, restaurants, galleries, and bars compete for attention. Many are housed in historic buildings, as this is one of the oldest parts of town. As you stroll, you can enjoy some of the sculptures, murals, and more than 20 totem poles that grace the area.

South Franklin starts right next to the cruise ship docks—there's room for only one street on this narrow peninsula of flat land between the Gastineau Channel and the mountainside. Just a few hundred yards north of the Goldbelt Tram, South Franklin hits the southeast corner of the downtown grid. The

**Goldbelt Tram**
- 490 S. Franklin St.
- 907-463-3412 or 888-461-8726 (shop)
- Closed late Sept.–early May
- $$$$$

goldbelttram.com

### Capital Contest

Sitka was the capital of Russian Alaska and early American Alaska, but by 1900 much of the region's commerce had moved to the area around Joe Juneau's former mining camp, causing officials to establish Juneau as the capital. However, after World War II, the population and much of Alaska's economic activity shifted northwest, and some residents wanted to move the state capital to Anchorage. The debate reached a peak in the 1970s, when a commission earmarked unused land just north of Anchorage for the new capital. But the hefty price tag of building a new capital repelled voters, and the movement collapsed.

**Sealaska Heritage Institute**

✉ 105 S. Seward St.

☎ 907-483-4844

sealaskaheritage.org

**Alaska State Capitol**

✉ 4th & Main Sts.

☎ 907-465-4648

🕑 Self-guided tours daily, guided tours daily May–Sept.

w3.legis.state.ak.us/docs/pdf/capitol_tour.pdf

grid runs about a mile (1.6 km) east to west and half a mile (0.8 km) north to south.

If you crave seafood, begin your wander up South Franklin just south of the tram at **Taku Fisheries** (550 S. Franklin St., tel 800-582-5122, takustore .com), aka Taku: Nature's Fish Store. Mainly a wholesale seafood-processing plant, Taku has a retail outlet where you can buy salmon caviar, king crab

---

**INSIDER TIP:**

Many towns, including Juneau, offer bike excursions—within five minutes you can be in untamed countryside on an adventure.

—EVERETT POTTER
National Geographic Traveler
magazine writer

---

legs, smoked sockeye fillets, and other local delicacies, and ship or carry them home. And who's to say you can't open that package of salmon jerky and devour its contents on the spot?

Several blocks north along South Franklin you'll find the **Senate Building Mall** (175 S. Franklin St., senatemall.com), an historic edifice that houses a number of local, independent stores selling goods ranging from children's books to fly-fishing gear. Most notable is the **Juneau Artists Gallery** (tel 907/586-9891, juneauartistsgal lery.org), a cooperative enterprise

managed and staffed by the few dozen local artists who sell their work here.

From here proceed north half a block and west on Front Street then turn left on Seward Street. As you walk down Seward toward the water, the **Sealaska Heritage Institute** looms on your right, taking up most of the city block; this is the headquarters of Sealaska, a major Alaska native corporation. The facade is adorned with artistic panels by celebrated Haida artist Robert Davidson, and three bronze totem posts, erected in 2018, stand by the entrance. Inside, the lobby displays a 40-foot-wide (12.2 m) carved Tsimshian house front, and you can enter to explore a stunning contemporary replica of a traditional clan house. Also on the ground floor is the **Sealaska Heritage Store** (tel 907-586-9114). This nonprofit art store carries authentic works by Alaska native artists. All the profits from the store go to the artists and to programs that promote Tlingit, Haida, and Tsimshian culture. Next, walk north along Seward Street. On the next block, **Annie Kaill's** (124 Seward Street, tel 907-586-2880, anniekaills.com) features fine arts and crafts created by some of Alaska's most renowned artists and some rising stars. Another 20 or so steps farther along, at **Wm. Spear Design** (230 Seward St., tel 907-586-2209, Ste. 201, wmspear.com), a universe of elaborate enamel pins awaits the collector. Designs include the expected—horned puffins, Alaska state flag—and the odd—Allosaurus skull, martini glass, and more.

## Historic Downtown

Thanks to good luck and decades of heroic work by the volunteer fire department, Juneau has suffered just one significant fire, and that 2012 blaze took out only a few buildings. In the seven-block radius of the original downtown, some 140 buildings dating from before 1914 still stand—scores of them go back earlier than 1904. If you don't mind giving your quadriceps a workout, browse the residential neighborhoods up the steep hills at the edge of downtown, where you'll see lovely historic homes.

An appropriate place to start a tour of Juneau's history is at the **State Capitol,** three blocks up Seward from the Sealaska building. Completed in 1931, the unassuming brick-faced building originally housed the territorial legislature (remember, Alaska didn't achieve statehood until 1959), governor, post office, courts, and numerous other territorial and federal agencies. The second floor displays historical photos.

Delve deeper into Juneau's past at the **Juneau-Douglas City Museum,** across Main Street from the capitol, with a 45-foot (13.7 m) Haida-style totem pole out front. Learn how two prospectors and a Tlingit chief together touched off one of the quickest gold rushes ever in 1880, with the first boatloads of would-be millionaires arriving about a month after Chief Kowee directed Joe

Juneau and Richard Harris to the mother lode above Gold Creek (now the Silver Bow Basin). In the end, millions of ounces of gold did indeed come out of the ground, but they had to be painstakingly extracted from low-grade ore, which required the efforts of big mining companies rather than independent miners. The mining heritage carries over into exhibits and activities in the hands-on history room. Displays cover many other aspects of the city's history, too, from shipwrecks to 19th-century domestic life.

More history can be glimpsed up steeply rising Seward Street, two blocks from the northeast corner of the capitol grounds. Huffing and puffing, you can rest when you reach **Wickersham State Historic Site,** known to most locals as the House of Wickersham. Built in 1898 for a mine superintendent, this handsome residence was bought in 1928 by Judge James Wickersham, a prominent Alaska lawyer, politician, author, historian,

### Juneau-Douglas City Museum

- 4th & Main Sts.
- 907-586-3572
- Closed Mon.–Wed.
- $$ summer only. Free rest of year

**juneau.org/library /museum/index.php**

■ Exhibits at the Alaska State Museum tell the story of the Great Land.

### Wickersham State Historic Site

- 213 7th St.
- 907-586-9001
- Closed Oct.–mid-May & Fri.–Sat. mid-May–Sept.
- $

**dnr.alaska.gov/ parks/aspunits/ southeast/wickshp. htm**

**Alaska State Museum**

✉ 395 Whittier St.
☎ 907-465-2901
🕐 See website for hours

**museums.alaska.gov/asm**

and, of course, judge. Wickersham was instrumental in the effort to make Alaska a territory, which finally succeeded in 1912. Soon after that victory, he began the drive to make Alaska a state, though he died 20 years before that happened. When docents are available, you can take a tour of his house and see details of the judge's illustrious past and some of his vast collection of Alaska artifacts plus his personal mementos.

## Alaska State Museum

The Alaska State Museum is a trove of interesting native artifacts, fine art, and natural history specimens. The easiest way to get there is to go down Main Street to Egan Drive, which hugs the waterfront, and proceed west about a quarter mile (0.4 km) to Whittier Street. Go right half a block and you'll arrive at this imposing, 118,000-square-foot (10,963 sq m) building, opened in 2016, that contains more than 30,000 artifacts. The excellent art collection showcases old Alaska masters such as Sydney Laurence and Eustace Ziegler as well as contemporary artists, including Alaska natives. Consider the modern rendition of a traditional Unangan hunting hat, its thin, steam-bent wood tapered like an Olympic cyclist's helmet, the outer surface replete with intricate designs, colorful beads, ivory carvings, and a fringe of sea lion

**INSIDER TIP:**

The Mendenhall trail on the west side of the glacier gives relatively easy access to the ice caves and terrain in front of the glacier.

—GREGORY WILES
*National Geographic field researcher*

■ Nugget Falls gushes down rocky slopes into the lake that has formed below Mendenhall Glacier.

whiskers. The museum's natural history collection also deserves high marks and includes fossils, seashells, minerals, and mounted animals. But human history is the museum's strong suit.

Start with the Alaska native exhibits, which represent native peoples from all over the state. The collection of Northwest and Eskimo baskets is among the finest anywhere and features some fragments from three recently discovered baskets that date back about 5,000 years, the earliest ever found in Alaska or along the Northwest Coast. Next comes the Russian era, highlighted by a bronze double-headed eagle emblem, one of only two known to exist. Elaborate religious icons, weapons, and a samovar the size of a potbellied stove also evoke the state's Russian years. Alaska's American history is likewise revealed by a broad range of items, such as gold rush tools, whaling gear, and objects from World War II's Aleutian campaign.

## Out the Road

Juneau's one highway, the **Glacier/ Juneau Veterans' Memorial Highway,** may be a dead end, but with so many worthy sites along the way, going up and back in a rental car is a worthwhile trip. The highway starts downtown as Egan Drive, which launches from South Franklin Street at the northern end of the cruise ship docks. The road runs west and then north along Gastineau and Favorite Channels. At Mile 9.3, it officially becomes the Glacier Highway. At Mile 12.1, it technically turns into the Juneau Veterans' Memorial Highway, but

## Glacier Adventures

If you're fit and have half a day, Juneau-based outfitter Above & Beyond Alaska, or ABAK *(tel 907-364-2333, beyondak.com)*, will take you on a fairly hard hike up to the Mendenhall Glacier and help you venture onto the river of ice. Guides provide crampons, ice axes, ropes, and other gear as well as an extensive safety lecture. On some trips, willing participants can rope up and try a little ice climbing under supervision.

most locals simply say they're going "out the road." By whatever name, the road continues on or near the scenic shoreline until it ends at Echo Cove, about 40 miles (64 km) from downtown.

The first quarter of this route passes through the Mendenhall Valley, home to Juneau's version of suburbia. At Mile 8, near the Fred Meyer store, visitors can poke around at the **Glacier Gardens Rainforest Adventure.** You can explore its 52 acres (21 ha) of rain forest with a guide along a 2-mile (3.2 km) loop, but flower-intensive gardens are perhaps the greater draw. In many places the logged trunks of big conifer trees, cut down to about 10 or 20 feet (3–6 m), have been rammed upside-down into the ground so the root masses stick up, forming platforms planted with abundant, overflowing flowers.

At Mile 9.3, the south junction of the Mendenhall Loop Road intersects the highway. This road leads 3.4 miles (5.5 km) inland to the visitor center at **Mendenhall Glacier,** one of the most popular attractions in Alaska. Spawned high in the mountains by the vast

### Glacier Gardens Rainforest Adventure
- 7600 Glacier Hwy.
- 907-790-3377
- Closed Oct.–April
- $$$$$

glaciergardens.com

### Mendenhall Glacier
- 8510 Mendenhall Loop Rd.
- 907-789-0097
- Closed Mon.–Thurs. Sept.–March
- $ in summer

fs.usda.gov /tongass

**Eagle Beach State Recreation Area**

☎ 907-465-4563

dnr.alaska.gov/
parks/brochures/
eaglebeachbrochure.
pdf

Juneau Icefield, this 13-mile-long (21 km), half-mile-wide (0.8 km) ribbon of blue and white ice snakes down the mountain to its present terminus, a little more than a mile (1.6 km) across Mendenhall Lake from the visitor center. The glacier has been melting rapidly in recent years, with the terminus shrinking an average of several hundred feet a year.

At the **visitor center,** exhibits and a film educate visitors on glaciers, outlining the relationship between the Juneau Icefield and the Mendenhall Glacier. Panoramic windows allow you to gaze at the glacier while staying warm. For a closer look, stroll along the easy 0.3-mile (0.5 km) **Photo Point Trail,** which winds out to the edge of the lake. To get closer still, take a kayak tour on the lake; there's even an outfit, **Alaska Tours** (888-317-3325, alaskatours. com), which transports people around the lake in a traditional Tlingit canoe. For the closest look of all, take a helicopter tour and

land on the glacier for a guided walk, or take a guided hike up to and onto the glacier. For a nonglacier activity, go to the end of the parking lot farthest from the visitor center and step onto the platform above **Steep Creek.** During the summer, sockeye and coho salmon spawn in this part of the creek. The salmon, a spectacle in themselves, also draw black bears to the area. Beavers favor the creek as well; look for their dams and lodges.

Several trails will take you into the surrounding landscape. The easy half-mile (0.8 km) **Trail of Time,** a self-guided nature walk, leaves from the center and weaves through the rain forest. One of the prettiest routes is the 3.5-mile (5.6 km), moderately difficult **East Glacier Loop,** which branches off from the Trail of Time. The loop passes through rain forest and yields views of the glacier, Nugget Falls, and alpine slopes.

Farther up the highway you'll encounter several other sites worth a look. At Mile 12.4 is **Auke Bay,** a harbor that offers kayak tours, whale-watching trips, and sport-fishing charters. The **Eagle Beach State Recreation Area** beckons at Mile 28 and includes a ranger station, trails, cabins, wetlands, and an expanse of old-growth forest. This area lay beneath thousands of feet of glacial ice until just 250 years ago, so this landscape is quite young. Use the spotting scopes by the interpretive signs to pull in the Chilkats from far across the waters of Lynn Canal or the bald eagles swooping above the estuary fed by Eagle River. ■

# ICY STRAIT POINT

**Icy Strait Point gives you a chance to experience Tlingit life and the natural environment in which that way of life is embedded—as well as the opportunity to have a lot of fun. This did not evolve organically, for Icy Strait Point is not a natural-born community; in fact, it's not a town at all. It is a destination created primarily for cruise ship passengers by the Huna Totem Corporation, an Alaska native corporation, and did not exist before 2004.**

■ Cruise ship passengers are brought ashore at the main building of Icy Strait Point.

The Tlingit people who conceived and constructed Icy Strait Point worked hard to make it authentic, to reflect their culture and to celebrate the beauty of the natural setting. These Tlingit live in or have ancestral ties to Hoonah, the community just 1.5 miles (2.4 km) from Icy Strait Point. With a population of about 750, it is Alaska's largest Tlingit village. More than 80 percent of Icy Strait Point staffers and guides are local Tlingits and Huna Totem shareholders.

You are welcome to mosey over to Hoonah to have a look around, maybe grab a bite, or buy a souvenir, but almost all the attractions, tours, shops, and eateries are in Icy Strait Point.

Catamarans take passengers from their anchored ships to the tender dock right in front of Icy Strait Point's main building. Now refurbished, this historic structure and a dozen smaller structures scattered nearby once constituted a major salmon cannery built by the Hoonah Packing Company in 1912 and operated until 1953. You can learn about this history in the main building at the **museum** and at the preserved canning line.

The local Tlingits moved to the area and founded Hoonah

**Icy Strait Point**

🗺 Map p. 67
✉ 108 Cannery Rd.
☎ 907-789-9600
🕐 Open whenever cruise ships are in port

**icystraitpoint.com**

## Flying High on Zip Lines

Over the last several years, zip lines have popped up all around Alaska, with perhaps the most famous one—the **ZipRider**—in Icy Strait Point (*tel 907-945-3141, icystrait point.com; book through your cruise operator*). Zip lines come in two distinct flavors. The ZipRider epitomizes the style that aims for a brief, pulse-pounding ride that stresses the "zip." The ZipRider operator takes you up to a cliff about 1,300 feet (400 m) above sea level, straps you into a chairlift-like seat, and sends you screaming down a heavy cable toward the shore just over a mile (1.6 km) away, which makes it one of the longest zip lines in the world. At times you are 300 feet (90 m) above the forest floor

and hurtling along at 60 miles an hour (97 km/h). Ninety seconds after you launch, you'll come to a stop at the beach and wobble away on shaky legs to boast of your adventure.

While hardly sedate, the other style of zip line emphasizes an exploration of the canopy of a forest. People don a harness and attach it to cables strung between platforms set in trees high above the forest floor. There's only a slight incline from one platform to the next, so you can move along slowly, even using a brake to stop and take a look at wildlife, seed cones, or whatever else the forest serves up. These journeys through the canopy can take as long as a couple of hours.

about 2,000 years ago, after an advancing glacier forced them to abandon their original village. For centuries they lived a subsistence lifestyle, which changed little until outside fur traders arrived in the 1880s. Soon stores, churches, schools, and other trappings of modern civilization reshaped Hoonah, though residents continue many subsistence pursuits. The arrival of a major-league cannery had a huge impact on the town, creating many jobs for cannery workers and fishers. In 1917, just five years after opening, the cannery churned out 7,320,240 one-pound cans of salmon. Naturally, such a big operation left a serious hole in the local economy when the cannery closed in 1953, and for decades the people of Hoonah looked for ways to fill that hole. The answer came when they decided to create a private cruise ship destination—the only

one in the United States—and in 2004 Icy Strait was born.

The main building also houses locally owned and operated shops whose goods range from straight-up souvenirs to products that reflect the land and people. Of all the stores, the one most at home in this former cannery is the **Salmon Shop,** where you can pick up all things salmon, from salmon caviar to, naturally, canned salmon.

## Cuisine & Excursions

If the salmon jerky didn't fill you up, you can get a meal at one of several establishments in some of the old cannery's outlying buildings—all within an easy 10-minute walk of the main building. You can combine great eating with a cultural experience by signing up for a 90-minute excursion called **In Alaska's Wildest Kitchen.** Held in Icy Strait Point by an expert Alaskan chef and commercial fisher, participants gather around a horseshoe-shaped counter and learn from a pro how to prepare and cook seafood the Alaskan way, all the while learning about local fishing and sampling a tasting menu of such culinary delights as grilled halibut, Dungeness crab, wild berries, and seasonal herbs and vegetables. The final exam comprises filleting your own catch of the day, grilling it over an alder-wood fire, and, of course, eating your own entrée.

The Wildest Kitchen is just one of about 20 excursions offered at Icy Strait Point. All but one expose you to Tlingit culture and the surrounding natural world, but that one is the most famous excursion of them all: the **ZipRider zip line** (see sidebar p. 92).

The more traditional excursions include kayaking the waterfront, taking a tram through the rain forest, halibut fishing, flightseeing over Glacier Bay, and hiking along the beach and in the forest. Some people opt for combo outings, such as the 2.5-hour **Hoonah Sightseeing & Tribal Dance.** A local guide takes you to the village and talks about the adventures of local fishers and how the residents rebuilt the village after it burned down in 1944. You'll return to the Heritage Center Native Theater at Icy Strait Point to watch Tlingit performers clad in traditional regalia use song, storytelling, and dance to convey their history and culture.

Another popular combo excursion is the five-hour **Whales, Wildlife, and Brown Bear Search.** Passengers take a high-speed catamaran through Icy Strait looking for marine wildlife, including seals,

---

**INSIDER TIP:**

During cruising season, humpback whales are *always* seen in Icy Strait: Whale-watch guides have not had a "no-show" since trips began in 2004.

—TOM O'NEILL
National Geographic
*magazine writer*

---

Steller sea lions, porpoises, and orcas. There are few places like this in the world, where you are guaranteed to spot humpback whales— a refund is offered if you don't see any. Back on land, you'll board a bus and drive through forest and muskeg to the Spasski River, where you're likely to see grizzlies feeding on migrating salmon. Throughout the excursion, your naturalist guide explains the biology and behavior of the animals you're watching. ∎

---

**NEED TO KNOW**

**Port Logistics: Icy Strait Point**
The cruise ship dock is right at Icy Strait Point, so you will come ashore at the tender dock in front of the main building, where the museum and shops orient you into the complex. This is a compact area, and you can easily walk around it at your leisure in a couple of hours. However, you'll probably want to venture on at least one of the many appealing cultural and natural excursions on offer. These vary in duration between 2 and 5 hours, so check return times against the time of your ship's departure.

# BUYING ALASKA NATIVE ART

All over Alaska, even in remote locations, visitors will encounter shops selling Alaska native art. The variety is wonderfully overwhelming, reflecting the array of styles, themes, traditions, and media that have developed in different regions. You will see the fine beadwork on moose hide characteristic of Athabaskan tribes, the etched walrus ivory produced by Inuit, and the intricately carved and brightly painted headdresses of the Tlingit, to name a few.

An ornamental visor from the Tlingit Nation, which is spread across much of Alaska's southeast

Along with the variety, the craftsmanship and natural materials that go into high-quality native art are sure to delight. These cultures have spent thousands of years refining their arts—and genuine native art can be dazzling. However, not all the items advertised as "native" art are genuine. Each year collectors and travelers spend millions of dollars on native art, and the temptation to cash in on that lucrative market has given rise to unscrupulous imitators, such as carvers who substitute resin for soapstone or stores that sell fake native art manufactured in China. The authenticity of a pair of $10 earrings may not matter to a buyer (then again, it may), but someone paying hundreds or thousands of dollars for a work they are told is by a native

artisan using traditional methods likely wants to ensure that it's the real McCoy.

How to know? One of the best (and easiest) ways is to look for the "silver hand" sticker, which bears a hand symbol and the words "Authentic Alaska Native Art From Alaska." Having been debated at length by the Alaska natives, the art community, and the Alaskan state legislature, the silver hand symbol carries considerable legal weight. In order to use the silver hand, artists must apply for a permit and demonstrate that they live in Alaska, create their work in Alaska, create their art by hand, and belong to a federally recognized Alaska native tribe. This method isn't foolproof, as occasionally stickers have been transferred to unqualified

◼ **Dorica Jackson colors a totem pole made by her Tlingit husband, Nathan Jackson.**

goods, but the silver hand is a good sign that the work is likely authentic. Note, however, that the absence of the silver hand by no means indicates that a piece is a fraud; some Alaska native artists refuse to use the silver hand for various reasons, such as a belief that separating artists according to their heritage is divisive or a strong conviction that the silver hand is mainly a marketing tool and its use belittles artists.

Probably the surest approach to taking home authentic goods from Alaska, short of personally knowing the artist, is to buy from a reputable shop. Of course, recognizing a reputable shop can be difficult, especially if you're not a local, but one good bet is to ask at visitor centers or chambers of commerce. Another reliable approach is to patronize gift shops at museums and cultural centers. For example, shops at the Alaska Native Heritage Center, in Anchorage, and the Alaska State Museum, in Juneau, are well known for selling authentic Alaska native artwork. For more information about the silver hand program, a list of trustworthy shops, and various other matters related to Alaska native art, contact the Alaska State Council for the Arts (907-269-6610, arts.alaska.gov).

## Buyer Beware: Protecting Yourself

Buying any work of art or any piece of crafted artifact—in Alaska or anywhere else—always involves an element of risk on the buyer's part. However you *can* take steps as an individual consumer to protect yourself.

If you visit an unfamiliar shop and see something you like that doesn't have the silver hand sticker, ask about the item's origins or request written proof of its authenticity. If the salesperson claims a seal figurine has been made of walrus ivory by a Yup'ik on St. Lawrence Island, ask the clerk to write that claim on your receipt. You should also carefully inspect the material from which the work is made. For example, genuine soapstone is cooler to the touch than resin, and soapstone is also heavier. An excellent brochure outlining such identification tips and supplying other valuable information is available online from the Federal Trade Commission (consumer.ftc.gov/articles/pdf-0055-alaska-native-art.pdf).

# GLACIER BAY NATIONAL PARK & PRESERVE

The heart of Glacier Bay National Park and Preserve is a new land. When Capt. James Cook sailed down this stretch of coastline in 1778, he encountered a sheet of glacial ice thousands of feet thick and several miles wide. But the Little Ice Age was fading fast, and by 1794, when Capt. George Vancouver passed through Icy Strait, a 5-mile-long (8 km) bay had appeared—the embryonic Glacier Bay. The ice has continued to melt over the years, and today the deep, double-armed bay extends about 65 miles (105 km) back into the Alaska mainland.

Calving ice from the Johns Hopkins Glacier flops into the waters of a remote inlet of Glacier Bay.

### Glacier Bay National Park & Preserve

- Map pp. 66–67
- Bartlett Cove
- 907-697-2230
- Closed early Sept.–late May

**nps.gov/glba**

Near the mouth of Glacier Bay, where the ice melted more than 200 years ago, mature forest has grown up. At the far end of the bay, where the ice did not recede until more recently, the early stages of recovery are evident, with colonizing plants like alder and flaming magenta-colored fireweed prospering. Here, scientists and visitors alike can witness the rebirth of a landscape.

The park boasts about a dozen tidewater glaciers (glaciers that reach the ocean), many of which calve slabs of ice into the water. Many of these glaciers lie deep in the bay, so cruise ships generally spend 9–10 hours sailing into and back out of the bay's farthest reaches, going almost to the ends of the **West Arm.**

**Reid Glacier** usually offers the first glimpse of a tidewater glacier. A few miles later you'll pass **Lamplugh Glacier,** with its castle-like turrets and spires of very blue ice. At this point your ship may cruise west into **John Hopkins Inlet** or north into **Tarr Inlet.**

## Identifying Icebergs

Icebergs are massive floating chunks of ice that have broken off from glaciers. In olden days, sailors had names that conveyed their size. For example, if the berg showed about 3 feet (1 m) of ice above water, it was called "growler ice," and if it showed 3 to 15 feet (1–4.5 m), it was a "bergy bit." The nature of an iceberg can be discerned by its color.

The bluer a berg is, the denser and more compressed the ice. A white berg has large numbers of air bubbles trapped inside it, and a greenish-black berg has been calved off the bottom of a glacier.

At the end of the former is the 300-foot-high (91 m), mile-wide (1.6 km) face of **Johns Hopkins Glacier,** the only glacier in the park that is still advancing. This glacier drops so much ice that large cruise ships must keep a distance and let passengers watch from Jaw Point, 5 miles (8 km) from the glacier's face. After 15 or 20 minutes of admiring Johns Hopkins from afar, many ships then head up to the end of Tarr Inlet and enjoy the active calving of mile-wide (1.6 km), 300-foot-high (91 m) **Margerie Glacier,** observable from as close as a quarter mile (0.4 km).

### A Closer Understanding

These encounters with glaciers are enhanced by the presence of National Park Service rangers, who board large cruise ships as they enter the bay. The rangers give presentations and often roam the outside decks, talking with passengers and pointing out wildlife, including whales, mountain goats, grizzlies, sea otters, puffins, bald eagles, and harbor seals hauled out on the icebergs. The Park Service website also offers lots of great information specifically designed to help cruise ship passengers make the most of their time in the bay.

There's much more to Glacier Bay than the stunning scenery, and rangers will help you understand the intriguing intricacies of an ecosystem that was buried under ice until the late 18th century.

Passengers of small tour boats will be lucky enough to have the chance to explore the terrestrial side of the park from the dock in **Bartlett Cove,** the site of **park headquarters,** the visitor center, **Glacier Bay Lodge,** and a modest **natural history museum.** From here you can hike the **Forest Trail,** a mile-long (1.6 km) loop that meanders through a verdant spruce-hemlock forest dotted with ponds and inhabited by bears, porcupines, and other critters. The trail returns to the developed part of Bartlett Cove along the shore, from which you may spot humpback whales. ∎

## NEED TO KNOW

### Port Logistics: Glacier Bay National Park & Preserve

Large cruise ships can't dock in Glacier Bay, but small vessels can, enabling exploration of the park. The mini-cruisers tie up at the dock in Bartlett Cove, the only developed part of the park and the site of park headquarters and the visitor center.

# HAINES

Home to a mere 2,500 people, Haines is comfy and unassuming, like a favorite flannel shirt. Yet surrounding the town's cozy cafés and little harbor is a flamboyant landscape of surpassing beauty: snowy mountains, waterfalls, forest, fjords, broad rivers, glaciers, and lakes. This landscape gets a mere 60 inches (152 cm) of precipitation a year on average, and these rugged environs have prompted Haines to call itself the "Adventure Capital of Alaska."

Bald eagles fish for their supper in a river near Haines.

**Haines**

Map p. 67

**Visitor Information**

✉ Haines Convention & Visitors Bureau, 122 2nd Ave.

☎ 907-766-6418

**visithaines.com**

**Alaska Indian Arts**

✉ 13 Ft. Seward Dr.

☎ 907-766-2160

🕐 Closed Sat.–Sun.

**alaskaindianarts.com**

Start your amble around Haines by marching about 300 yards (274 m) straight up Portage Street to the gleaming white, well-kept frame buildings of **Fort William H. Seward National Historic Landmark.** Fort Seward was an active U.S. Army outpost from 1904 to 1947. Many of the former officers' houses are now private homes, but a variety of businesses occupy other buildings in the complex, including **Alaska Indian Arts,** housed in the former base hospital. This nonprofit is dedicated to the preservation of the crafts and culture of the Northwest Coast tribes, and at their shop you can buy silk screen prints bearing

traditional designs and sometimes watch master carvers working on totem poles.

From Fort Seward, go three blocks north on Second Avenue until it hits the Haines Highway. Just a few steps to your right, down the highway toward the waterfront, takes you to the **American Bald Eagle Foundation,** which houses a natural-history museum and a raptor center. It's no coincidence that an institution devoted to bald eagles is located in Haines, for just 10 miles (16 km) up the highway from town sprawls the 48,000 acres (19,424 ha) of the **Alaska Chilkat Bald Eagle Preserve.** More than 3,000 of these iconic raptors overwinter here—perhaps the largest gathering of bald eagles in the world. The foundation celebrates the eagles and the entire preserve's ecosystem with an enormous diorama featuring more than 200 wildlife specimens, such as grizzlies, moose, and mountain goats. The foundation also provides a home for numerous birds in its live raptor center, including not only bald eagles but owls, hawks, falcons, and even a Eurasian eagle owl.

---

**INSIDER TIP:**

Drive slowly on Lutak Road and you'll spot harbor seals, bears feeding on salmon, mountain goats, and of course, bald eagles.

—PETER GWIN
National Geographic
*magazine writer*

---

The **Hammer Museum,** the result of one local man's inordinate and idiosyncratic enthusiasm for hammers, waits three blocks north on Second Avenue and one block east on Main Street. The collection of more than 1,500 hammers conveys a rich history. The Tlingit Warrior's Pick "Slave Killer," an 800-year-old hammer found in the ground right under the museum, was used to sacrifice slaves. The oldest hammer, dating from 2500 B.C., was used by ancient Egyptians in association with the building of the third pyramid at Giza.

Continue half a block on Main Street and you'll come to the **Sheldon Museum and Cultural Center,** notable for its collection of Alaska native artifacts, especially those from the local Tlingit. You'll see fine displays of beadwork and spruce-root basketry as well as some outstanding Chilkat Tlingit blankets, highly prized by Alaska natives and often sought out by nobility and the wealthy to use as ceremonial robes.

The visitor center can point you to guided tours outside of Haines or help you rent a car. Drive out on **Lutak Road:** This byway skirts Chilkoot and Lutak Inlets and ends at the **Chilkoot Lake State Recreation Site** *(dnr .alaska.gov/parks/aspunits/south east/chilkootlksrs.htm),* with trails along the lake shore and to the summit of Mount Riley (1,760 feet/536 m). Bald eagles, harbor seals, bears feeding on salmon, mountain goats on the slopes—it's hard to know where to point your binoculars first. ∎

**American Bald Eagle Foundation**
- ✉ 113 Haines Hwy
- ☎ 907-766-3094
- 🕐 Closed Sat.–Sun.
- 💲 $$, free with military ID

**baldeagles.org**

**Hammer Museum**
- ✉ 108 Main St.
- ☎ 907-766-2374
- 🕐 Closed Oct.– April & Sun. May–Sept.
- 💲 $

**hammermuseum.org**

**Sheldon Museum and Cultural Center**
- ✉ 11 Main St.
- ☎ 907-766-2366
- 🕐 Closed Sun.
- 💲 $

**sheldonmuseum.org**

---

**NEED TO KNOW**

**Port Logistics: Haines**
Cruise ships tie up right in town at the Port Chilkoot Cruise Ship Dock; schedules are arranged so there is only one large ship at a time in port. Haines can be seen in 2–3 hours on foot, or you may choose to rent a car and take a tour out of town. An 11-mile (18 km) drive down Lutak Road offers some spectacular wildlife-spotting opportunities and leads to the Chilkoot Lake State Recreation Site.

# WHITE PASS & YUKON TRAIN RIDE

During the Klondike gold rush, the narrow-gauge White Pass & Yukon Route was blasted and chiseled 110 miles (177 km) through the mountains to connect Skagway (which had ocean access) to Whitehorse, Yukon (which had river access leading to the interior goldfields). Begun in 1898, it took tens of thousands of laborers 26 months and 450 tons (408 tonnes) of explosives to finish "the railway built of gold."

The White Pass & Yukon Route runs through the high country above Skagway.

In recognition of this accomplishment, the route is now designated an international Historic Civil Engineering Landmark. Today passengers board vintage railcars and travel various distances along the route. The most popular excursion, described here, takes you 20 miles (32 km) up to **White Pass Summit** and back, a scenic 3- to 3.5-hour journey.

This narrated trip is very popular, so book well in advance (tel 800-343-7373, wpyr.com). It starts in Skagway at the **depot** ❶ on the corner of Second Avenue and Spring Street. (If you book through your ship, you can board at the dock.) For the best views, get a seat on the left side going up and the right coming back. You can stand on the outside platforms—great for photos. And bring a coat—it can get cold out there.

**NOT TO BE MISSED:**

Rocky Point • Bridal Veil Falls • Inspiration Point

The train eases out along the east side of town, passing the **Gold Rush Cemetery** ❷ at railroad Mile 2.5. Here rest the bones of gold rush gangster "Soapy" Smith and Frank Reid, the man who shot him.

Continuing above the Skagway River, steadily gaining elevation, the train chugs up to **Denver** ❸ at Mile 5.8. On the train's morning runs backpackers often get off here to head up the Denver Glacier Trail. The train crosses the Skagway River East Fork and about a mile (1.6 km) later reaches **Rocky Point ❹**, which yields great views down the valley to Skagway, the harbor, and beyond.

The hardship of gouging this route out of these rugged mountains is grimly memorialized at Mile 10.4, **Black Cross Rock,** where a blasting accident buried two workers under the 100-ton (91 tonne) hunk of black granite by the tracks; altogether 35 laborers died during the two years of construction. Hundreds of horses used to haul equipment also perished, earning one stretch of the route the nickname "Dead Horse Gulch." A profusion of waterfalls grace the route as it proceeds, topped at Mile 11.5 by spectacular **Bridal Veil Falls ❺**, fed by nearby glaciers.

At Mile 16, just before entering **Tunnel Mountain ❻**, the train crawls across a bridge 1,000 feet (305 m) above Glacier Gorge. Shortly after the long tunnel, at Mile 17, arguably the finest vista of the route appears: **Inspiration Point ❼**. The views down the valley stretch to Skagway, out to the Lynn Canal (a natural body of water), and far out to the Chilkat Range, some 20 miles (32 km) farther south. Finally, after huffing and puffing, the engines pull the railcars up to their destination, **White Pass Summit ❽**, 2,865 vertical feet (873 m) higher than sea level, where the train started.

| | |
|---|---|
| 🅰 | See also area map p. 67 |
| 🅿 | Skagway |
| 🕛 | 40 miles (64 km) round-trip |
| 🕒 | 3–3.5 hours round-trip |
| 🅿 | Skagway |

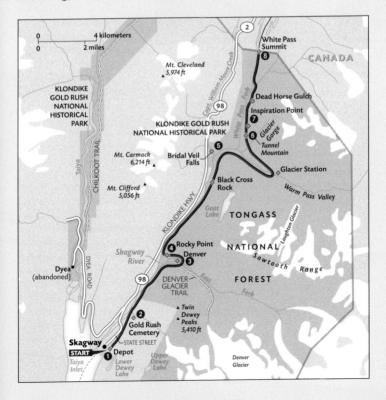

# SKAGWAY

Skagway is an unabashed tourist town, evoking the life and times of the Klondike gold rush with an exceptional array of about 100 preserved and restored buildings from that era. Much of downtown Skagway is maintained as part of the Klondike Gold Rush National Historical Park, absorbing the daily summer flood of thousands of visitors.

■ Historic downtown Skagway has become a shoppers' paradise within a backdrop of natural beauty.

**Skagway**

Map p. 67

**Visitor Information**

Skagway Convention & Visitors Bureau, 245 Broadway

907-983-2854 or 888-762-1898

**skagway.com**

**Klondike Gold Rush National Historical Park**

2nd Ave. & Broadway

907-983-9200

Closed Sun.

**nps.gov/klgo**

In 1895 the town of Skagway didn't exist. The future site of this settlement lay at the northern-most point of the Inside Passage but was still a remote wilderness inhabited by a few scattered Tlingits and Euro-American settlers. But by 1897 and 1898, at the height of the gold rush, about 10,000 people lived here. Skagway was the favored terrestrial starting point for tens of thousands of stampeders, who shipped into town, stocked up on supplies, and then tried to make the arduous trek over the coastal mountains to the interior of Canada, where gold had been discovered near the Klondike River.

Almost all the main sights of Skagway lie conveniently within

the four-by-seven-block down-town, just north of the docks, so exploring on foot is easy. You can see most of the main attractions simply by walking half a dozen blocks up Broadway.

Start at Broadway and Second Avenue, at the **Klondike Gold Rush National Historical Park** visitor center, housed in the large, colorful former depot of the White Pass & Yukon Railroad. (The new, still active depot of the railroad is a couple of doors to the east; see pp. 100–101.) The park service staff answers questions, shows a 30-minute film, and offers a variety of 45-minute ranger presentations. Note the reproduction of the *Seattle Post-Intelligencer* for July 19, 1897, which announces the discovery of that seductive yellow metal with huge bold letters in a headline that screams "Gold! Gold! Gold!"

An adjacent part of the visitor center showcases exhibits on the gold rush, including evocative photographs that reveal the hardships the prospectors endured. One image shows dozens of gold seekers on the beach with their mountains of gear that needed to be hauled up and over the daunting Chilkoot Trail. The center displays some examples of that gear, too, such as dog packs, snowshoes, and, of course, gold pans.

## Broadway & Beyond

As you stroll the wooden side-walks of the next two blocks of Broadway, nearly every building you see was built between 1897 and 1900. One of the most popular for having a beer or taking a tour is the **Red Onion Saloon,** a brothel during gold rush times that was moved to its current location diagonally across from the national park visitor center in 1914. Upstairs is now a brothel museum, little changed from Klondike times, although now mannequins cast come-hither looks onto the street below. Female docents in flousy period costumes give tours.

Just a few steps farther up Broadway stands the **Arctic Brotherhood Hall,** former home of a pioneer fraternal organization and currently home to the **Skagway Convention & Visitors Bureau**'s visitor center. The distinctive facade is an attraction all its own, fashioned from 8,883 pieces of driftwood, most of them original sticks from 1900.

The interior of the **Mascot Saloon,** at Broadway and Third Avenue, remains much the same as when the saloon was built in 1898, when men bellied up to the bar, and, as one interpretive sign notes, whiskey was a drink, beer a mere chaser. The Mascot was one of some 80 saloons that helped make 19th-century Skagway "little better than hell on Earth," as one Canadian police superintendent wrote in 1898.

After wandering farther along Broadway, turn right on Seventh Avenue and walk one block to the 1899 granite-faced building that houses city hall and the **Skagway Museum.** Check out its eclectic collection, ranging from a Tlingit canoe to a stuffed brown bear to the July 15, 1898, edition of the *Skagway News,* which reports the gunfight that resulted in the death of notorious Skagway crime boss Jefferson "Soapy" Smith. ∎

### Red Onion Saloon

- 201 Broadway
- 907-983-2414
- Closed Oct.–March

redonion1898.com

### Skagway Museum

- 700 Spring St.
- 907-983-2420
- $

skagway.org/museum

## NEED TO KNOW

### Port Logistics: Skagway

The main cruise ship terminal borders the center of Skagway, where most of the attractions are located, so walking into town is easy. Passengers whose ships tie up at the Railroad Dock have a half-mile (0.8 km) stroll to reach downtown. City buses meet the ships and take you there for a few dollars; an all-day pass is the best deal. Skagway can be seen in 2–3 hours.

### Skagway Highlights

You could profitably spend more time at any of these places of interest, but here are some attractions with suggested visiting times:

- Klondike Gold Rush National Historical Park: 1–2 hours
- Lower Dewey Lake Trail: 2–3 hours. While this is only 0.7 mile (1.1 km) long, it rises 600 feet (183 m) to the lake; it begins on Spring Street between Third and Fourth Avenues.
- Smuggler's Cove Trail: 1–2 hours. This easy stroll along the ocean heads out to Yakutania Point.
- White Pass & Yukon Route: 3–4 hours. A great train ride (see pp. 100–101).

Stunning parks to explore on land and water, awe-inspiring landscapes and wildlife, a dream highway, and an angler's paradise

# SOUTH-CENTRAL COAST

A sea otter floats in Resurrection Bay near Seward, Alaska. Opposite: Sea of ice in Prince William Sound

# SOUTH-CENTRAL COAST

**Variety is a defining characteristic of the civilized aspects of the south-central coast. The ports range from Whittier, a drab, utilitarian town of about 200 souls that mainly serves as a gateway to Prince William Sound, to Homer, a charming enclave of 5,000-plus known for its free-spirited ways and odd blend of fine art and great fishing.**

The region's other three ports—Cordova, Valdez, and Seward—are similar in population, running from about 2,000 to about 4,000 people, but they differ considerably in character. Cordova is a rough-hewn, isolated commercial fishing center that can only be reached by boat or plane. Valdez is the terminus for the Trans-Alaska oil pipeline and the port for the massive tankers that haul oil around the globe. It becomes quickly apparent, however, that this port town is also home to a thriving outdoor recreation industry that takes advantage of the scenic surroundings. Seward is the terminus for the Alaska Railroad, which connects to Anchorage and points north, and also functions as the gateway to Kenai Fjords National Park.

Relations with large cruise ships also vary among the five ports: Numerous large cruise ships call on Seward, a fair number depart from Whittier, only a handful reach Homer, and none at all venture to Valdez or Cordova. Medium and small adventure cruise ships go to some of the towns, but only the Alaska Marine Highway ferries regularly visit all these ports.

Variety is likewise a defining characteristic of the natural aspects of Alaska's

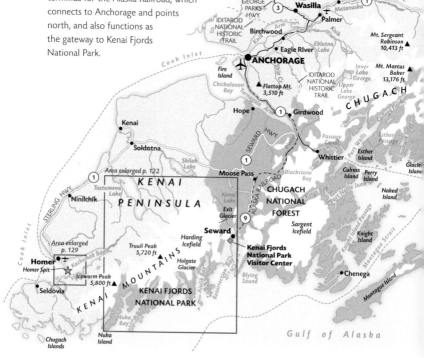

south-central coast. On display are rocky shores, mossy rain forest, gleaming glaciers, high mountains that often hover right above the coastline, rushing rivers, subalpine meadows painted by wildflowers, and alpine tundra. However, the region does share one wonderful trait: The whole place is drop-dead beautiful and richly endowed with wildlife. The cold, clear coastal waters teem with fish and harbor some of the world's finest commercial salmon fisheries. Sportfishing draws boatloads of visitors, too; Homer bills itself as the "Halibut Capital of the World" and Seward hosts a major fishing derby every year. Fleets of tour boats also venture into these waters to give passengers a look at the whales, sea lions, dolphins, seals, otters, and seabird colonies that throng offshore pinnacles.

The Copper River Delta, a vast maze of sinuous channels, grassy wetlands, and fertile mudflats, constitutes one of the world's great bird migration stopovers; millions of sandpipers, dunlins, phalaropes, and other shorebirds check in every spring and fall to rest and refuel.

## NOT TO BE MISSED:

**Driving the scenic Richardson Highway** 114–115

**Watching the puffins fly and the sea lions slither at the Alaska SeaLife Center** 118–119

**Touring Kenai Fjords National Park by powerboat** 121–123

**Browsing Homer's art galleries** 125–126

**A nature tour of Kamechak Bay with the Center for Alaskan Coastal Studies** 127

The wildlife smorgasbord continues on land, though the terrestrial critters often are harder to spot. Homer is a major jumping-off point for grizzly-viewing trips. Both grizzlies and black bears roam the rain forests. The moose of the Kenai Peninsula are famed for their giant size. Mountain goats scale steep slopes in the high country, and equally nimble Dall sheep clamber about on rocky outcroppings. And, even far inland, salmon make the scene pushing upstream to their spawning ground. All five species of Pacific salmon swarm up the rivers and creeks of the south-central coast by the millions, providing an iconic wildlife spectacle not to be missed. ∎

# CORDOVA & COPPER RIVER DELTA

Cordova is a fishing town. Its permanent population of about 2,300 more than doubles in the spring and summer when visitors pour in for the fishing season. But most aren't tourists looking to do a little sportfishing; these are seasonal workers coming to crew fishing boats or labor in seafood processing plants. Cordova is, above all, a *commercial* fishing town.

Angling for a prize catch, fishermen head upriver along a slow, smooth stretch of the Copper River.

**Cordova**

🏔 Map p. 107

**Visitor Information**

✉ Cordova Chamber of Commerce, 401 1st St.

☎ 907-424-7260

**cordovachamber.com**

The logical place to make the acquaintance of a fishing town is at its harbor. From the Alaska Marine Highway ferry dock, walk south along Alaska Route 10, the only street that runs past the ferry terminal. You'll pass piers stacked with shipping containers and warehouses. As you near downtown you may see fishing nets drying in front yards.

After about a quarter of a mile (0.4 km) on Route 10, turn right on the short stub of Cannery Row, which leads to **Copper River Seafoods.** This major Alaskan company was founded in Cordova in 1996 by four fishermen. The retail outlet is next to the office in the processing complex—this is no tasting room in Napa—so look for signs to the office, ask

around, and watch your step as you traverse this industrial area. Once you find the shop, you can buy a jar of smoked Copper River sockeye, some frozen king crab legs and claws, or splurge on a gift box that includes Copper River king, sockeye, and coho salmon. You'll find similar local and Alaskan seafood treats nearby at the little retail outlet attached to the processing plant at **60° North Seafoods.** To find 60° North, walk on down Route 10 from Cannery Row and turn right on the next street (there's no street sign). Follow this road as it almost immediately curves to the left, at which point you're on Jim Poor Avenue. Go two blocks to the intersection with Haida Lane and you'll be there.

Laden with bags of salmon and halibut, labor on down Jim Crow Avenue (aka Seafood Lane) for about 300 yards (274 m) to the intersection with Breakwater Avenue, on the harborfront. Immediately in front of you are two short piers, with one slanting diagonally off to your right at the harbor's mouth. Amble out to the blue-roofed building, home to the **Prince William Sound Science Center.** Outside you'll find a covered observation deck from which to take in the fishing fleet and watch for sea otters swimming in the harbor; the Cordova area is packed with these crowd-pleasing members of the weasel family. Founded in April 1989, one month after the *Exxon Valdez* oil spill (see p. 33), the center is today a leading research and education facility in the local environment, climate change, and human impact. It has educational programs and interpretive signs around the deck.

The fishing fleet may be out chasing salmon, but when the boats are in port, you'll notice that these are *boats,* not ships—not 120-foot (37 m) corporate-fleet trawlers. These 30- and 35-foot (9.1 and 10.7 m) vessels are the tools of independent fishers, men, women, and families who live in Cordova and operate their own boats, with maybe one or two hired crew members during high season.

Now walk east along the harborfront and turn right on Railroad Avenue; after 100 yards (91 m), turn left onto Council Avenue for First Street, the next block and the city's main drag. For information

about the town, walk north up First one block to the **Cordova Chamber of Commerce.**

Back at the corner of First and Council, it's time to mosey down First Street, the heart of Cordova's **downtown,** which consists of just a few square blocks of local businesses, such as **Copper River Fleece** *(504 First St., tel 907/424-4304, copperriverfleece.com),* which makes and sells colorful hand-crafted garments inspired by Alaska's cultural heritage. Relatively few historic buildings remain from a century ago. Not least, a major fire in 1963 destroyed the entire block on First between Council and Browning Avenues. However, one block down First is a local hangout that survived the conflagration and has been around since the dawn of Cordova's creation in 1907, following the discovery of copper and development of the Northwestern Railway, which serviced what

**Copper River Seafoods**

✉ 300 Cannery Row

☎ 907-424-3721

copperriverseafoods.com

**60° North Seafoods**

✉ 210 Jim Poor Ave.

☎ 907-424-7755

sixtynorth seafoods.com

## Wild Salmon

Alaska is bullish on wild salmon. Its commercial wild salmon fishery is the largest in the world, hauling in about 160 million salmon a year. The state doesn't allow fish-farming, and it passionately promotes the health, economic, and conservation benefits of wild salmon. (In fishing towns like Cordova, you'll notice bumper stickers and signs in windows celebrating wild salmon.) The **Alaska Seafood Marketing Institute** *(alaskaseafood.org)* is the source for all things salmon, from recipes to information on the salmon life cycle.

**Prince William Sound Science Center**

✉ 300 Breakwater Ave.

☎ 907-424-5800

🕓 Closed Sat.–Sun.

pwssc.org

## Cordova Center & Cordova Historical Museum

✉ Cordova Center, 601 1st St.

☎ 907-424-6665

🕐 Closed Sun. Memorial Day–Labor Day & Sun.–Mon. rest of year

💲 $

cordovamuseum.org

## Ilanka Cultural Center Museum

✉ 110 Nicholoff Way

☎ 907-424-7903

🕐 Closed Sat.–Mon. & Wed.

eyak-nsn.gov/culture/#museum

## Copper River Highway/Delta

🗺 Map p. 107

Visitor Information

✉ Cordova Ranger District, Chugach National Forest, 612 2nd St.

☎ 907-424-7661

fs.usda.gov/chugach

was at the time the world's largest copper mine. The well-worn **Alaskan Hotel & Bar** (600 1st St., tel 907-424-3299), patronized by locals still wearing their work boots, proudly displays its sign upside down. Its near-twin next door, the beloved "CoHo," or Cordova Hotel & Bar, was demolished in 2016.

In stark contrast, the sleek, contemporary **Cordova Center** rises on the other side of the street. Opened in 2015, this 34,000-square-foot (3,159 sq m) complex houses city offices, a library, conference halls, performance spaces, and—across the street—the **Cordova Historical Museum.** The museum covers in depth the 196-mile (315 km) railroad that was miraculously built in the early 1900s from the copper mines in what is now Wrangell–St. Elias National Park through forbidding mountains to the port of Cordova. A little bit of everything Cordovan is here: photos of the Iceworm Festival through the years, an Eyak canoe, a small painting by local artist Sydney Laurence, fishing gear, and the museum's beloved stuffed leatherback sea turtle, Prince Willy.

Take the path around the outside of the Cordova Center and follow the stairs down the hill to Railroad Avenue and its intersection with Nicholoff Way, which borders the south side of the harbor. A few minutes' walk on Nicholoff will bring you to the high-windowed **Ilanka Cultural Center Museum,** which serves the area's Alaska natives. Its small but elegant museum displays

historical and contemporary cultural and natural artifacts, such as a purse made of swan's feet and one of the world's few complete killer whale skeletons. It also is the home of a famous "shame" totem pole created by local Tlingit carver Mike Webber. Unveiled on March 24, 2007—the 18th anniversary of the Exxon Valdez oil spill—it depicts a sea otter, a bald eagle, and sea ducks floating dead in the water. A huge black tongue of oil runs from the mouth of an upside-down face atop the pole—

---

**INSIDER TIP:**

As you watch Childs Glacier calving at the Million Dollar Bridge, be wary of waves. Keep to the high ground.

—ROWLAND SHELLEY
National Geographic field researcher

---

a depiction of Lee Raymond, the longtime CEO of Exxon. His disembodied head is carved with dollar signs for eyes and a long Pinocchio nose to convey what locals viewed as the corporation's failure to fully compensate locals for the damage. Go another block along Nicholoff, and the street ends and the boardwalk **Breakwater Trail** begins, leading out along the breakwater on the west side of the harbor.

## Copper River Highway

You'll need to rent a car for this journey out of town on Route 10. Construction on this route began in 1945 with the intent to go far north to link up with Alaska's highway system, but the 1964 earthquake put an end to that idea after just 49 miles (79 km) had been built. That 49-mile remnant is today's Copper River Highway, curving across the bountiful **Copper River Delta,** one of the stopovers for millions of birds migrating along the Pacific Flyway. This is the largest continuous wetland on the Pacific coast of North America. You'll hit the western edge of the delta at about Mile 7, where the highway emerges from mountains and forest into open delta country. This is mostly flat wetlands greened by alder, willow, and grass populated by moose, bears, beavers, and trumpeter swans. At Mile 10.7 there's a Forest Service pavilion with interpretive signs.

For a look at **Sheridan Glacier,** turn off at Mile 13.6 and drive to the end of the 4-mile (6.4 km) spur road, where you'll find two trailheads. Take the **Sheridan Mountain Trail** only if you're up for a long, strenuous trek. Otherwise, choose the **Sheridan Glacier Trail;** after negotiating loose rock on a bit of a slope right at the beginning, it's an easy 30- to 45-minute hike to the glacier. Back on the highway, at Mile 16.8, take the 3-mile (4.8 km) spur road to **Alaganik Slough,** a classic slice of delta made accessible by an elevated boardwalk, interpretive signs, and wildlife-viewing blind. In summer, bears, eagles, and other animals come to feed on spawning candlefish. The **Haystack Trail,** at Mile 19.1, is a moderate 0.8-mile (1.3 km) hike through a spruce-hemlock forest. It ascends a knoll

■ A maze of waterways and marshes, the vast Copper River Delta drains the Wrangell and Chugach Mountains.

that rewards your effort with terrific views of the delta and the Gulf of Alaska.

Near Mile 27 the highway starts crossing the main channels of the Copper River on bridge after bridge. Unfortunately, Mile 36 is permanently closed, and the highway beyond is no longer driveable. However, you can take a jet-boat ride (*$$$$$*) from here to the "Million Dollar Bridge," at the terminus of **Childs Glacier;** contact Childs Glacier Lodge (*childs glacierlodge.com*). ■

## NEED TO KNOW

### Port Logistics: Cordova

No cruise ships stop here. Ferry passengers arrive at the Alaska Marine Highway ferry dock, about 0.75 mile (1.2 km) out of town. Fast ferries make several runs a week to Cordova from both Whittier (3.25 hours) and Valdez (2.75 hours). Walk south along Alaska Route 10 into the town center. To go out into the Copper River Delta from Cordova, you'll need to rent a car (*tel 907-424-4277, chinookautorentals.com*).

# VALDEZ

Historically, Valdez is a tale of two cities—the one prior to the 1964 Good Friday earthquake and the one that emerged since then. Situated at the end of a fjord at the northeastern edge of Prince William Sound, the town grew into a modestly important port, especially after the Richardson Highway linked Valdez to Anchorage in 1913.

A moose dwarfs visitors to the Valdez Museum.

On Good Friday 1964, a massive earthquake and ensuing tsunamis obliterated much of Valdez. Citizens rebuilt the town on higher, more stable ground 4 miles (6.4 km) to the west. Growth accelerated after the oil industry and the Trans-Alaska Pipeline came to Valdez in the 1970s. Today Valdez is a prosperous town of about 4,000 that serves as a terminal for oil tankers and a recreation hub for sportfishing, kayaking, flightseeing, river rafting, hiking, wildlife-viewing, winter sports, and boat tours of the sumptuous eastern end of the sound.

Now and then a cruise ship steams into Valdez, but the vast majority of waterborne visitors arrive by the marine highway and tie up at the dock at the south end of the little downtown. As you exit the dock area, take a left on Hazelet Street for about 100 feet (30 m) to **Remembering Old Valdez,** a unit of the Valdez Museum that recollects the pre-earthquake community. A scale model faithfully details the town's appearance, right down to the window design on the Alaskan Hotel. The other main exhibits recall the earthquake and tsunami of 1964, including harrowing video clips.

To visit the main **Valdez Museum,** continue up Hazelet

Street a few blocks to Egan Drive. Turn right and walk on Egan one block to reach this well organized facility, which displays a mix of Alaska native, gold rush, early settlement, and oil-industry artifacts. To counterbalance a romanticized view of the gold rush, take a look at the museum's evocative photos

## Trans-Alaska Pipeline

**The 1,000 acres (405 ha) of the Trans-Alaska Pipeline terminal sprawl on the south side of the bay, across from Valdez. Huge tankers dock here to ingest the oil that has flowed 800 miles (1,287 km) through 4-foot-diameter (1.2 m) pipes south from the fields in Prudhoe Bay, on the Arctic Ocean. Completed in 1977, the pipeline crosses three major mountain ranges and 34 major rivers, and has a linefill capacity of 9,059,057 barrels.**

of the 19th-century stampeders struggling to the goldfields, accompanied by quotes that make plain the extreme hardships faced by contemporaries forced to haul heavy loads. The existing museum is scheduled to be demolished and replaced by a new, larger, state-of-the-art structure, to be completed by about 2023. (It will also house Remembering Old Valdez.)

Downtown offers yet another worthy museum, this one

adjacent to the Prince William Sound Community College campus. Retrace your steps to Hazelet, go north six blocks to Lowe Street, and go right one block on Lowe to the **Maxine & Jesse Whitney Museum,** which boasts one of the largest private collections of Alaska native art and artifacts in the state. Don't miss the fantastic parkas, such as the one made from 40 murre breasts with wolverine lining. Another highlight of the museum is the scrimshaw—birds, dolls, ships, whales, and other figures carved from walrus ivory.

For a look at contemporary Valdez, return to the Valdez Museum and continue one block down Egan to Meals Avenue. Turn right, walk two blocks, then turn left on **North Harbor Drive,** which runs along the picturesque **Small Boat Harbor.** This is the main waterfront; the downtown side of this short street is lined with gift shops, motels, kayak tour outfits, and cafés, and the harbor side is devoted to a promenade. Get a look across the 3 miles (4.8 km) of the fjord at the Trans-Alaska Pipeline terminal—not to mention the town's generally beautiful setting—by going to the east end of the Small Boat Harbor to **Dock Point Park** and walking the easy **Dock Point Trail,** a 0.75-mile (1.2 km) loop.

To see more scenery but without the pipeline terminal, consider taking one of the numerous tour boats based in Valdez, the gateway to eastern

*(continued on p. 116)*

### Valdez

🗺 Map p. 107

**Visitor Information**

✉ Valdez Convention & Visitors Bureau, 309 Fairbanks Dr.

☎ 907-835-2984

**valdezalaska.org**

### Remembering Old Valdez

✉ 436 Hazelet St.

☎ 907-835-5407

💲 $

**valdezmuseum.org**

### Valdez Museum

✉ 217 Egan Dr.

☎ 907-835-2764

💲 $$

**valdezmuseum.org**

### Maxine & Jesse Whitney Museum

✉ 303 Lowe St.

☎ 907-834-1690

💲 Donation

**mjwhitney museum.org**

# DRIVE: EXPLORING THE RICHARDSON HIGHWAY

The scenic Richardson Highway connects Prince William Sound and Valdez to points north. Tracing a 19th-century gold rush route, the road follows a dramatic river up into the coastal mountains to a high pass and a state recreation site that provides a close-up look at a glacier.

The view from Thompson Pass stretches for miles across the Chugach Mountains.

Known as Alaska's first road, the Richardson opened to motor vehicles in 1913. For a few years prior it was traversed by horses and livestock-drawn wagons; in its earliest years it was known as the Valdez-to-Eagle Trail. Today the highway runs 366 miles (589 km) to Fairbanks, but this driving tour only covers the first 29 miles (47 km) out of Valdez (see pp. 112–113, 116); fortunately, they're the prettiest miles of the entire route.

Note that the mileposts along the Richardson were erected prior to the 1964 earthquake, which leveled Old Valdez and forced the town to a new site 4 miles (6.4 km) farther away. So when you see, for example, mile marker 26 at Thompson Pass, that means you're 26 miles (42 km) from Old Valdez but 30 miles (48 km) from present-day Valdez. This entry uses the

## NOT TO BE MISSED:

**Keystone Canyon • Thompson Pass • Worthington Glacier**

same mileage figures as the mileposts, so if you want to know exactly how far you are from Valdez, add 4 miles (6.4 km).

Around Mile 4 you'll travel alongside the **Lowe River ❶**, whose braided channels are gray with glacial silt from the mountains you're about to head into. At Mile 13, the Richardson swings northeast and enters the narrow confines of **Keystone Canyon ❷**. Seemingly at every bend, waterfalls cascade from towering cliffs into the Lowe. Turn out at Mile 13.4 to contemplate **Horsetail Falls** ❸ and about half a mile (0.8 km) later to savor **Bridal Veil Falls** ❹. If you want to stretch your legs, from the turnout at Bridal Veil you can head up the 2.5-mile (4 km) Valdez Goat Trail, which follows an old Alaska native route that figured prominently in getting gold seekers and military personnel from the coast to the interior before the Richardson was built. This trail saved the lives of countless stampeders by opening a route that didn't cross any glaciers. If you prefer not to hike the whole trail, a quarter-mile (0.4 km) uphill walk will take you to a scenic overlook.

Near Mile 16 you'll begin to emerge from Keystone Canyon, and a few miles later the highway starts to climb in earnest. After several miles you'll rise above tree line into the wide-open vistas of the alpine tundra. At Mile 24, a 1-mile (1.6 km) spur road leads to **Blueberry Lake State Recreation Site** ❺, which has a campground, picnic tables, and fine fishing. Take the time here to scan the lake and ponds for trumpeter swans, or just listen for their resonant calls. And there are indeed blueberry bushes here for the picking, ripe in late summer or early fall.

## Thompson Pass & Beyond

At Mile 26, you reach the highest point in this stretch of the highway: **Thompson Pass** ❻, elevation 2,678 feet (816 m). This is one of the snowiest places in all of Alaska, having recorded 5.1 feet (1.5 m) of snow in one day and almost 84 feet (25 m) in one year. All this snow has long attracted winter sports enthusiasts, and major skiing and snowboarding competitions are regularly held in this area. There's something truly irresistible about those steep, untracked, mile-long (1.6 km) runs to lovers of adventure sports.

The drive ends near Mile 29, where a half-mile (0.8 km) paved side road winds uphill to the parking lot at **Worthington Glacier State Recreation Site** ❼. There's a visitor center and a short trail to the face of the glacier, where visitors are urged to stay back a safe distance due to the dangers of falling ice.

---

🏔 See also area map p. 107
🅿 Valdez
🚗 67 miles (108 km) round-trip
🕐 2 hours (without stops)
🅿 Valdez

---

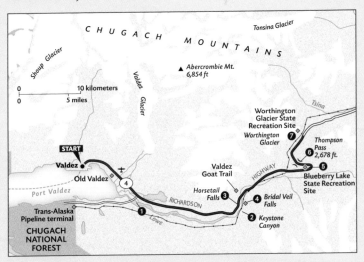

**Whittier**

Map pp. 106

**Visitor Information**

907-472-2327

**whittieralaska chamber.org**

**whittieralaska.gov**

Prince William Sound. A typical full-day trip will cruise through the upper reaches of **Valdez Arm,** staying about 200 yards (183 m) off the forested northern shore. Dozens of waterfalls course down the green tundra of the steep mountain slopes. You're almost sure to see sea otters, bald eagles, and sea lions, and you're likely to spot humpback whales, tufted puffins, mountain goats, and harbor seals. At the far reach of the voyage, you'll enter **Columbia Bay,** where luminous blue icebergs will start appearing, evidence that you're nearing **Columbia Glacier,** one of the largest and most active glaciers in Alaska. Sometimes these icebergs become so thick that the boat must stop miles from the face of the glacier, but usually you can motor up to within a mile (1.6 km) or even half a mile (0.8 km) and watch as giant slabs of ice shear off with gunshot-like bangs and thunder into the water.

## Whittier

Multitudes of travelers come to this tiny utilitarian town, 110 miles (177 km) west of Valdez, where function trumps form. Nearly all of its 200-some residents live in a couple of drab high-rises built in the 1950s to house military personnel. It has no visitor center, no notable attractions, and just a few unremarkable restaurants and shops. So why the crowds? Whittier is the gateway to western Prince William Sound, a place of unsurpassed beauty. And large numbers of people can get to the sound via Whittier not only on cruise ships but also by the road to Anchorage, about 60 miles (96 km) away, via the **Anton Anderson Memorial Tunnel.** During World War II, Army engineers blasted a 1-mile (1.6 km) tunnel through Begich Peak and a 2.5-mile (4 km) tunnel through Maynard Mountain. Dimly lighted and enclosed by dripping rock walls, this narrow tunnel is not for the claustrophobic. ■

## NEED TO KNOW

### Port Logistics: Valdez & Whittier

Whittier is regularly visited by cruise ships; Valdez is served mainly by ferries, with an occasional cruise ship stopping. Whittier's cruise ship terminal is on the waterfront; from the cruise ship dock at the west end of town, walk east along the waterfront, and you'll quickly encounter the many tour companies and charter outfits that can take you into western Prince William Sound. One popular site is Blackstone Bay, home to towering waterfalls, tidewater glaciers, and a host of wildlife. Many tours head for Esther Passage, easing by a Steller sea lion rookery and passing 26 glaciers.

The ferry dock in Valdez is downtown, so walking is easy, but you will have to rent a car to take the Richardson Highway tour.

### Valdez & Whittier Highlights

Here are some suggested times:
- Boat tour to Columbia Glacier (Valdez): 7 hours
- Maxine & Jesse Whitney Museum (Valdez): 1–2 hours
- Boat tour in Prince William Sound (Whittier): 4–6 hours

# SEWARD

**The town of Seward overlooks Resurrection Bay, a svelte finger of the Gulf of Alaska. Framed by rugged peaks and dark spruce forests, it is a pleasant port of about 2,700 residents, roughly divided into two parts: the relaxed, older downtown and a busy cluster of new development centered around the harbor, a mile (1.6 km) north of downtown.**

Seward is a coastal haven for vessels of all sizes in the summer months.

Seward is a transportation center. It's the southern terminus of the **Seward Highway,** a scenic byway that runs 127 miles (204 km) north to Anchorage and connects to the rest of Alaska's main road system. Seward also is the southern terminus of the **Alaska Railroad,** which takes travelers north to Anchorage, Denali National Park and Preserve, and Fairbanks. All this comes together at the port, where the cruise ship and railroad passengers share the **Dale R. Lindsey Seward Intermodal Facility,** and the highway is just a couple of blocks away. Many cruise ship passengers disembark in Seward to catch trains, board buses, or drive themselves

from Seward to points north, or they arrive back in Seward and immediately board their cruise ships. However, travelers shouldn't be in a hurry to leave; this charming little town has much to offer, not to mention that Kenai Fjords National Park (see pp. 121–123) lies nearby.

Despite its unprepossessing designation as an "intermodal facility," the terminal itself has some charm in the form of murals. The governor of Alaska has officially proclaimed Seward to be "The Mural Capital of Alaska," and a number of artists and art lovers in town have formed the **Seward Mural Society** (*sewardmuralsociety.com*);

**Seward**

- Maps pp. 106, 122

**Visitor Information**

- Seward Chamber of Commerce–Convention & Visitors Bureau, 2001 Seward Hwy.

- 907-224-8051

**seward.com**

■ A playful Steller sea lion swooshes past delighted visitors at Seward's Alaska SeaLife Center.

## Seward Community Library & Museum

✉ 239 6th Ave.
☎ 907-224-4082
🕐 Library: Closed Sun. Museum: Closed Mon.
💲 $$$$

**cityofseward.us/ departments/ library-museum**

## Alaska SeaLife Center

✉ 301 Railway Ave.
☎ 907-224-6300 or 800-224-2525
💲 $$$$$

**alaskasealife.org**

their website features an interactive map of Seward's more than 30 mural locations (mostly downtown).

Cruise ships dock on the east side of the **Seward Small Boat Harbor,** a bustling mix of commercial fishing vessels, pleasure craft, and tour boats. The harbor also attracts a surprising amount of wildlife, in part because the nearby seafood processing plant discharges some tasty leftovers into the water. Look for bald eagles, harbor seals, terns, kittiwakes, sea otters, and Steller sea lions, then walk around to the west side of the harbor and check out the upscale restaurants, galleries, souvenir shops, and cafés. The westside dock is also thick

with sportfishing charter outfits. Stroll through as the boats return at day's end and watch happy anglers string up their catch. The dock houses the **Kenai Fjords National Park Visitor Center** *(tel 907-422-0500)* and several companies offering boat tours of the park and other areas.

The harbor is about a mile (1.6 km) north of downtown, via a paved **shoreline path** that runs from the west side of the harbor along the shore of Resurrection Bay to the southern end of downtown. Scattered along the trail are a couple of parks and numerous interpretive displays on topics such as temperate rain forest flora, commercial fishing, and the history of the Alaska Railroad.

Just beyond the children's playground, turn inland on Adams Street and go one block to the intersection with Sixth Avenue, the location of the **Seward Community Library & Museum,** in a handsome contemporary building faced with multihued metallic tiles. This cultural combo features paintings by leading Alaska artists, a 19th-century cannon, a collection of Russian icons, and the original Alaska flag, designed in 1927 by a boy from a local orphanage. Check out the gripping video of the 1964 Good Friday earthquake, which hit Seward hard.

Walk down 6th Avenue one block and turn right on Railway Avenue to the **Alaska SeaLife Center,** a superb aquarium and research institution devoted to educating the public about Alaska's marine ecosystems and to rehabilitating marine wildlife. The aquarium presents meaty information about such topics as research on the Bering Sea and the ongoing ramifications of the 1989 *Exxon Valdez* oil spill, but the SeaLife Center also knows how to elicit a "gee whiz."

Generous underwater viewing galleries let visitors press their faces against the glass to watch harbor seals and sea lions zip by with astounding speed and grace. In the Discovery Touch Pool, kids can run their fingers over sticky sea anemone tentacles or a sea star's smooth rays. Check out the monitors that show what's happening in the rehabilitation facility (the "I.Sea.U."); you may witness blood being drawn from a puffin or anesthesia being administered to a sea otter.

For an extra fee, you can participate in some special programs. Take a 60-minute **behind-the-scenes tour** to learn even more fascinating facts about marine life as you visit parts of the aquarium closed to the general public. For example, did you know that giant Pacific octopuses can squeeze through a 2-inch (5 cm) hole, that they display emotions, and that they recognize individual human beings? Two educational **Encounter Tours** get you up close and personal with marine critters. The first is the Sea Otter Experience, which lets you see how aquarium staff feed and care for these adorable marine mammals, abundant in local waters. The Puffin Encounter takes you into the aviary to meet puffins and other seabirds.

## Downtown

Immediately north of the Alaska SeaLife Center is downtown Seward, a compact district of a few dozen square blocks graced by many historic commercial buildings and homes. If you start walking straight up from the SeaLife Center, you'll be on **Fourth Avenue,** which is the main drag. You'll find appealing shops and galleries, but downtown is not a tourist area like the west side of the Seward Small Boat Harbor; most of its restaurants, clothing stores, and the like are geared toward locals, making a visit a very good way to sample a slice of Alaskan life.

If you'd like a close look at one of those historic buildings, walk two blocks up Fourth Avenue and go left a few steps on Adams Street to the **Van Gilder Hotel.** Built in 1916 and decorated today

### Van Gilder Hotel

✉ 308 Adams St.
☎ 907-224-3079
**vangilderseward.com**

## Mount Marathon Race

Most people wouldn't look at a 3,000-foot-plus (915-plus m) peak and think "Let's run up and down that mountain as fast as we can!" Then again, most people aren't from Seward. Every Fourth of July since 1915, runners starting at sea level in downtown Seward have raced 1.5 miles (2.4 km) up Mount Marathon and 1.5 miles back down. The slopes are so steep in spots that contestants must use their hands to haul themselves up. Add gullies, loose shale, ice, and snow, and it's no wonder that bloodied knees are par for the course. The record run is 41 minutes, 26 seconds. The race has become a major event that draws 900 participants (the maximum allowed) and thousands of onlookers from all over Alaska and beyond.

## Resurrect Art Coffee House Gallery

⊠ 320 3rd Ave.
☎ 907-224-7161

**resurrectart.com**

## Lowell Point State Recreation Site

☎ 907-262-5581

**dnr.alaska.gov /parks/aspunits /kenai/lowellptsrs .htm**

## Caines Head State Recreation Area

⊠ Alaska State Parks, Kenai/ PWS Area Office
☎ 907-262-5581

**dnr.alaska.gov /parks/aspunits/ kenai/cainesheadsra. htm**

## Seavey's Ididaride Sled Dog Tours

⊠ 312820 Old Exit Glacier Rd.
☎ 907-224-8607
🕐 Check website for tour times
$ $$$$$

**ididaride.com**

much like it was at its inception, the Van Gilder welcomes visitors. The corridors are lined with an extensive collection of historical photographs with explanatory captions. For example, a photo of the massive 1941 downtown fire reveals that soldiers took a military approach to extinguishing the blaze. Unfortunately, when they dynamited the building in which the fire started, the explosion blew flaming debris all over town.

For a taste of contemporary life in Seward, go one block west on Adams, turn right on Third Avenue, and proceed less than a block to the **Resurrect Art Coffee House Gallery.** A favorite local hangout set in a historic former church, it offers espresso, tasty pastries, and a fine helping of local art, ranging from simple crafts to expensive paintings.

## Outside Seward

A short drive in a rental car will take you to several worthy sites close to Seward. A couple of miles south on shore-hugging Lowell Point Road is **Lowell Point State**

**Recreation Site.** This 20-acre (8 ha) spread offers beach access to Resurrection Bay and is a jumping-off point for kayak trips and the trailhead for the 4.5-mile (7.2 km) hike to **Caines Head State Recreation Area.** The scenic path follows the western shore of the bay along a beach backed by mountains. Check with park staff to time your hike, as portions are passable only at low tide. At the recreation area you can explore **Fort McGilvray,** a strategic command center built during World War II. Take a flashlight and wander the subterranean passageways or enjoy views from the artillery batteries atop the 650-foot (198 m) promontory.

A ten-minute drive north from Seward takes you to **Seavey's Ididaride Sled Dog Tours,** which gives tours of the kennels and lets visitors ride on a sled with wheels that is used to keep the dogs fit during the summer. The Seaveys are the first family of mushing. Dan Sr. was one of the founders of modern Alaskan sled-dog racing and the famed Iditarod race. Once a decade or so he does the grueling race again, finishing 50th in 2012 at the age of 74. His son Mitch won the Iditarod in 2004 and again in 2013, and 2017 at age 56, making him the oldest winner ever. Mitch's son Dallas won in 2012, at age 25, making him the youngest winner ever, and then won again in 2014, 2015, and 2016. But even these guys are upstaged by the dogs, especially the puppies, which visitors get to play with. ∎

---

## NEED TO KNOW

### Port Logistics: Seward

Seward's cruise ship dock is at the small boat harbor. You can get the train and buses to Anchorage and points north, take tour boats to Kenai Fjords National Park and other sites, and find rental cars, water taxis, terrestrial taxis, etc. Downtown is about a mile (1.6 km) south, easily reached on city streets or via a shoreline path. The highlight local attraction is undoubtedly the Alaska SeaLife Center, which will take about 2–3 hours to visit.

# KENAI FJORDS NATIONAL PARK

Kenai Fjords is a primordial place. Nature in the raw. A world where you can witness fundamental geological processes in action. Except for a fringe of temperate rain forest, the park is a rugged land of rock and ice—especially ice, which sheathes a large majority of Kenai Fjords's 670,000 acres (271,139 ha). The Harding Icefield alone buries more than half the park beneath hundreds and thousands of feet of ice.

A breaching humpback whale in Kenai Fjords National Park

The best way to visit is with a guide. A cadre of experienced tour operators have set up shop in the gateway town of Seward. The Park Service also offers a handful of guided tours. If you haven't already made reservations, stroll the dockside companies and find out what they offer.

The quickest means to a literal overview of Kenai Fjords is in a bush plane or helicopter. Though you won't see things up close—unless you arrange a glacier landing or such—you will see remote spots that boat tours can't reach.

Within minutes you can be buzzing above the 300-square-mile (777 sq km) **Harding Icefield,** skimming over snowfields and aqua-tinted crevasses. Watch for the stony tips of mountains that peek up from the ice; Eskimos call these *nunataks,* meaning "lonely peaks." Here on the icefield, hundreds of inches of annual snowfall compact into dense ice that fuels some 40 glaciers. However, these rivers of ice are retreating faster than they're being replenished, as happened in the last ice age, when withdrawing glaciers left behind

**Kenai Fjords National Park**

⛰ Maps pp. 106, 122

**Visitor Information**

✉ Kenai Fjords NP Visitor Center, 1212 4th Ave., Seward

☎ 907-422-0500

🕐 Center closed Oct.–April

**nps.gov/kefj**

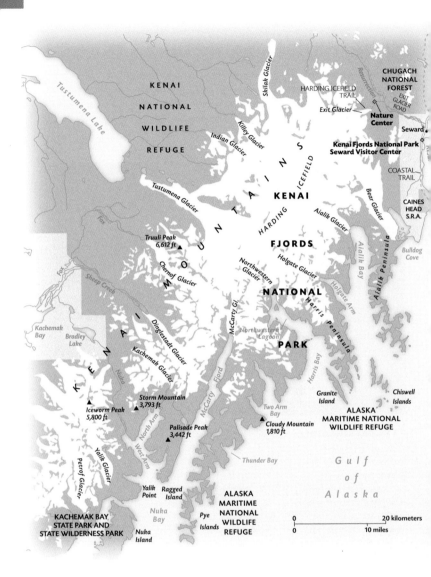

the deep, narrow, U-shaped fjords that gave this park its name.

## Boat Tours of the Park

These sublime fjords are best approached from the sea. Most visitors choose a powerboat tour, whether aboard a smaller vessel with 20 passengers or a multideck cruiser that holds hundreds of people. Others opt for guided kayak trips, usually power-boating out to a starting point for a day trip.

The powerboat tours range from three-hour loops of **Resurrection Bay** to trips lasting ten hours. Dress warmly, as even on a sunny day the combination of a fast-moving boat and the proximity of all that ice can make things chilly out on deck.

A typical full-day trip heads out of the Small Boat Harbor and south along the western shore of Resurrection Bay. Soon you'll see bald eagles and sea otters. Rocky cliffs and forest mountains rise steeply from the shore. The summer snowmelt revs up a multitude of waterfalls and nearly vertical streams that gush down these slopes, bright white streamers running over the dark stone. Less than 10 miles (16 km) out of Seward, you'll come to the boundary of the park, at **Bear Glacier.**

These cold, fertile waters support an abundance of life, including a host of marine mammals. Humpback whales are commonly spotted, usually eating, as they feed for up to 23 hours a day to bulk up for the migration back to Hawaii, where they breed. You'll often see harbor seals pop their heads out of the water to watch your boat pass. Dall porpoises, which look like miniature orcas due to their black-and-white markings, also frequent these waters.

About 10 miles (16 km) south of Bear Glacier, many boats loop around the end of the Aialik Peninsula and head into the rugged confines of **Aialik Bay,** either going up **Holgate Arm** to see the **Holgate Glacier** or continuing to the end of the bay to spend some quality time with the Aialik Glacier.

## Exit Glacier

Exit Glacier, the only part of the park accessible by road, is a 12-mile (19 km) drive from Seward. If you don't have a car, you can get there by taxi, bus, or with a number of tour companies, even if you're not officially on one of their tours. However, you might want to consider taking a tour, as a couple operators will take visitors out onto the ice for a little glacier trekking, even some ice climbing.

If you're on your own, start at the **Nature Center** and ask about the short trails leading to views of Exit Glacier, including some close-ups. If you have more time (6–8 hours) and lots more energy, you can try the **Harding Icefield Trail,** an 8-mile (13 km), 3,500-foot (1,067 m) elevation-gain round-trip that follows one flank of the glacier up to a point where you can see the icefield. ∎

### NEED TO KNOW

**Port Logistics: Kenai Fjords National Park**

Start at the Kenai Fjords National Park Visitor Center, at the Seward Small Boat Harbor, a short walk across from the cruise ship terminal. Here you can pick up a list of authorized tour operators, including some boat trips that have park interpreters on board. In addition, dozens of private tours are run out of a long row of buildings adjacent to the visitor center.

# HOMER

Homer was a remote outpost until the Sterling Highway arrived in the early 1950s and initiated the town's modern era. Not that millions flocked here—even today the population is only a little more than 5,000—but a diversity of newcomers has kept trickling in: artists, charter boat captains, Russian Old Believers, '60s dropouts, naturalists, and commercial fishers.

There's always time for chess, coffee, and ice cream in Homer.

**Homer**

🗺 Maps pp. 106, 129

**Visitor Information**

✉ Homer Chamber of Commerce & Visitor Information Center, 201 Sterling Hwy.

☎ 907-235-7740

**homeralaska.org**

## The Spit

The best place to start exploring Homer is at the harbor, located near the end of the Homer Spit, where the Alaska Marine Highway ferry and the cruise ships pull in. This is the literal and figurative end of the road, where the town began. This legendary 4.5-mile (7 km) sand-and-gravel finger pokes into

Kachemak Bay, curving halfway to the far shore. These days the spit is quite narrow, maybe a few hundred yards across in some places, barely 100 yards (91 m) in others at high tide. Once it was broader and higher, with groves of spruce and meadows bright with wildflowers, but the spit dropped about 7 feet (2 m) in the 1964 Good Friday quake, and the ocean reclaimed the lower elevation margins.

The spit is a busy, densely developed place, especially out near the end. On the skinny beaches, which fill out a bit at low tide, you'll see people flying kites, kayaking, fishing, grilling salmon, and licking ice cream cones. The **harbor** is jammed with hundreds of commercial fishing boats, sportfishing charter boats, tour boats, and water taxis. On the highway side of the harbor and along the highway itself, you'll find the little offices of maritime businesses ready to help if you want to do some deep-sea fishing or tour beautiful Kachemak Bay.

Along with the tour operators you'll find souvenir shops, art galleries, a hotel, candy stores, restaurants, RV parks, bars, a community theater, campgrounds, and other local businesses along the highway.

One apt enterprise is the **Kachemak Shellfish Growers Co-op,** which sells the products of 14 (and counting) local oyster growers. The cold, clean waters of Kachemak Bay are ideal for raising plump, juicy oysters that are safe from the infections that plague oyster growers in warmer waters. You'll find their retail outlet and processing facility on the highway just northwest of the harbor. Also on the highway, alongside the harbor, stop by **Hands of Alaska's Local Showcase** to see a range of art and crafts handmade by locals, including ivory sculptures, masks, and artifacts from the gold rush and homesteading days.

## The Alaska Islands & Ocean Visitor Center

This is a good, central starting point in Homer, right on the Sterling Highway just a minute's walk east of Main Street. This elaborate high-tech facility is actually a natural history and cultural museum with a specific mission: to study the Alaska Maritime National Wildlife Refuge and share the findings with the public. This unusual refuge comprises a constellation of 2,500 far-flung islands and coastal havens that host marine mammals and some 40 million seabirds—more than in the rest of North America put together. To get a feel for the refuge, go to the **Seabird Experience Theater.** Towering above you are realistic, fake-guano-stained artificial rocks inhabited by more than 120 sculpted puffins,

auklets, cormorants, and other seabirds. At the press of a button, the simulated colony springs to life, as huge screens amid the rocks erupt in a swirl of birds. Other exhibits are devoted to humans' past and present relationship with the refuge. Rangers give nature talks and lead guided walks and even tide-pooling at Bishops Beach.

## The Art of Homer

In Homer many galleries carry local art. One of the best, **Bunnell Street Arts Center,** lies less than five minutes' walk from the Visitor Center; take the highway to Main Street and go left on Main a couple of blocks to West Bunnell Street, then right just a few steps. You'll find this nonprofit arts center in Homer's oldest commercial building, the Inlet Trading Post, yet the center's emphasis is on cutting-edge contemporary art.

---

**Kachemak Shellfish Growers Co-op**

✉ 3851 Homer Spit Rd.

☎ 907-235-1935

**alaskaoyster.com**

**Hands of Alaska's Local Showcase**

✉ 4246 Home Spit Rd.

☎ 907-235-8415

**handsofalaska.com**

**Alaska Islands & Ocean Visitor Center**

✉ 95 Sterling Hwy.

☎ 907-235-6546

**islandsandocean.org**

**Bunnell Street Arts Center**

✉ 106 W. Bunnell St.

☎ 907-235-2662

**bunnellarts.org**

---

## Barefooters

In the 1950s the Barefooters came to Homer. Their official name was the Wisdom, Knowledge, Faith, and Love Fountain of the World, so it's not exactly surprising that this group had a cultish whiff to it, yet they also were serious back-to-the-land farmers and engaged in community service. They went about their business in robes and never wore shoes, even in the Alaskan winter—hence the nickname "Barefooters." After a few years the colony crumbled, but some members remained in the area. One, Asaiah Bates, grew to be a beloved Homer character and served on the city council. It was he who created the town's alternative moniker: "Cosmic Hamlet by the Sea."

**Ptarmigan Arts**

- ✉ 471 E. Pioneer Ave.
- ☎ 907-235-5345

ptarmiganarts.com

**Fireweed Gallery**

- ✉ 475 E. Pioneer Ave.
- ☎ 907-235-3411

fireweedgallery.com

**Pratt Museum**

- ✉ 3779 Bartlett St.
- ☎ 907-235-8635
- 🕐 Closed Mon. mid-Sept.–mid-May
- 💲 $$$

prattmuseum.org

**Carl E. Wynn Nature Center**

- ✉ Mile 1.5 E. Skyline Dr.
- ☎ 907-235-6667 or 907-235-5266 (summer)

akcoastalstudies.org

Other notable galleries are strung along Pioneer Avenue, including a pair on East Pioneer between Svedlund Street and Kachemak Way. Go about half a mile (0.8 km) up Main Street from the arts center to Pioneer and then head right about a quarter of a mile (0.4 km). Here **Ptarmigan Arts,** a local artists' cooperative whose works range widely, displays fiber art, paintings, hats, glass, and ceramics, to name but a few. Next door, **Fireweed Gallery** shows high-end Alaska work from grand oil paintings to serigraphs to old-fashioned engravings.

The Pioneer Avenue area is also home to the **Pratt Museum,** one of Alaska's best small-town museums. To get there from Gallery Row, go half a mile (0.8 km) back down Pioneer and turn right on Bartlett Avenue; the museum is a quarter mile (0.4 km) up the road. The Pratt focuses on life around Kachemak Bay—past, present, and future.

If you have a car, drive up to the plateau that rises more than 1,000 feet (305 m) above town. To get there from the Pratt Museum, go east on Pioneer, which soon turns into East End Road, and drive about 1.5 miles (2.4 km) to the intersection with East Hill Road. Go left and climb the steep switchbacks for about 2 miles (3.2 km) until you hit Skyline Drive. Go right for 1.5 miles (2.4 km) to reach the **Carl E. Wynn Nature Center.** The center's 140 acres (56 ha) shelter wildflower meadows, spruce forest, and a migration corridor for bear and moose. ■

**INSIDER TIP:**

Almost every port visited by cruise ships has outfitters offering mountain bike, hiking, and kayak tours—often at better prices than what the ship offers.

—EVERETT POTTER
National Geographic Traveler
*magazine writer*

## NEED TO KNOW

### Port Logistics: Homer

Homer's harbor is a hub, serving cruise ships, the state ferry, charter fishing vessels, tour boats, water taxis, and boats that cross Kachemak Bay, as well as flightseeing trips. It is 4.5 miles (7 km) from downtown, so to see the rest of the town, you'll need to get a taxi, rent a car, or catch the Homer Trolley. Cruise ships typically provide transportation for their passengers from the spit to downtown.

You may want a rental car to explore Homer, as it's not a compact city, and it lacks in public transportation. However, if you're willing to walk 2 or 3 miles (3–5 km), you can reach most of the main attractions. Another option for traveling between the spit and downtown is the Homer Trolley *(tel 907-299-6210, homer trolley.com, $$$$$ day pass).* This privately owned, hop-on/hop-off sightseeing bus has a driver and guide.

# ACROSS KACHEMAK BAY

**This alluring slice of Alaska doesn't have an official name, so most people refer to it as "across Kachemak Bay," or simply "across the bay," meaning on the other side of the bay from Homer. Broadly, the area includes everything on the northwestern half of the 20-by-60-mile (32 by 96 km) protrusion of land at the tip of the Kenai Peninsula.**

Not surprisingly, no roads lead to this side of the bay. You can set down a bush plane on one of several landing strips, but boats are the usual mode of transportation. Travelers will find a flotilla of watercraft choices in Homer harbor. The **Center for Alaskan Coastal Studies** *(708 Smoky Bay Way, Homer, tel 907-235-6667, akcoastalstudies.org)* offers excellent half-day to full-day boat tours of the bay (see pp. 128–129). You can hire a water taxi and go just about anywhere; some of these are military-style landing craft that will motor right up onto a beach.

There are several ways to journey to **Seldovia,** the main settlement, from Homer. Several days a week the **Alaska Marine Highway** ferry makes the 75- to 90-minute run. The ferry stays for between 75 minutes and 4.5 hours before returning, giving you time to look around. If you prefer a tour to mere transportation, try the seven-hour trips to Seldovia run by either **Central Charters & Tours** or **Seldovia Nature Tours.** Unlike the ferry, they take the scenic, wildlife-rich route down the coast and past island seabird colonies on the way to Seldovia, where they spend about three hours. The quickest trip is the 45-minute ride on the 150-passenger *Kachemak Voyager* (see p. 131), which twice a day scoots over and back at nearly

■ Colorful sea stars huddle on rocks in Halibut Cove.

30 miles an hour (48 km/h).

Seldovia is a quiet little fishing village, but it's the big city in these parts, the only place across the bay that sports even a few streets. Sportfishing is huge here. Most anglers go out on charter boats, but when the king salmon are running, you can hook one right from the **Seldovia Slough Bridge,** at the south end of town. Visitors also come to dig for clams, go whale-watching, take a kayak tour, or go flightseeing.

From the harbor, near the south end of Seldovia, you can stroll along the half mile (0.8 km) or so of Main Street, which traces the waterfront. (If you come on the ferry, you'll dock *(continued on p. 131)*

**Seldovia**
🗺 Map p. 106
**Visitor Information**
☎ 907-234-7612
youotterbehere.com

**Alaska Marine Highway System**
☎ 800-642-0066 or 907-465-3941
$ $$$$$
dot.state.ak.us/amhs

**Central Charters & Tours**
☎ 907-235-7847
$ $$$$$
centralcharter.com

**Seldovia Nature Tours**
☎ 907-231-6891
$ $$$$$
seldovianature tours. com

# BOAT TOUR OF KACHEMAK BAY

**Though Kachemak Bay has plenty of personality, it could get by on its looks alone. About 30 miles (48 km) long and 5 to 10 miles (8–16 km) wide, the bay cuts deep into the southern end of the Kenai Peninsula. If you're looking from a vantage point at the end of the Homer Spit, halfway across the bay, you'll be surrounded by cold, clean, dark blue waters that harbor diverse wildlife and some of the best oysters you'll ever taste.**

Tours of the bay reveal its wildlife, striking scenery, and fascinating natural history.

To the northeast you'll see the tapering end of the bay, home to Fox River Flats Critical Habitat Area. To the east and south are the glaciers, lakes, rivers, forests, and snowbound summits of the Kenai Mountains and Kachemak Bay State Park. Looking west, you'll see Cook Inlet and, across its waters, the peaks of the Alaska Peninsula, including the Augustine Volcano.

The Center for Alaskan Coastal Studies (akcoastalstudies.org), based in Homer, offers a full-day guided tour (typically limited to a maximum of nine participants) that will introduce you to the diverse natural beauty and ecology of Kachemak Bay. When cruise ships are in port, the center also runs a five-hour tour designed for cruise ship passengers with tight schedules.

The journey begins in the harbor, near the

> **NOT TO BE MISSED:**
>
> **Gull Island • Peterson Bay field station • China Poot Bay**

end of Homer Spit. Watch for sea otters as the boat motors out of the harbor. You'll reach **Gull Island ❶** in about 20 minutes. The boat may spend time slowly circling these few acres of rock, which in summertime host thousands of nesting seabirds, including black-legged kittiwakes, tufted and horned puffins, cormorants, and gulls. Sometimes bald eagles swoop in and stir up the colony as they search for prey. From Gull Island it's about a mile (1.6 km) to the center's **Peterson Bay Coastal Science Field**

**Station ❷**, tucked among trees on a hill overlooking Peterson Bay. If weather allows, visitors sit on the deck of the log building for a briefing by a naturalist. Because much of the hike will involve tide-pooling, the group also spends time at the touch tanks inside the field station, where you can see and handle such intertidal critters as a fish-eating sea star, a decorator crab, and a gumboot chiton.

## Hiking & Kayaking

As you begin the moderate **forest hike ❸**, notice the diversity of the plant life; this area is a transition zone between coastal temperate rain forest and interior boreal forest. As you drop down from a hill into the flats bordering a nearby bay, the trail tiptoes through a ghost forest of dead spruce, killed when the 1964 Good Friday earthquake dropped the land 6 feet (1.8 m), allowing seawater in. The trail emerges onto the cobble shore of **China Poot Bay ❹**, where the retreating tide reveals the mysterious world of tide pools. Kachemak Bay has a huge tidal range, which means that at low tides you'll see things that would otherwise be hidden by the water. You'll spend an hour or two peering into crevices and under rocks, ferreting out anemones, clams, limpets, snail eggs, and the occasional octopus. After a hike back to the center, you'll gather for 30 minutes of kayak instruction. Some tours head to Gull Island, others deeper into **Peterson Bay ❺**, to spot sea otters and see an oyster farm. After two or three hours, kayakers return to the dock and return to Homer in a bigger vessel. Overnight stays in yurts can be reserved, and you can even volunteer to help in chores such as trail construction and maintenance.

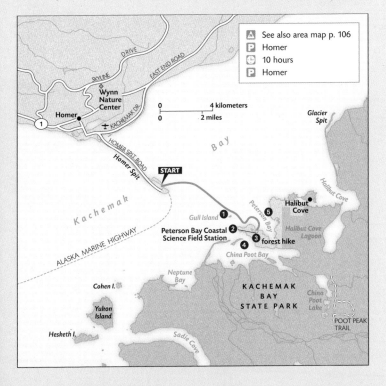

Black Kittiwake

Bald Eagle

Lynx

Wolves

Orca

Dall Porpoise

Aleutian Tern

Red-faced
Cormorant

Tufted
Puffin

Sandhill
Crane

Sea Otter

Common
Murre

Ancient
Murrelet

Horned Puffin

Chinook Salmon

Eider Drake

Painted
Anemone

Yellow
Zoanthid

Orange Ochre
Sea Star

Painted Star

Sunflower
Sea Star

Pacific Herring

Black Bear

Moose

Harbor Seal

Western Sandpiper

**Residents of
Kachemak Bay**

near the north end of Main Street.) Right across from the harbor on Main is the modest **Seldovia Visitor Center and Museum,** which tells the story of Seldovia's heritage. On a small hill above Main Street near its north end perches **St. Nicholas Russian Orthodox Church,** built in 1891, a reminder that Russian fur traders settled here some 140 years ago.

To reach Halibut Cove, you either take a water taxi or board the *Danny J,* an old fishing boat that is part ferry and part tour boat. Most of its passengers are heading over for a meal at **The Saltry Restaurant,** a famed dining establishment associated with the *Danny J.* Twice a day the boat takes up to 30 people from Homer to the cove, where they have three hours before the return trip to wander this town: There are no roads; residents kayak or take a skiff across the lagoon or stroll the raised boardwalk. Stop in at the **Halibut Cove Experience Gallery,** which shows the work of 15 to 20 local artists—about a third of Halibut Cove's residents. ∎

**Kachemak
Voyager Seldovia
Bay Ferry**
☎ 907-435-3299
💲 $$$$$
seldoviabayferry.com

**Seldovia
Visitor Center
and Museum**
✉ 206 Main St.
☎ 907-435-3266
🕐 Closed Sat.–Sun.
Oct.–May
svt.org/seldovia-
visitor-center-and-
museum

**Danny J/
The Saltry
Restaurant**
☎ 907-226-2424
🕐 Open seasonally,
call for hours
thesaltry.com

**Halibut Cove
Experience
Gallery**
☎ 907-296-2215
🕐 Closed mid-
Sept.–mid-May
halibutcove
experience.com

## NEED TO KNOW

### Port Logistics: Homer Harbor

Homer's harbor is a hub for boats going across Kachemak Bay. Depending on the itinerary, tours of Kachemak Bay run from an hour to all day. Options include trips offered by the Center for Alaskan Coastal Studies, water taxis, charter boats, kayaking, and the state ferry. The Homer Chamber of Commerce *(tel 907-235-7740, homeralaska.org)* can help.

Urban Anchorage, the delights of Denali National Park, and a wild
archipelago stretching nearly 1,500 miles (2,414 km) into the Pacific

# ANCHORAGE & BEYOND

Shooting stars bloom on Kodiak
Island. Opposite: Grizzly bears
feed at a salmon run in Katmai
National Park and Preserve.

# ANCHORAGE & BEYOND

Visits to Anchorage, Denali National Park and Preserve, and the Alaska Peninsula and Aleutian Islands will leave the traveler with lasting impressions of many aspects of Alaska. With its high-rises, malls, traffic, galleries, suburbs, and shops, Anchorage will feel familiar to most travelers. A four-hour drive north of Anchorage, Denali is a huge, wild slice of the interior, but it also offers campgrounds, tour buses, and other amenities. The Alaska Peninsula and the Aleutians are coastal Alaska at its most remote.

In contrast to the somewhat developed park lands of Denali, the 1,500-mile-long (2,414 km) arc of the Alaska Peninsula and Aleutian Islands presents travelers with almost uninterrupted nature; some of the wildlife refuges are visited by only a few dozen people a year, so don't expect to find a gift shop. The farthest reaches of this windswept area lie just a couple hundred miles from Russia, nearer to Asia than to the rest of Alaska.

About 300,000 people call Anchorage home, making it a modest urban center by lower 48 standards. But that 300,000 represents almost half of Alaska's population, which means that Anchorage is by far the state's largest city and the hub of most of its commercial and cultural activity. Here you can enjoy sophisticated restaurants, outstanding museums, a highly regarded performing arts center, avant-garde art galleries, a lovely botanic garden, five-star hotels, and other civilized amenities. It also has a quality no big city in the lower 48 can claim: close proximity to deep wilderness. Bears and moose occasionally wander through Anchorage, even downtown, and unspoiled expanses of mountain and forest tightly embrace the city, with wilderness just a 20-minute drive away.

Even grander wilderness awaits in Denali. It welcomes people with an elaborate visitor center, snack bars, guided hikes, theater programs, and other niceties, but these exist only in the front country. The vast majority of the park lies

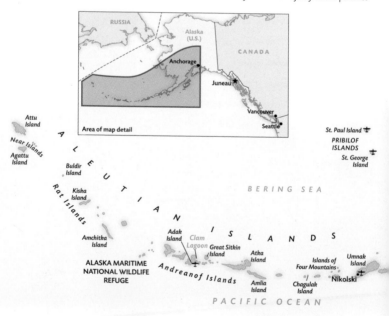

in the almost entirely undeveloped backcountry. The one main road into Denali's untamed heartland gives visitors a relatively easy way to taste the backcountry, to glimpse the woods and tundra, the broad braided rivers and blue-slitted glaciers, the bears and moose and wolves and golden eagles and caribou and snowshoe hares, and, if the clouds that often crown it allow, the towering bulk of Mount Denali, the continent's highest peak.

Even more remote than Denali, the Alaska Peninsula and the 1,100-mile-long (1,770 km) string of Aleutian Islands follow the westward curving Ring of Fire, a chain of volcanoes that frames most of the North Pacific. The northern arc—the spine of southwestern Alaska—contains more than 60 fire-breathing mountains, many still active. The forests and mountains of the peninsula harbor wolves, moose, massive salmon runs that attract famed gatherings of grizzlies, and other landbound wildlife. The tundra-greened Aleutians boast marine wildlife, such as whales, sea otters, seals, porpoises, and some of the world's largest seabird colonies. The Unangan and Alutiiq have occupied this region for ages, with Russians and

### NOT TO BE MISSED:

**An introduction to the Great Land at the Anchorage Museum** 139–140

**Learning about native culture at the Alaska Native Heritage Center** 141

**A flightseeing tour around Mount Denali** 148

**Bear-watching at Hallo Bay, McNeil River, or Brook Falls** 150–151

**Journey through the Aleutians on the M.V. Tustumena ferry** 161

Americans adding to the mix over the last 250 years. Still, only about 25,000 people live in the entire region and most of them inhabit the only two significant ports: Kodiak and Unalaska/Dutch Harbor. ■

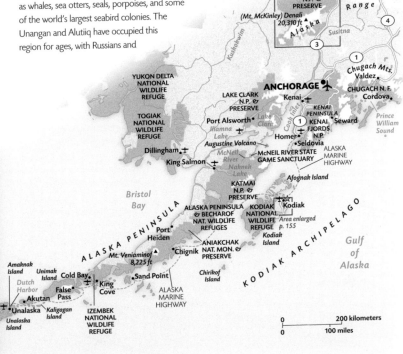

# ANCHORAGE

Home to about 300,000 people, Anchorage is Alaska's largest city. Travelers who have been cruising past uninhabited islands and visiting remote villages may experience culture shock when they encounter its urban bustle. They also may be surprised by Anchorage's mild summer weather; only about 17 inches (43 cm) of rain fall on the city in an average year, and summer temperatures often allow visitors to wear short sleeves.

Downtown Anchorage represents Alaska's only big-city skyline, looking onto Cook Inlet.

**Anchorage**

🗺 Maps pp. 135, 137

**Visitor Information**

✉ 524 W. 4th Ave.

☎ 907-276-4118

**anchorage.net**

**Alaska Center for the Performing Arts**

🗺 Map p. 137

✉ 621 W. 6th Ave.

☎ 907-263-2900

🕐 Closed Sept.– late May

💲 $$

**alaskapac.org**

Anchorage's civilized amenities notwithstanding, the great outdoors is never far away. Many city residents have a tale to tell of their encounters with a bear or moose right there in town—not that charismatic megafauna lurk around every corner. Visitors and residents alike appreciate the fact that even when they're stuck in traffic or emerging from a shopping mall, they're greeted by views of the mountains and forest that ring the city.

Anchorage has no dedicated facilities for cruise ships; they just dock at the industrial port along with the freighters and tankers. The port is only a 20-minute walk north of downtown, but unless you want to dodge semitrucks it's best to take the shuttle provided by your cruise ship or grab a taxi. The shuttles typically drop their passengers in the middle of downtown, often at the **Egan Civic and Convention Center,** so start your walkabout from there. Though Anchorage is a big city, many of its attractions can be found in a central 8 x 10 block area, so you can see a lot if you walk 2 or 3 miles (3–5 km).

South across Fifth Avenue from the convention center is **Town Square Park,** a festive space of fountains and flowers. Bordering the park to the west is the **Alaska**

**Center for the Performing Arts.**
In the center's Sydney Laurence Theatre you'll be transfixed by AurorA—Alaska's Great Northern Lights, an hourly 40-minute show of coruscating aurora borealis images set to music.

Next walk diagonally across from the center, near the intersection of Fifth and G Streets, to the Glacier Brewhouse building, where you can browse high-end art at **Aurora Fine Art Gallery.** It carries a range of Alaskan artists working in a variety of media, such as Timber Vavalis, who creates traditional Tlingit-style carvings out of yellow cedar. Aurora also offers works from internationally known figures,

such as Gail Niebrugge, a pointillist whose vibrant watercolors capture scenes from the Alaskan wilderness. In the same building, **Alaska Max Gourmet** (tel 907-274-0238) sells fireweed honey, birch syrup, reindeer sausage, and other Alaskan fare.

Another high-end gallery, **Stephan Fine Arts Gallery,** is located a couple of blocks down on Fifth Avenue in the Hotel Captain Cook. You can't miss this iconic Anchorage hotel, as its three highrise towers occupy an entire city block. While Stephan Fine Arts carries mostly painters, including both Alaskan and international artists, it also represents artists

**Aurora Fine Art Gallery**

🗺 Map p. 137
✉ 737 W. 5th Ave.
☎ 907-274-0234

**aurorafineart-alaska .com**

**Stephan Fine Arts Gallery**

🗺 Map p. 137
✉ Hotel Captain Cook, 939 W. 5th Ave.
☎ 907-274-5009
🕐 Open daily noon–7 p.m.

**stephanfinearts.com**

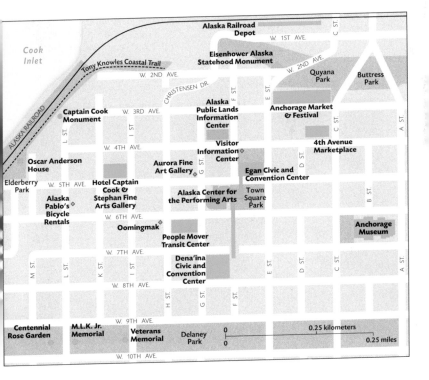

**Oscar Anderson House**

🗺 Map p. 137

✉ 420 M St.

☎ 907-929-9870

🕐 Open Tues.–Sun. 12 p.m.–4 p.m.

💲 $$

**oscaranderson housemuseum.org**

**Alaska Pablo's Bicycle Rentals**

🗺 Map p. 137

✉ 415 L St.

☎ 907-274-1600

🕐 Closed Oct.–April

**pablobicycle rentals.com**

who work in other media, such as glass sculpture. While you're in the hotel, you might want to head up to the **Crow's Nest Restaurant** for views as expansive as the name implies.

Continue two blocks west on Fifth and you'll hit Elderberry Park, which sits above Knik Arm, an appendage of Cook Inlet. Near the north end of the park is the **Oscar Anderson House**, one of the few historic buildings left in Anchorage; many were destroyed by the 1964 Good Friday earthquake. Built in 1915, this modest home was erected in what was then only a year-old railroad construction port. Now a museum, it displays Anderson family belongings.

## Tony Knowles Coastal Trail

A few steps west from the Oscar Anderson House and Elderberry Park will lead you to the Tony Knowles Coastal Trail, which runs south and west for 11 miles (18 km) along the shore of Knik Arm and Cook Inlet. This broad, paved path's central city stretches are packed with runners, cyclists, in-line skaters, and people out for a stroll to enjoy the views. Watch for beluga whales, particularly just south of downtown. The more distant stretches of the trail, starting around Mile 4, become wilder, and you may encounter moose and occasionally bears, so stay alert.

If you want to rent a bike to go farther along the trail, Anchorage has numerous bike rental businesses, including **Alaska Pablo's Bicycle Rentals**, on L Street, just a block from Elderberry Park. About a mile (1.6 km) down the trail from the park lies **Westchester Lagoon**, where you may spot Canada geese or red-necked grebes in their floating nests. Not far past the lagoon you'll cross the

▪ The Anchorage Museum offers insight into many ages of Alaska's history.

aptly named **Fish Creek Bridge;** look down into the water in late summer and you may see migrating salmon heading upstream.

A couple of miles (3.2 km) farther brings you to **Earthquake Park,** untouched since the 1964 quake broke it into massive, uplifted blocks. The Good Friday quake–at magnitude 9.2 Richter, the largest ever recorded in North America– hammered Anchorage. Coastal areas just south of town dropped about 10 feet (3 m), enabling tides to wash over the railroad tracks. In a westside neighborhood, houses were tossed upside down, yet, astoundingly, the quake killed only nine people in Anchorage. An interpretative trail through the forested park leads past rippling hills and a sharp drop-off that speak of the geological forces at play that fateful day.

Head a few blocks back into town from Elderberry Park to the corner of Sixth Avenue and H Street. Here, in a little old house amid the downtown towers and shops, you'll find a store as unusual as its name: **Oomingmak.** This is a co-op that sells sweaters, hats, baby booties, and other clothing hand-knitted by Alaska native craftspeople, most in remote communities, using qiviut, the ultrawarm inner hair of musk oxen. Villages have their own copyrighted knitted patterns developed from traditional roots, such as the Lacy Harpoon pattern from Mekoryuk, on Nunivak Island in western Alaska. This pattern was derived from a 1,200-year-old walrus ivory harpoon head found on the island.

## Saturday Market

Hankering for some homemade Alaskan jam or a fur coat? If you're in Anchorage on a summer Saturday or Sunday, try the Anchorage Market & Festival *(anchorage markets.com),* spread out in an open space next to Third Avenue between C and E Streets. Known to locals as the Saturday Market, this is not a farmers market so much as an outdoor bazaar. More than 300 local merchants and craftspeople sell an amazing array of goods, including smoked salmon, ivory jewelry, coonskin and skunk-skin caps, and wallets made from duct tape. Street performers add a festive air; occasionally a phalanx of bagpipers will march up one of the walkways.

## Anchorage Museum

Six short blocks east on Sixth awaits what many consider the city's premier attraction: the Anchorage Museum. Vastly expanded in 2017, its new 31,000-square-foot (2,973 sq. m.) Rasmuson Wing combines 21st-century styling with an exterior clad in Alaskan Yellow cedar and zinc.

The wing houses the new **Art of the North** galleries, displaying some 200 works in various media representing perceptions of the Alaskan landscapes and people.

The Rasmuson's **Alaska Gallery** employs a blend of art and artifacts to depict the long history of Alaska from ancient times to the 21st century. Much of this section focuses on the past lives of Alaska natives, such as the cutaway diorama of a traditional Unangan house, and the ingenuity, technology, and knowledge

### Oomingmak

🅰 Map p. 137
✉ 604 H St.
☎ 907-272-9225 or 888-360-9665
🕓 Closed Sun. in winter

**qiviut.com**

### Anchorage Museum

🅰 Map p. 137
✉ 625 C St.
☎ 907-929-9228
🕓 Closed Mon.– Wed.
💲 $$$$

**anchoragemuseum .org**

## Alaska Native Heritage Center

✉ 8800 Heritage Center Dr.
☎ 907-330-8000 or 855-330-8085
💲 $$$$$

**alaskanative.net**

## Alaska Aviation Museum

🅰 Map on inside front cover
✉ 4721 Aircraft Dr.
☎ 907-248-5325
🕐 Closed. Sat.–Mon.
💲 $$$$

**alaskaairmuseum.org**

that have allowed people of the North to survive and thrive. Watch for the little things, too, like the photo taken during a 1908 Nome parade of men in white top hats herding reindeer through town. Among the many notable works of art is a whole hall devoted to Sydney Laurence, the state's most renowned painter.

Another of the museum's highlights is the **Arctic Studies Center,** which has an extensive exhibit on Alaska native cultures, anchored by more than 600 artifacts provided by the Smithsonian Institution. If you're interested in knowing more about, say, an 1893 Tlingit war helmet, you can use a touch screen to scroll through all sorts of historical and cultural information, check out related images, or listen to pertinent oral histories. As you wander the 10,000-square-foot (929 sq m) center, you'll encounter various art pieces, too,

such as a 3-D sound art installation that uses natural sounds and recordings by Alaska native storytellers to transport you to the Arctic.

If you or your kids feel the need to be more active, head for the museum's newly expanded **Discovery Center,** where visitors of all ages can learn by playing. At the Tsunami Tank, you can command the seas to hurl tidal waves at a miniature coastal community, or move to the touch tank to gently handle crabs and sea stars. Among the other offerings, you can envelop yourself in a giant bubble in the aptly named Bubble Space or learn about wind by shooting an air cannon in the Kinetic Space.

## Downtown & Beyond

Head north from the museum on C Street two blocks and turn left on Fourth Avenue. In a few steps you'll reach the **4th Avenue Marketplace.**

By taxi or rental car you can venture beyond downtown to several compelling attractions. About 10 miles (16 km) to the northeast lies the **Alaska Native Heritage Center,** set

## Qiviut

As you peruse the Anchorage shops, look out for gifts made of qiviut. This ultra-warm animal hair, which comes from musk oxen, is used by some Alaska natives to knit cozy clothing. Qiviut insulates so wonderfully because the musk ox is a denizen of the Arctic and has evolved to withstand fierce winters. Weighing as much as 800 pounds (363 kg), these burly beasts sport excessively shaggy coats that make them look like mops with four legs and horns. They're one of only a handful of large animals from the mammoth and mastodon era that still exists, though they were hunted out of Alaska and had to be reintroduced from Greenland in the 1930s.

on 26 wooded acres (10 ha). In midsummer you can get there on a free shuttle from several downtown sites. The center is an excellent place to learn about Alaska native culture and history. Although the Heritage Center displays wonderful artwork and historical artifacts, it is emphatically not a museum with static displays. People representing the state's native cultures gather here to preserve their traditions.

Staffers greet visitors at the **Welcome House.** From there, a half-mile (0.8 km) trail leads around a small lake to several "village" sites, each depicting a particular culture or group of cultures. Guided tours of just more than an hour are often run, but you also can make the rounds on your own. The **Hall of Cultures** brims with art and crafts both historic and contemporary, and native artists from around the state are often working on-site, eager to speak with visitors and offer their art for sale. In addition, the **Gathering Place** hosts storytellers, dancers, athletes, and other performers.

Small planes, almost universally called "bush planes" by locals, are integral to life in Alaska. In the United States as a whole, about one in 1,400 people owns a small plane—compared with one in 70 in Alaska. Understanding the allure of bush planes for Alaskans will help you appreciate the **Alaska Aviation Museum,** situated just north of Anchorage International Airport, about 4 miles (6.4 km) from downtown. Sure,

■ **A Tlingit dancer dresses in traditional garb for a performance at the Alaska Native Heritage Center.**

the museum has a 1928 Stearman biplane, a U.S. Air Force F-15 fighter jet, and other nonbush aircraft, but the historic bush planes seem most dear to its heart. To see some contemporary small planes in action, spend some

## Alaska Botanical Garden

✉ 4601 Campbell Airstrip Rd.

☎ 907-770-3692

🕐 Closed. Sun.-Mon. mid–May to mid-Sept.

💲 $$$ (by donation in winter)

**alaskabg.org**

## Chugach State Park

☎ 907-345-5014

**dnr.alaska.gov/parks /aspunits/chugach/ chugachindex.htm**

time on the **observation deck** overlooking adjacent Lake Hood, the world's largest and busiest floatplane base.

To find out more about Alaska's native plants, as well as some flora from around the globe, head southeast about 5 miles (8 km) from downtown to the **Alaska Botanical Garden.** The plantings are organized into some ten distinct gardens, such as the **Herb Garden,** with its medicinal and culinary herbs, and the **Lower Perennial Garden,** known for its bountiful summer eruptions of peonies and Himalayan blue poppies. The **Rock Garden** features more than 350 plant species adapted to alpine conditions, including native Alaskan flora and plants from the alpine regions of Norway, China, and other countries. The 110-acre (44 ha) property also harbors some trails, such as the **Wildflower Trail** and the **Lowenfels Family Nature Trail.** Along the former you'll see bluebell, fool's huckleberry, and various native Alaskan blooms.

The latter curves for about a mile (1.6 km) down to Campbell Creek, which hosts spawning king salmon in summer. Pick up a printed trail guide at the trailhead for information keyed to the 22 interpretive signs along the path. But remember that this is Alaska, and watch out for bears and moose.

That warning goes double for **Chugach State Park,** the half-million-acre (202,343 ha) playground and wilderness in Anchorage's backyard. The park's western boundary lies a couple of miles (3.2 km) east of the botanical garden. Another popular access point is just south of the city along the Seward Highway, flanking the shore of Turnagain Arm. You can hike, fish, pick berries, mountain bike, and enjoy this nature sanctuary. Backpack for a day in the park or drive 20 minutes from downtown, walk a short trail, and be treated to a 360-degree panorama of the city, Cook Inlet, the park, and mountains in all directions. ∎

## NEED TO KNOW

### Port Logistics: Anchorage

Anchorage has no dedicated dock for cruise ships, so they tie up at the industrial port. (Most cruise ship visitors are arriving from ships in Whittier or Seward; few sail into Anchorage.) It's about a 20-minute walk north of downtown, but it's best to take a cab or shuttle if your ship provides one, rather than wade through the port's heavy industrial traffic. Once you're downtown, 2 or 3 miles (3–5 km) of walking will get you to most attractions. To

reach outlying sites you'll need to take a taxi, a city bus, or rent a car. Note: During midsummer the Alaska Native Heritage Center runs a free shuttle from several downtown sites.

### Anchorage Highlights

• Anchorage Museum: 2–4 hours
• Tony Knowles Coastal Trail: 1–5 hours
• Alaska Native Heritage Center: 2–4 hours
• Chugach State Park: 3 hours to 1 week

# DENALI NATIONAL PARK & PRESERVE

**Denali is enormous—at more than 6 million acres (2.4 million ha), it's larger than Vermont. Glaciers dozens of miles long. Braided rivers half a mile (0.8 km) wide. Moose that stand 7 feet (2.1 m) at the shoulder. And, above all, 20,310-foot (6,190 m) Mount Denali, the continent's highest point. Many locals call it simply "the mountain."**

Located deep in Alaska's vast interior, Denali's huge appeal inspires many cruise ship passengers to make their way to the park before or after their cruises, often on excursions organized by the cruise companies. Occasionally a ship will dock in Anchorage, but more typically they land in either Whittier or Seward, and passengers board buses or take the train to travel to Denali.

More than 2 million of Denali's acres (800,000 ha) are designated wilderness, and nearly all of the remaining 4.1 million acres (1.65 million ha) are eligible for wilderness protection and likewise show little evidence of human presence. It's no wonder grizzly bears and wolves thrive here. In fact, the presence of bears, wolves, and big-game animals such as caribou, Dall sheep, and moose was a key to the establishment of the park. A nearby gold rush in the early 1900s brought hordes of market hunters to this part of Alaska, and they began killing game at an unsustainable pace to provide meat to the stampeders, crews building the Alaska Railroad, and the growing town of Fairbanks. This led to a long effort to create a park to protect the area from commercial hunting, a mission that

Mount Denali dominates this section of the Alaska Range.

## Denali National Park & Preserve

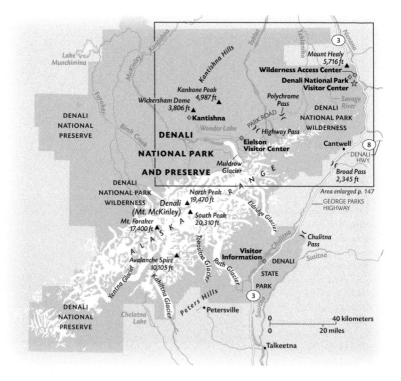

📍 Maps pp. 135 & this page

**Visitor Information**

✉ Mile 237 Parks Hwy.

☎ 907-683-9532

💲 $$$ (park entrance fee)

**nps.gov/dena**

finally succeeded in 1917, when President Woodrow Wilson established Mount McKinley National Park. The park was expanded and renamed "Denali" in 1980.

Being so big and wild, Denali is more difficult to tour than, say, Yosemite or Great Smoky Mountains National Parks, but with some effort casual visitors can at least make Denali's acquaintance. The park comprises two main areas: the front country and the backcountry. The vast majority of the park is backcountry, and for the most part only backpackers set foot out there. However, one road, the 92-mile (148 km) **Park Road** (see drive, pp. 145–147), reaches

far into this wilderness. All but the first 15 miles (24 km) are closed to private vehicles, so drivers/guides authorized by the Park Service take buses varying distances out this road; some go all the way to the end and back. To get a good look at the natural beauty of the park, take a bus at least halfway.

The front country has its own charms, evident even amid the sprawl of roadside services near the park entrance. Note the **promenade** above the rushing **Nenana River** and the excellent views from some of the restaurants and hotels.

Several tour operators around
(continued on p. 148)

# DRIVE: DENALI NATIONAL PARK

The 92-mile (148 km) Park Road extends into Denali's otherwise wild heart. It slips through spruce and aspen forests, tightropes along mountainsides above broad river valleys, crosses vast expanses of alpine tundra, and provides ample opportunities to view the park's resident wildlife.

A park-operated shuttle bus rolls along the restricted road through Polychrome Pass.

Access beyond the first 15 miles (24 km) is by shuttle bus only. Passengers are free to hop off the bus at certain spots, see the sights, then take a different bus either farther into the park or back to the entrance. If you opt for a walkabout, prepare to spend at least an hour in the wilderness. At a minimum, carry rain gear and insect repellent and know the ABCs of dealing with bears.

For information and to catch a bus, head to the **Wilderness Access Center ❶** (WAC; see map p. 147), a half mile (0.8 km) from the park entrance. In busy summer season it's best to make reservations weeks ahead (*tel 907-272-7275 or 866-761-6629, nps.gov/dena/planyourvisit/shuttles.htm and reservedenali.com*).

First decide whether you want a tour or

**NOT TO BE MISSED:**

Views of Mount Denali
• Polychrome Pass • Wonder Lake • Kantishna Roadhouse
• Grizzly sightings

shuttle bus. Both stop at key points along the road and make unscheduled stops to take advantage of wildlife sightings. Tour buses provide full service and popular itineraries. The Tundra Wilderness Tour, for example, features a naturalist guide, a box lunch and drinks, pickup at places besides the WAC, and service to and from the Teklanika or Toklat Rivers (Mile 31.3 or Mile 53).

At Mile 14.7 the **Savage River** marks the boundary between the park's front country and backcountry. Here, buses pass a checkpoint beyond which private vehicles are not permitted, and pavement gives way to gravel. For the next 8 miles (13 km), the road parallels **Primrose Ridge,** mostly above the tree line in the tundra. Passengers enjoy unobstructed views of the Alaska Range to the south. Open views of the river valleys and tundra-covered slopes offer excellent wildlife-watching opportunities.

The stretch from Savage River to Polychrome Pass, at Mile 45.9, offers even better odds for spotting the park's bears. Soon after bridging the **Sanctuary River** at Mile 22, the road turns south and runs about 17 miles (27 km) along the Teklanika River to Sable Pass. Wolves sometimes roam this river valley, and people have spotted them near or even on the road. Moose favor ponds and willow thickets in the forested bottomland. Scan surrounding snow line slopes for Dall sheep; passengers often spot herds grazing on precipitous meadows as casually as cows feed on Wisconsin flatland. Though grizzlies range widely and unpredictably, sows and their cubs have been repeated visitors over the years around **Sable Pass** (Mile 39.1). Also favoring the pass at times is a wolf pack—one of about a dozen that roam the park.

Backpackers head toward Polychrome Pass.

Choose from a list of half a dozen distances and destinations, ranging from a two-hour round-trip that turns around at Mile 15 to a 13-hour round-trip that goes to the end of the road, Mile 92. For the best views, grab a window seat that will face south—and bring binoculars.

## Toward Polychrome Pass

The first 15 miles (24 km) of road to Savage River is paved, skirting the base of **Healy Ridge** and threading two river valleys. After a few miles the road climbs, and the predominant white spruce and accompanying aspen, paper birch, and balsam poplar diminish in both number and stature. Higher elevations bring successively harsher growing conditions and sparse vegetation.

## Spectacular Scenery

The dramatic landscape takes center stage as the road rises to **Polychrome Pass ❷**. Passengers may feel the urge to flee their south-facing seats as the narrow road negotiates dizzying drop-offs, although the views usually keep even white-knuckled passengers riveted. Everyone can breathe easy and savor the vistas as buses linger at the Polychrome Pass rest stop. If time permits, take the short hike up to the overlook above the road that enhances the fantastic view. In addition to the mountains, sprawling river valleys, and glaciers, you'll be treated to the orange-, yellow-, red-, purple-, black-, and white-banded Alaska Range foothills for which the pass is named.

Both wildlife and scenic beauty abound along the 20 miles (32 km) from Polychrome Pass to the Eielson Visitor Center. Amid open tundra the road crests **Highway Pass** at 3,980 feet (1,213 m) with a panorama to match its lofty status. Watch for soaring golden eagles and scan nearby rock piles for the pikas and marmots those eagles are hunting. Also scope out the ridgetops and remnant snowbanks, where caribou hide to escape swarming bugs.

The **Eielson Visitor Center** ❸ is all about location, location, location. Opened in 2008, it features exhibits, a short interpretive trail, a ranger desk, and guided outings. From this perch, visitors get a top-to-bottom view of **Mount Denali**—that is, if the weather cooperates. Summer showers account for most of the park's 16 inches (41 cm) of annual rainfall, and clouds often obscure all or part of the mountain, even on fairly clear days. But if you beat the one-in-three odds of seeing the summit, the view will knock your socks off.

From Eielson the road descends along the Thorofare River, past Muldrow Glacier, then follows the McKinley River to **Wonder Lake** ❹.

Watch for moose in the roadside ponds—not to mention beaver, muskrat, and waterfowl. At Mile 84.6, most buses take the short spur to **Wonder Lake Campground,** a beautiful spot to picnic. This is the closest (27 miles/43 km) the road comes to Mount Denali.

A few buses continue to **Kantishna** ❺ (Mile 91), a mile from road's end. This area was absorbed into the park in a 1980 expansion—along with 4.2 million other acres (1.7 million ha). Several preexisting, privately owned lodges remain here, deep in the otherwise lodge-less park. These provide a more comfortable alternative for visitors who long to be in the backcountry but prefer not to camp. In the Kantishna District, the buses come to the end of the road, and then turn around and head back, granting you the joy of seeing all 92 miles again.

---

🄰  See also area maps pp. 135 & 144

🄿  Wilderness Access Center

ⓘ  106 to 184 miles (170 to 296 km) round-trip

🕒  5 to 13 hours

🄿  Wilderness Access Center

---

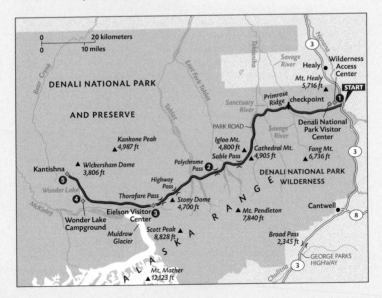

## Denali Blooms

Plants tend to get short shrift when grizzlies ramble into view or the mountain emerges from the clouds, but during the summer, Denali puts on a wildflower show that deserves your attention. The park is home to nearly 450 species of flowering plants, including blue kitten tails, pink and white fireweeds colonizing eroded riverbanks, white Alp lilies, the lovely deep purple of poisonous monkshoods, and the brilliant blue of mountain forget-me-nots, the Alaska state flower. You may see 50 or 60 species on a single hike.

the entrance offer guided excursions into surrounding wildlands and one into the park itself.

**Flightseeing trips** are a popular, though pricey, option. These bush planes tour the park and, weather permitting, circle the mountain. Buzzing around Mount Denali imparts a visceral sense of its magnitude. At 20,310 feet (6,190 m), it's the undisputed champion of North America, but in a very real sense it's even bigger than that. While 9,000 feet (2,743 m) short of Mount Everest in elevation above sea level, Denali is 6,000 feet (1,829 m) taller than Everest when measured from the flats below it. Denali towers higher above its surroundings than perhaps any mountain in the world.

### Visitor Center & Beyond

When you've passed the entrance, you can then get your bearings 1.5 miles (2.4 km) into the park at the **Denali Visitor Center,** which presents exhibits on the natural and cultural history of the park. Check out the visually stunning films on the big screen in the spacious theater. Interpretive hikes and a free shuttle bus to the park kennel leave from here. But don't expect to board Fido at this kennel; it's for the park's sled dogs, which rangers use to patrol Denali during the winter. In summer the rangers stage sled-dog demonstrations three times a day.

Near the visitor center you'll also find the **Murie Science and Learning Center.** Though many of its programs are aimed at organized groups, a fair number are offered to casual visitors. It hosts regular public evening presentations on scientific research taking place in the park. The truly gung-ho traveler can sign up for three- to five-day field seminars on such topics as the wolves of Denali and glaciers of the Alaska Range.

Though the backcountry has very few established trails, hikers can choose from a variety of well-maintained trails in the front country. Denali is so wild that even here you need to watch out for wildlife, particularly bears and moose. Make sure you observe them from a safe distance; the Park Service recommends a minimum of 25 yards (23 m) for a moose, double that if it's a cow with calves, and 300 yards (274 m) for a bear. Rangers advise maintaining that 25-yard minimum even for large mammals that aren't so dangerous, for their own protection and comfort. Stretch that to at least 100 yards (91 m) for nesting raptors or when you're in the vicinity of large-mammal dens.

The **Savage River Loop Trail** (2 miles/3.2 km round-trip) begins at Mile 15 on Park Road. All other trails start at or near the visitor center. If you don't fancy anything too strenuous, one of the easiest is the **Taiga Trail** (2.6 miles/4.2 km round-trip), which winds through subarctic forest and connects with three other trails. Another gentle route is the **McKinley Station Trail** (1.6 miles/2.6 km one-way), which leads you through spruce forest from the visitor center to the **Riley Creek Campground,** passing several historic sites. Perhaps the most popular walk is the **Horseshoe Lake Trail** (a gentle round-trip of 1.4 miles/2.3 km), which meanders past a river, creek, ponds, and the eponymous lake. And of course, all that water hosts plenty of natural life, from tiny flowers to beaver, muskrat, and moose.

**INSIDER TIP:**

Unlike the park transit buses, tour buses offer narration throughout your journey. Although you can't disembark en-route, they're a great way to learn as you "ooh!" and "aah!"

—CHRISTOPHER P. BAKER
*National Geographic author*

Those with strong legs should consider the **Mount Healy Overlook Trail** (4.5 miles/7.2 km round-trip from the Taiga Trail or 5.5 miles/8.9 km from the visitor center). This lively hike takes you through the park's primary habitats and puts you atop a ridge offering expansive views of the front country. To reach the trailhead from the visitor center, walk half a mile (0.8 km) on the Taiga Trail. When you finally reach the overlook, scan for Dall sheep and golden eagles. ■

## NEED TO KNOW

### Port Logistics: Denali National Park & Preserve

Located about 275 miles (443 km) by road or railway from the nearest port, Denali nonetheless is on the itinerary of many cruise ship passengers. By train, bus, plane, and rental car, you can travel north into Alaska's interior, usually on an excursion arranged by your cruise ship. Typically you'll stay in a hotel near the park's entrance, but if you want to get a good look at Denali, make sure you go beyond the entrance clutter, and head out Park Road on one of the tour or shuttle buses. These get extremely busy during the summer, so reserve well in advance. The park's website has lots of helpful information.

### Denali National Park Highlights

• Bus tour of Park Road: 5–13 hours
• Flightseeing around Mount Denali: 1–2 hours
• Polychrome Pass (by shuttle bus): 5–6 hours round-trip
• Eielson Visitor Center (by tour bus): 8 hours round-trip

# BEAR-WATCHING

Ten people stand very quietly on a slope overlooking the river, all eyes on an approaching grizzly. Walking along on all fours, the huge male comes within 100 feet (30 m)—much closer than recommended by bear safety experts, given that a bear can run 100 feet in less than three seconds. For a moment the grizzly pauses right below the group, and then it wades into the river, a salmon dinner on its mind.

Before the salmon begin their runs in Alaska rivers, bears often graze on grass.

Other grizzlies are already out in the water fishing, and the two juveniles in this big male's path aren't about to tangle with him. They move aside. About 50 feet (15 m) from the bank, the dominant bear finds a spot to his liking atop the rim of a head-high rocky ridge that spans the river, creating a barrier over which migrating salmon must jump. He crouches at the edge of the cascade, facing downstream, and waits. Suddenly, a 10-pound (4.5 kg) coho launches itself upriver and over the ridge, but this salmon isn't destined to reach its spawning ground. With unnerving quickness the grizzly pivots and

snatches the fish out of the air. Ripping off strips of flesh, the bear devours the salmon rapidly and readies itself to catch the next unlucky fish.

For hours this group of people watches the big male and the 15 to 20 other grizzlies working this stretch of river. Some of the bears fish below the falls in the shallows, splashing around as they use their dinner plate–size paws and claws to try to pin elusive salmon. A sow and her two cubs lurk around the edges of the prime fishing grounds, looking for opportunities without exposing the cubs to attack. With so many bears in such a small area, disputes are inevitable. Every so often the bears woof and grunt at each other, occasionally things escalate to roars and bluff charges, and once in a great while full-contact fights break out.

Because these ten people are on a reputable, organized bear-watching trip, they aren't taking any greater risk than someone who goes river rafting or flightseeing. Were they on their own, it would be foolhardy to get so close to bears, but these excursions operate under tight safety restrictions laid down by the government agency that oversees the public land where the bear-watching takes place. The trips are led by experts who know how to behave around bears and who make sure tour participants follow the rules. And for that rare confrontation, these guides come prepared with guns, pepper spray, and/or flares.

## Right Guide, Right Place

Choosing a guide and a place is difficult, because Alaska has scores of both. Many of the best places to observe bears can be found on public lands with easy access from Alaska's ports. Southeast Alaska is rich with established bear-viewing places, and Kodiak Island and the Aleutians have some too, but perhaps the greatest concentration of outstanding sites is at the northern end of the Alaska Peninsula, especially in and around Katmai National Park and Preserve. Most of the outfitters authorized to lead trips to Katmai and vicinity fly out of south-central Alaska, notably Homer and Anchorage. To find out more about sites and

guiding outfits, contact the public lands involved, the visitor information centers in the port cities, and peruse the websites of the Alaska Public Lands Information Centers (alaskacenters.gov) and National Park Service (nps.gov/subjects/bears/safety.htm), where you'll find bear-viewing etiquette and bear safety information.

---

**INSIDER TIP:**

Know the basics of bear safety before you enter their territory; bears won't wait while you consult your smartphone.

—JUSTIN KAVANAGH
*National Geographic Travel Books editor*

---

Given that some 50,000 black bears and 35,000 to 45,000 grizzlies roam the wilds—and sometimes the cities—of Alaska, you don't have to be on an organized bear-watching trip to see a bear. You're likely to find them, particularly grizzlies, concentrated near rivers and creeks during salmon runs, which mainly occur in summer and fall. Grizzlies also spend a lot of time in the spring on mudflats digging for clams, and in coastal meadows eating sedges; they're hungry after emerging from hibernation, and they need something to eat until the salmon start returning from the sea. Black bears don't tend to congregate like grizzlies and usually are spotted by themselves in forests and meadows, though they won't turn down a salmon dinner.

## McNeil River State Game Sanctuary

For superb bear-watching, no place surpasses McNeil River State Game Sanctuary, a small enclave adjacent to Katmai National Park and Preserve. People go to great lengths to enjoy the privilege of being in close quarters with McNeil River grizzlies, sometimes as breathtakingly close as 10 feet (3 m). First, would-be visitors must enter a lottery before March 1

in hopes of being one of the lucky few to win a permit; if they win, they pay hundreds of dollars for the permit and hundreds more to fly to the site. They camp there in primitive conditions and hike 4 miles (6.4 km) round-trip to the 10-by-10-foot (3 by 3 m) gravel viewing pad. They remain there for six to eight hours to get this close to the bears.

# KODIAK ISLAND ARCHIPELAGO

The 16 major islands and numerous smaller ones of the Kodiak Island archipelago are scattered across the Gulf of Alaska for nearly 200 miles (322 km). Kodiak Island accounts for nearly three-quarters of the archipelago's dry land. Though this windswept island realm is most famous for its hulking brown bears (usually called "Kodiak bears"), it is also the most accessible and developed part of southwestern Alaska. Roughly 15,000 people live in the archipelago.

■ A thick understory of devil's club carpets the rain forest.

**Kodiak Island**

Ⓜ Maps pp. 135 &
   155

**Visitor Information**

✉ Kodiak Island
   Convention &
   Visitors Bureau,
   100 Marine Way
☎ 907-486-4782
🕐 Closed Sat.–Sun.
   Oct.–April;
   closed Sun.
   May–Sept.

**kodiak.org**

**Kodiak History
Museum**

✉ 101 E. Marine
   Way
☎ 907-486-5920
🕐 Closed Sun.
💲 $$

**kodiakhistory
museum.org**

## Kodiak Island

The city of Kodiak is tucked into a few square miles of the northeast corner of Kodiak Island, sheltered from the tempestuous Gulf of Alaska by nearby islands. About 6,500 folks inhabit this commercial fishing center, making it the largest community in the region. About 100 miles (160 km) of scenic gravel roads fan out from Kodiak; you can rent a car to explore some of these roads and the grand landscape they infiltrate.

From Pier 2, begin exploring the island with a short walk along Shelikof Street. You'll quickly get a sense of the importance of commercial fishing as you pass the island's big seafood-processing plants. This is reinforced as you skirt **St. Paul Harbor** and see some of the hundreds of fishing boats that operate out of Kodiak. At the north end of the harbor, Shelikof dead-ends on West Marine Way, where you turn right and walk along the east side of the harbor for a couple of minutes until West Marine Way curves almost 90 degrees and becomes East Marine Way.

Near this curve you'll see the **Trident Seafoods** plant, and notice something a little different: the 441-foot (134 m) *Star of Kodiak.* The last Liberty ship, this World War II vessel has been absorbed into the other Trident buildings over the decades. After a monstrous tsunami generated by the 1964 Good Friday earthquake wiped out much of downtown, including several canneries, the mothballed ship was towed up to Kodiak to serve as a fish-processing plant. More than 50 years later, it still handles about 1.5 million pounds (680,389 kg) of seafood a day.

A few minutes along East Marine Way brings you to Center Street and the **Kodiak History Museum.** The oldest Russian building in the U.S., it was constructed in 1808 by the Russian-American Company to store sea otter pelts. Inside is a wealth of artifacts from Alaska's Russian era, including dazzling Easter eggs. The museum also houses Alutiiq artifacts, notably a 19th-century kayak made of wood and sea lion skins that is 26 feet (7.9 m) long.

Immediately west of the museum, the **Kodiak National Wildlife Refuge Visitor Center** provides information for travelers who want to explore the

---

**INSIDER TIP:**

If you rent a car on Kodiak, ask that it be cleaned of fish remains.

—DAVID GRIMALDI
*National Geographic field researcher*

---

refuge, which encompasses most of Kodiak Island. It also presents various exhibits and a short film. There are specimens of Kodiak bears and a complete skeleton of a 36-foot (11 m) gray whale.

Just north of the refuge visitor center, go right on Mission Road and proceed a block to the **Holy Resurrection Cathedral** *(tel 907-486-5532).* This is the third Russian Orthodox church built on this site; the first dates back to 1794. From the robin's-egg blue onion domes to the ornate interior, this 1945 edifice is a visual feast. Tours are available.

Just down Mission Road from the church is the **Alutiiq Museum.** This appealing facility houses more than 100,000 artifacts that evoke the lives of the Alutiiq and other Inuit peoples

over the past 8,000 years, including an ancient kayak. You can listen to oral histories, and kids can dress up in Alutiiq clothing and enter a replica Alutiiq house.

## Beyond City Limits

If time allows, head northeast on Rezanof Drive (which turns into Monashka Bay Road) about 4 miles (6.4 km) to **Fort Abercrombie State Historical Park.** The old concrete bunkers of this World War II–vintage artillery emplacement are interesting, but sightings of sea otters, puffins, whales, and more will enthrall.

Finally, there are the 1.9 million acres (769,000 ha) of **Kodiak National Wildlife Refuge,** which occupy the southwest two-thirds of the island. Its most celebrated denizens are its 3,000 or so Kodiak bears, the gargantuan grizzly subspecies. Various tours will take you to view bears and more in this scenic blend of mountains, tundra, and deep fjords. ∎

**Kodiak National Wildlife Refuge Visitor Center**

- ✉ 402 Center Ave.
- ☎ 907-487-2626
- 🕐 Closed Sun.–Mon. in winter

fws.gov/refuge /kodiak

**Alutiiq Museum**

- ✉ 215 Mission Rd.
- ☎ 844-425-8844
- 🕐 Closed Sun.–Mon.
- 💲 $$

alutiiqmuseum.org

**Fort Abercrombie State Historical Park**

- ✉ 1400 Abercrombie Dr.
- ☎ 907-486-6339
- 🕐 Closed Sun.–Mon.
- 💲 $$

dnr.alaska.gov/parks /aspunits/kodiak/ fortabercrombieshp. htm

---

## NEED TO KNOW

### Port Logistics: Kodiak Island

Smaller cruise ships and the occasional big cruise ship call on Kodiak. The Alaska Marine Highway terminal is downtown, but cruise ships usually dock at Pier 2, about half a mile (0.8 km) west. While it's an easy walk, some ships provide a shuttle into town.

To visit Kodiak National Wildlife Refuge, you'll need about 4 hours. Kodiak-based Kingfisher Aviation *(tel 907-486-5155, king fisheraviation.com)* offers tours focused on bear-viewing. Andrew Airways *(tel 907-487-2566, andrewairways.com)* also offers short trips to fit cruisers' schedules.

# DRIVE: KODIAK'S CHINIAK HIGHWAY

This route traces the scenic northeastern shore of Kodiak Island, slaloming around three deep bays before swinging east to end at Cape Chiniak. It passes through a variety of landscapes, including temperate rain forest, alpine meadows flush with wildflowers, rolling tundra, stands of alder and cottonwood, and coastlines subject to pounding waves and turbulent tides.

Cliffs on Kodiak Island

Rent a car in Kodiak to take to the Chiniak Highway, where you'll encounter bits of rural Alaska, such as a roadhouse, some cattle and bison ranches, and countless fishing holes frequented by locals chasing steelhead, Dolly Varden, and all five species of salmon. The first 31.5 miles (50.7 km) of the highway are paved; the last 11 (17.7 km) are decent gravel. Some stretches have sharp curves that should make you slow down to 10 miles an hour (16 km).

The drive begins at the corner of Marine Way and Rezanof Drive in **Kodiak ❶**, at the north end of St. Paul Harbor. Head southwest on Rezanof, which soon turns into the Chiniak Highway. At Mile 2.4, enjoy the panorama of Kodiak's harbors, Chiniak Bay, and some of the archipelago's islands that opens up at **Deadman's Curve**. To fully appreciate the view, stop at the roomy pullout, which is enhanced by benches and telescopes.

**NOT TO BE MISSED:**

Buskin River State Recreation Site • Pasagshak Bay Road

Continue on the highway to Mile 4.1, where you'll see the sod-roofed headquarters of the Kodiak National Wildlife Refuge. This is the turnoff to the **Buskin River State Recreation Site ❷**. A one-mile (1.6 km) drive on a side road takes you to the site, which has a day-use area near the beach, a campground, and some of the most popular fishing on the island; big runs of sockeye, coho, and pink salmon throng the river in summer. You'll likely see lots of bald eagles, too, swooping down to grab the fish.

About half a mile (0.8 km) farther along the highway is the turnoff for **Anton Larsen Bay Road,** an 11.7-mile (18.8 km) dead end that leads northwest through mountains, valleys, and forests to the bay. All but the first 3 miles (4.8 km) are gravel, and in places there are tight switchbacks, so take it slow. Then again, considering the scenery, the berry-picking, the fishing, the bird-watching on the tidal flats, and sightings of wildlife like fox, river otters, and deer, you'll likely want to take it easy regardless.

Back on the highway and heading south, at various points from about Mile 6 to Mile 7 you'll see **Coast Guard Air Station Kodiak,** the largest Coast Guard base in the United States. From some vantage points you can see the Coast Guard cutters tied up to the pier, and at times Coast Guard helicopters and aircraft will buzz overhead. Around the middle of this stretch, look for a pullout above **Women's Bay**

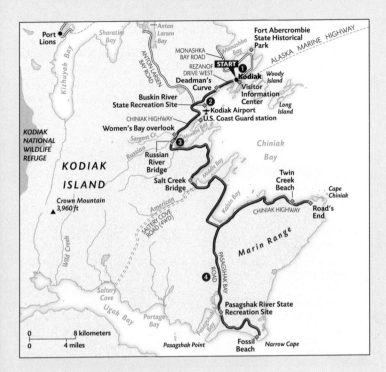

that has informative signs and picnic tables. The bay was so named because Alutiiq women favored it as a place to hunt, fish, and gather food. For several miles the wilds will be interrupted by civilization, including a roadhouse, the island's fairgrounds, and a raceway.

If it's August or September, stop near Mile 10 and stand on the **Russian River Bridge 3** to watch spawning salmon swarming below. Near Mile 13, a turnout at the Heitman Lake trailhead serves grand vistas and, if you scan the mountains, sightings of mountain goats. The wildlife theme continues between Miles 18 and 20, with looks at shorebirds on the mudflats near **Salt Creek Bridge** and eagles and their nests in the cottonwoods along **Middle Bay.**

Drive along the highway to Mile 30.5, where you'll hit the junction for the **Pasagshak Bay Road 4.** This 16.5-mile (26.5 km) spur leads to the private Pacific Spaceport aerospace

> 🗺 See also area map p. 135
> 🅿 Kodiak
> 🚗 85.6 miles (137.8 km), out and back, without spur roads
> 🕐 4 hours plus stops
> 🅿 Kodiak

facility and **Fossil Beach,** where at low tide you can see marine fossils embedded in the cliffs.

Back on the highway for the stretch run, around Mile 39 you can walk out to some World War II sites high above the ocean; look for sea otters in the kelp below. Another few hundred yards down the road, you can enjoy the dark sands, tide pooling, and more sea otters at **Twin Creek Beach.** At Mile 42, the highway ends at Road's End. From here you can hike out on unmaintained roads to great viewpoints, including a World War II bunker, and look for sea lions, whales, seabirds, and seals.

# ALASKA PENINSULA & ALEUTIANS

A few cruise ships call on Unalaska. They sail west along the south side of the Alaska Peninsula and Aleutians to reach this port on Unalaska Island, which lies partway along the Aleutian chain as it arcs across the North Pacific. But to see this stark realm Alaskan style, to cozy
up to the seabird colonies, fishing villages, tundra-clad islands, and volcanoes, take Tusty.

Hundreds of thousands of fur seals breed around coastal Alaska.

**Alaska Marine
Highway System**

Visitor Information

☎ 907-465-3941
or 800-642-
0066

**dot.state.ak.us/amhs**

"Tusty" is the nickname for the
**M.V. Tustumena,** the Alaska
Marine Highway ferry that twice a
month during spring and summer
goes from Homer to Cold Bay,
and once a month to Unalaska,
and back. The round-trip voyage
takes a week, so travelers often
make it a one-way, three-and-
a-half-day journey by flying in
or out of Unalaska. Those passengers who do the round-trip
have six or seven hours to check
out **Unalaska** (see pp. 158–160)
before heading back to Homer.
Visitors who choose the one-way
option often stay in Unalaska for
a day or two to experience the

Aleutians' only town of any size.
    Aside from Unalaska and
Kodiak, this voyage is not about
the ports so much as the journey
aboard Tusty. Homer and the
first destination, **Kodiak** (see
pp. 152–153), are larger towns
with ample attractions, but once
Tusty gets to the Alaska Peninsula
and turns toward the Aleutians,
the ports are just little fishing
villages at which the ferry stops
only for about an hour. The most
populous village, Akutan, barely
cracks the 1,000 mark, while
the smallest, False Pass, claims a
grand total of 35 residents. Take
**Chignik,** the first of the villages

that Tusty visits on its westbound run. The ferry ties up at the dock of one of the two fish-processing plants, where a couple of boats may be off-loading the day's catch.

Along with commercial fishing, most of Chignik's inhabitants lead a subsistence lifestyle that includes fishing for their own larder plus hunting caribou and moose. Part of the ramshackle town of about 90 (the population roughly doubles during the summer fishing season) spreads out behind the docks on the little patch of flat ground that lies below tundra-sheathed mountains; the town's other two parts lie on buildable land nearby. Though Chignik is not geared to visitors, Tusty pauses here for 90 minutes so you can wander amid the storage sheds, weathered houses, fuel tanks, and drying nets and see a no-frills village in a setting of surpassing beauty.

The one town that breaks the mold—well, maybe cracks the mold—is **Cold Bay,** where the ferry stops for three hours in a harbor surrounded by snow-topped volcanoes. It's an isolated fishing village much like the rest, but Tusty passengers can enter a lottery to win a seat on an old bus that takes the winners on a two-hour tour of **Izembek National Wildlife Refuge.** Here they'll see huge flocks of birds and perhaps spot bears, caribou, wolves, and other refuge denizens.

Aside from the Izembek tour, most of the scenery- and wildlife-viewing takes place from Tusty's

deck or through the generous windows of the forward observation lounge. The opportunities are abundant, as the ferry passes all sorts of wildlife sanctuaries, critical habitat areas, and waters rich with marine mammals—not to mention all the islands, rocky outcrops, islets, and sea stacks that are part of the vast **Alaska Maritime National Wildlife Refuge,** summer home to tens of millions of seabirds. Avid birders often travel on Tusty, enticed by the likelihood of spotting tufted puffins, harlequin ducks, whiskered auklets, marbled murrelets, gyrfalcons, and many

---

**INSIDER TIP:**

Mosquitoes don't handle salty water well, so you don't need quite as much insect repellent along the coast.

—SARAH ROESKE
*National Geographic field researcher*

---

other species that bird-watchers lust after. Passengers get to see places that few other travelers see. Consider that one of the public lands you'll pass, **Aniakchak National Monument and Preserve** (nps.gov/ania/index .htm), gets only about 30 visitors in an average year.

All that wildlife and natural beauty are the reasons to take Tusty to Unalaska—people sure don't do it for the onboard entertainment. The *Tustumena* is basic transportation, a lifeline for

## Izembek National Wildlife Refuge

🗺 Map p. 135

☎ 907-532-2445
  or
  877-837-6332

**fws.gov/refuge/ izembek**

## Alaska Maritime National Wildlife Refuge

🗺 Map p. 134

✉ Alaska Islands & Ocean Visitor Center, 95 Sterling Hwy., Homer

☎ 907-235-6546

🕐 Closed Sun.– Mon.

**fws.gov/refuge/ alaska_maritime**

**Unalaska/
Dutch Harbor**

📷 Map p. 135

**Visitor Information**

✉ Convention &
Visitors Bureau,
487 Salmon Way

☎ 907-581-2612
or
907-581-2613

**unalaska.org**

the local communities it connects. It has a few amenities, such as a small movie theater, showers, and a full-service dining room. Most passengers sleep in their seats, on benches, or in their free-standing tents in the solarium. Tusty does offer 26 staterooms of various types, but they're extremely popular, so if you're interested, reserve many months in advance. Some adventure cruise specialists offer nature-focused expeditions to the Aleutians, including National Geographic Expeditions (*nationalgeographic.com*).

## Unalaska/Dutch Harbor

Unalaska is the hub of the Aleutians. About 4,700 people live there year-round, and 5,000 to 10,000 temporary workers stay during the fishing season (Nov.–April), which makes it the largest town in these islands. Many people refer to Unalaska as "Dutch Harbor" or simply "Dutch," but Dutch Harbor is actually the name of the main harbor, not the city.

The town straddles two islands: Unalaska and its much smaller

neighbor, Amaknak, where Dutch Harbor is located. The islands are connected by a 500-foot (152 m) span officially named the Bridge to the Other Side.

A few small cruise ships and the occasional large one make it out to Unalaska, but most seafaring visitors arrive via the **Alaska Marine Highway** (see pp. 156–157). Both ferry and cruise ships tie up at the Unalaska Marine Center, which locals call the city dock, so this is the logical place to start exploring. Unalaska is fairly spread out but walkable. However, even if you're up for a long walk, the weather may convince you to take a taxi or rent a car. Even during the summer, the weather can be stormy; the confluence of the mild Kuroshio, or "Japan Current," and the frigid Bering Sea creates a lot of wind and rain.

From the ferry dock you'll head south into town along the western shore of Dutch Harbor, where you'll see some of the commercial fishing boats, seafood-processing plants, cranes, warehouses, and other development that goes into making Dutch the

## The Less Deadly Catch

The popular TV series *Deadliest Catch* follows the harrowing fishing adventures of several crab boat crews based in Dutch Harbor. Though it's still one of the most dangerous jobs around, fishing for crabs is less deadly than it used to be. In the bad old days, authorities set a quota for the whole crab fleet, and as soon as that quota was reached, often in just a few days, the fishery was closed. This system caused hundreds of crab boats to race to sea the

moment crab season started, regardless of the weather, often overloaded with heavy traps. Typically crews worked with little or no sleep, which led to accidents. Nowadays a new system gives each boat a quota and months to fill it, so they can take their time and exercise caution. In the 1990s an average of seven crab fishers a year died doing their job; but since the new system was implemented, only one crab fisher death was reported in the first six years.

A crabber shows off his catch near Unalaska's Russian Orthodox Church of the Holy Ascension.

number one fishing port by volume in the United States (about 700 million tons/635 million tonnes a year), an honor it has held for a couple of decades. Until the 1960s, Unalaska was a village of maybe 400 people, but during that decade, the crab fishery took off, followed in the 1980s by the boom in the pollock fishery, and rapidly the village added a zero to its population count and became the thriving hub it remains today.

About a mile (1.6 km) south of the ferry dock, near the airport, stop at the **Aleutian Islands World War II National Historic Area.** It's a little-known fact that the Japanese invaded America in 1942, capturing a couple of the Aleutian Islands. Though they didn't land on Unalaska Island, they did initiate their invasion of two more westerly islands by bombing Unalaska, site of a major U.S. naval base and carrier fleet. The Allies recaptured the two

islands in 1943, after a notoriously bloody battle in which both sides suffered thousands of casualties. Housed in a World War II–era building, the historic area's visitor center museum explores that yearlong struggle. If you drive around town and the surrounding area, you'll see concrete bunkers, Quonset huts, barracks, and other leftovers from the war.

Another mile south brings you to the **Museum of the Aleutians,** a 9,250-square-foot (859 sq m) facility that covers Unangan history and culture, Russian-American history, and the World War II campaign, though the Unangan occupy center stage. More than two dozen known Unangan prehistoric sites lie within 3 miles (4.8 km) of the museum, the earliest dating back 9,000 years, making it one of the oldest sites in Alaska. No wonder the museum harbors hundreds of thousands of Unangan artifacts.

**Aleutian Islands World War II National Historic Area**

- ✉ Visitor Center, 2716 Airport Beach Rd., near airport
- ☎ 907-581-9944
- 🕐 Closed Sat.–Sun. in summer; open by request Oct.–May (tel 907-581-1276)

nps.gov/aleu

**Museum of the Aleutians**

- ✉ 314 Salmon Way
- ☎ 907-581-5150
- 🕐 Closed Sun.–Mon.
- 💲 $$

aleutians.org

**Holy Ascension
of our Lord**

✉ W. Broadway
Ave.

☎ 907-359-2509

oca.org/parishes/
oca-ak-unahak

In more recent times, Unalaska was an early center for the Russian fur trade, as evidenced by the Russian Orthodox **Holy Ascension of Our Lord Cathedral,** on the downtown waterfront on the Unalaska side of the Bridge to the Other Side, about 2 miles (3.2 km) from the Museum of the Aleutians. This beautiful building topped by twin green onion domes was completed in 1896, but the first Russian Orthodox

■ Drama king: The male harlequin's brightly colored costume is reflected in its scientific name *(Histrionicus histrionicus)*.

chapel to occupy this site dated back to 1808. The cathedral houses more than 600 historic relics, icons, and books, some dating back to 16th-century Russia. This house of worship remains very active and is a center of the local Unangan community; services are held in the Unangan language, Slavonic, and English.

The lands and waters beyond town also offer many adventures for travelers. As you might guess, sportfishing is wildly popular

here, as visiting anglers seek halibut, salmon, cod, and other fish to ship home. Less expected is the large number of birders, who come to Unalaska looking for whiskered auklets and some of the other rarities that make birdwatchers swoon. Many travelers opt for general tours that include natural history, great scenery, World War II history, and Unangan culture.

## Adak Island & Attu Island

Lying 445 miles (716 km) west of Unalaska, half of **Adak Island** is a wilderness section of the maritime refuge. This exceedingly remote place is accessible by twice-weekly flights from Anchorage, and ashore by roads and trails established when Adak was home to a big military base. The base closed in 1997 and now about 80 people live there, giving it a ghost-town feel. Stop at the refuge headquarters in town to find out how to explore this starkly beautiful place, with its 2,000-foot (609 m) sea cliffs and mountains.

Don't miss the 6-mile (9.6 km) wildlife drive around pretty **Clam Lagoon,** where you should spot sea otters, seals, and all sorts of birds, including sought-after Asian rarities. At **Finger Bay,** a dramatic, fjord-like cut in the island, you can take an easy, 1-mile (1.6 km) hike up to and along **Lake Betty.** Right outside of town are the black sands of **Kuluk Bay beach,** a good place to watch seabirds and, if it's clear, to gaze 20 miles (32 km) across the water to the 5,704-foot (1,739 m) volcano that is Great Sitkin Island.

**Attu Island,** 450 miles (724 km) west of Adak, is the westernmost point of land in the United States, a roughly 400-square-mile (1,036 sq km) island at the far end of the Aleutian chain. Treeless, mountainous, often foggy, rainy, and buffeted by fierce winds, it comes as no surprise that Attu is uninhabited and rarely visited.

Yet on May 11, 1943, some 15,000 U.S. soldiers stormed ashore to retake the island from Japanese troops, who had invaded this island in June 1942. The only World War II land battle fought on American soil was also one of the most ferocious of the entire war. Those rare visitors to Attu these days still come across rusted-out jeeps, collapsed Quonset huts, bullet casings, and other wartime debris, but military history is generally not what brings today's travelers to this quintessentially remote island. Usually they come for the birds.

Attu is hallowed ground for serious birders, especially those who will go to almost any lengths to add new species to their North American lists. Attu is very close to Asia, so Asian bird species sometimes stray to this speck of North American territory. So if, say, a Siberian blue robin is spotted on Attu, it can go on the list, while if the birder spots that same species while in Asia, it can't. Hence, birders will endure arduous travel, often miserable weather, and spend big bucks to get to Attu. Visitors typically fly to Adak and take a special charter boat from there, sometimes pounding through heavy seas for the two-day voyage. Zugunruhe Birding Tours (*zbirdtours.com*) runs an annual spring birding trip, taking a maximum of ten birdwatchers plus guides for a week of chasing birds on Attu in the hopes of spotting an Oriental turtledove or Siberian rubythroat. Aurora Expeditions (*auroraexpeditions.com.au*) and National Geographic Expeditions (*nationalgeographic.com*) also visit Attu on their Aleutian Islands itineraries. ∎

## NEED TO KNOW

### Port Logistics: Alaska Peninsula & Aleutians

The Alaska Peninsula and the Aleutians are off the beaten path for most cruise ship lines, but some small and medium adventure cruise ships and an occasional large cruise ship stop in Unalaska. The cruise ship terminal is not close to downtown, and if there's no shuttle, you'll want to get a cab when you dock.

If you want to take the Alaska Marine Highway ferry on one of its semimonthly trips (spring–summer only) along the Alaska Peninsula and the eastern Aleutians,

make reservations (*dot.state.ak.us/amhs*). If you want a cabin, make reservations months ahead. On Attu, which is uninhabited, there are no cabs, terminals, or shuttles. If you take one of the rare cruises to Attu, everything will be arranged by the tour company.

### Alaska Peninsula & Aleutians Highlights

- Aleutian World War II National Historic Area (Unalaska): 1 hour
- Museum of the Aleutians (Unalaska): 2 hours

# TRAVELWISE

Northern lights over a cruise ship

## PLANNING YOUR TRIP

### Climate

Encompassing the weather with a single generalization in a state as big as Alaska is a tall order—except to note that even in the summer it can be volatile, and you should always be prepared for changes. That said, a few broad comments about the climate can be useful.

During the mid-May to late September cruising season, travelers typically enjoy mild temperatures, with highs ranging from about 50 to 65°F (10–18°C), except on the Alaska Peninsula and in the Aleutians, where highs hover in the 40s (4–9°C). Rainfall varies dramatically, with Anchorage and northern Inside Passage ports receiving only 1–3 inches (2.5–7.6 cm) of precipitation a month during the summer, while southern Inside Passage and Prince

William Sound ports get more like 7–10 inches (17.7–25.4 cm) per month in June, July, and August, and as much as 20 inches (51 cm) in September. Whatever the amounts, there is a monthly pattern for rainfall in most areas: less during May, June, and July; a bit more in August; and lots more in September. Pretty much anywhere in the region storms can roll in on short notice, especially in the tempestuous Aleutians.

### What to Take

This section covers a few items that will enhance your enjoyment of Alaska, not what will enhance the time you spend inside the ship. Whether you bring that tux or slinky evening gown is up to you.

Given that the weather can vary hour to hour, bring layers of clothing so you can make adjustments. Be sure some of those layers are very

warm, not only because storms and winds can drop those usually mild temperatures drastically, but also because you may spend time out on the deck of your ship or on an excursion boat—maybe even around some glaciers—and it can get extremely chilly. And be sure your outer layer is waterproof.

During the cruising season you're likely to enjoy many days with highs of 50, 60, or even 70°F (10, 16, and 21°C). But Alaska can also be cold and wet any time of the year, so bring the right gear. A rain jacket is a must, and a rain hat and rain pants are advisable. Before you travel, make sure your gear is actually waterproof; a hose can provide a robust test. Too often clothing you think is waterproof is only water-resistant, which could lead to discomfort or even danger if you get wet in the wild.

Because you'll be on the water, you should also bring sunscreen and polarized sunglasses. You also may want some kind of seasickness remedy; even if you don't get seasick on large cruise ships, an excursion on a small boat or in a bush plane will be a lot less stable than a 1,000-foot (305 m) vessel. Because you'll also spend time on land, bring along some effective insect repellent. Depending on your excursions, you may want to pack some hiking boots, too, or at least some sturdy walking shoes. Finally, bring some binoculars so you can get a close look at those grizzlies, sea otters, glaciers, whales, etc.

## Safety

Let's start with bears, as they're often at the top of the safety concerns for visitors to Alaska (see pp. 150–151). Both grizzlies (aka brown bears) and black bears can be dangerous, so keep your distance, especially if cubs are in the picture. (For details, visit the National Park Service's "Bear Safety" web page, *nps.gov/subjects/bears/safety.htm.*) Moose are perhaps more dangerous than bears, in part because visitors underestimate their strength. Again, keep your distance, especially if calves are around. To learn more, visit the Alaska Department of Fish & Game webpage: *adfg.alaska.gov/index.cfm?adfg=livewith.moose.*

Probably the most dangerous thing in Alaska, particularly if you're spending time in small boats, kayaks, and canoes, is cold water. If you fall into the sea, you'll need to get warm and dry quickly to avoid hypothermia. Worse, if you take a plunge, you may experience cold-water shock. Some authorities say serious cold-water shock might take you down before you can swim even 10 feet (3 m), if you aren't wearing a flotation device. Prevention is best. Wear a flotation device, never go out alone, and watch children carefully. For more information, see the Alaska Marine Safety Education Association website, *amsea.org.*

## PRACTICAL ADVICE
### Money

U.S. dollars will suffice unless you spend time in a Canadian port, in which case you'll need Canadian dollars. Major credit cards are accepted in Seattle, Vancouver, and most Alaska ports, but in some of the smaller towns, and at some of the smaller businesses, you'll need cash.

### Passports & Visas

Foreign visitors coming to Alaska must have valid passports, visas, or other acceptable documents. American citizens embarking or disembarking in Vancouver, British Columbia, need a valid passport. American citizens who embark and disembark in an American port and are taking a cruise ship can get by with various documents instead of a passport, but it is strongly recommended that they bring a valid passport. Whatever travel documents you intend to use, it is advisable to check with your cruise line to make sure your documents will suffice.

### Phones

Your cell phone should work in Seattle, Vancouver, and most Alaska ports, but don't count on it in some of the back-of-beyond sites. In the U.S. and Canada, dial 911 for emergencies, though the call may not get through in remote areas.

### Rental Cars

Even the small ports usually have rental cars available, although there may be only one outfit in the little towns. Your ship concierge or the town visitor center can be helpful in locating these, and you may want to book in advance.

### Car Travel

Most people who drive to Alaska cross over from Canada via the **Alaska Highway**—aka "the Alcan." The Alaska Highway is paved and offers ample services, though it still passes through wilderness for most of its 1,390 miles (2,237 km) between Dawson Creek, British Columbia, and Delta Junction, Alaska. Travelers who'd like to drive the highway only one direction can take their vehicle one way on the ferry.

### Driving Tips

Alaska has all the usual driving hazards, such as teenagers, but the state also presents motorists with some unusual issues. Frost heaves, for example, turn some highway stretches into roller coasters. Caused by the freezing and thawing of the soil, these speed bumps on steroids are especially common in the interior. Watch for moose. Much bigger and longer-legged than deer, moose stand taller than the front end of a typical passenger car, so if a sedan hits a moose, the moose's body will often come right through the windshield.

The most prevalent concern while driving in Alaska is remoteness. While most of Alaska lacks roads, the south-central coast and parts of the interior include a handful—most of them paved, all of them scenic. However, scenery means you're driving in remote, wild country, so bring emergency gear, including ample clothing, food, water, spare tires, and tools in case you get stuck. To check road conditions and other driving information, dial 511 or visit *511.alaska.gov.*

### Reservations

For fine-dining restaurants, it's best to make reservations. Rental cars sometimes get snapped up during the summer, so reserve them well ahead to be safe. If particular shore excursions are important to you, reserve them well in advance. Most of the large cruise ships let you reserve these several months before your trip, and typically you can cancel without penalty up until 24 hours before the excursion.

## Time Zones

Almost all of Alaska is in the Alaska Time Zone, which is one hour earlier than pacific standard time and four hours earlier than eastern standard time. The exception is the western stretch of the Aleutian Islands that lies in the Hawaii-Aleutian Time Zone, one hour earlier than the rest of Alaska. Alaska uses daylight saving time during summer.

## Maps

State and city maps are available from local tourism offices and visitor centers. For more details of the entire state, try the *Alaska Atlas & Gazetteer* (by DeLorme). All public lands are plotted on map brochures or detailed topographic maps. Contact one of the Alaska Public Lands Information Centers *(alaskacenters.gov)* for assistance.

## Taxes & Tipping

For tipping waitstaff, taxi drivers, hotel staff, etc., follow the same rules as in the lower 48: 10–15 percent for waitstaff, 10–15 percent for taxi drivers, and $1–$5 a day for hotel maids. Guidelines for tipping tour operators are less standardized, but if you're on a small, personalized trip, a tip for good service is appropriate—perhaps 10 percent of the tour's overall cost. Shoppers will be happy to learn that Alaska has no state sales tax, though some boroughs impose their own taxes.

## Travelers With Disabilities

Major tour companies and government operations offer reasonable access and appropriate facilities. But in small towns and remote villages, travelers with disabilities will encounter many obstacles. For more information, contact Access Alaska *(tel 907-248-4777 in Anchorage, 907-479-7940 in Fairbanks, 907-357-2588 in Wasilla, 907-262-4955 in Soldotna; accessalaska.org).*

## Visitor Information

The main statewide tourism information entity is the **Alaska Travel Industry Association** *(610 E. Fifth Ave., Ste. 200, Anchorage, AK 99503, tel 907-929-2842, travelalaska.com).* Before leaving home, ask the TIA to mail you its vacation planner, which has useful information.

More intel can be gathered from the **Alaska Public Lands Information Centers** (APLIC; *alaskacenters.gov*). There are centers located in Anchorage *(605 W. 4th Ave., Suite 105, tel 907-644-3680),* Fairbanks *(101 Dunkel St., Ste. 110, tel 907-459-3730),* Ketchikan *(Southeast Alaska Discovery Center, 50 Main St, tel 907-228-6220),* and Tok *(Milepost 1314 Alaska Hwy., tel 907-883-5667).* The interagency APLIC allows visitors one-stop shopping for information on state and federally managed public lands. Recreation permits and reservations for backcountry cabins may also be made at these centers. In each of these locations, the **Alaska Natural History Association** has outlets, selling natural history books, maps, and guides to all areas of Alaska.

## GETTING AROUND

### Air Travel

**Ted Stevens Anchorage International Airport** is Alaska's air transportation hub *(tel 907-266-2525, dot.state.ak.us/anc).* It lies 3 miles (4.8 km) southwest of downtown. Other major airports include **Fairbanks International Airport** *(tel 907-474-2500, dot.state.ak.us/faiiap),* 3 miles (4.8 km) southwest of downtown, and **Juneau International Airport** *(tel 907-789-7821, juneau.org/airport),* 9 miles (14.5 km) northwest of downtown.

Because this state has so few roads relative to its magnitude, airplanes of all sorts and sizes play a prominent role. Remote Arctic towns like Kotzebue offer daily jet service. More remote and smaller settle-

ments, like Adak, in the Aleutians, welcome twice weekly Alaska Airlines flights. Smaller airlines with smaller planes regularly service many otherwise isolated communities. Check with a travel agent, local visitor center, or chamber of commerce about flight availability to your chosen destinations if you wish to travel more before or after your cruise.

### Bush Planes

Bush planes—commonly three- to six-passenger propeller planes, some on wheels or tundra tires, some on floats, and some on skis—offer scheduled flights or are available for charter. Bush planes can go almost anywhere, landing on lakes, riverbed gravel bars, beaches, and even glaciers. However, they are expensive—perhaps $200 to $600 an hour for the plane. Hours add up quickly.

Some travelers harbor concerns about small plane travel that are entirely appropriate. Crashes do occur now and then, usually from foul weather. While even experienced pilots with shipshape planes sometimes have accidents, more crashes stem from careless operators who are cavalier about dangerous weather or proper maintenance.

Choosing a reliable operator is more art than science, but you can take several steps to improve your odds. If the National Park Service, a cruise ship company, or other discerning entity regularly uses the operator, it's likely among the best. If the company is recommended by the local chamber of commerce, has been around for a decade or two, and can demonstrate a good safety record, it's also a good bet. Don't be embarrassed to ask a company about its safety record or its pilots' levels of experience. Use your instincts and common sense, too. You can also search for an operator's safety record on the National Transportation Safety Board website *(ntsb.gov).*

As a passenger on a chartered flight, you play an important safety role. First, urge your pilot to err on the side of caution if the weather seems risky. Pay attention to the safety lecture at the start of the flight and take note of the location of flotation devices and survival kit. Bring survival gear of your own, such as clothing to keep you warm and dry if the pilot has to make an emergency landing in the wilderness. If you're carrying bear spray or compressed gas for a backpacking stove, ask the pilot to store it safely. Bring earplugs in case the pilot doesn't supply ear protection, and carry your gear in smaller soft bags, not big, hard-shelled suitcases. Small planes adhere to space and weight restrictions, and cargo and passengers must properly balance.

## Boat Travel

Alaska includes islands galore, more coastline than the lower 48 combined, and long navigable rivers that meander through vast expanses. Thus, boat travel is very popular. Large cruise ships account for the lion's share, each year hauling hundreds of thousands of people to and around Alaska. These 2,000- to 3,000-passenger behemoths are balanced by smaller cruise ships that accommodate up to 250 passengers, plus smaller ships and boats that usually focus on the nature experience.

Overseeing the state ferries, the **Alaska Marine Highway System** (AMHS; *7559 N. Tongass Hwy., Ketchikan, AK 99901; tel 907-465-3941 or 800-642-0066, ferryalaska. com*) is the other big player, taking tens of thousands of people along the southeastern and south-central coasts, even into the Aleutians. Providing access to dozens of Alaska communities, the AMHS is an essential resource for exploring the Inside Passage.

If you want to transport your vehicle from the lower 48 to Alaska, start on the Washington State and British Columbia ferries and cross to Prince Rupert, British Columbia,

where you can pick up the Alaska Marine Highway.

Operating on a much smaller scale are water taxis, which can take travelers to places not served by the cruise ships or ferries. While a few water taxis operate on more or less regular schedules, nearly all are for hire. Weather and tide allowing, they'll drop you off at a little fishing village, a remote trailhead, or a public-use cabin. Water taxis are especially common in the southeast and in Kachemak Bay. To locate them, contact the local visitor center or chamber of commerce. Be sure to ask questions to ensure your water taxi company is reliable.

## Bus Travel

Public buses and shuttles are scarce in Alaska, though tour buses are common. Ask at visitor centers or browse the Alaska Travel Industry Association website *(travelalaska.com)* for a listing of companies.

## Train Travel

Train travel in Alaska is limited, but the two existing options both follow scenic routes. In fact, the **White Pass & Yukon Route,** which runs between Skagway and Fraser, Bennett Lake, and Whitehorse, Canada, is primarily a tourist train (see pp. 100–101).

The main train service is run by the state-owned **Alaska Railroad** *(tel 907-265-2494 or 800-544-0552, alaskarailroad.com).* In summer it goes daily between **Anchorage, Fairbanks,** and **Seward;** a 7-mile (11 km) spur leads from Portage to Whittier. You can also take such unique trains as the **Hurricane Turn Train,** running between Talkeetna and Hurricane—55 miles (89 km) one-way, most along the beautiful Susitna River. The Hurricane is one of the nation's last flag-stop trains; you can flag it down and hop on board.

## FURTHER READING

Updated annually, *The Milepost (themilepost.com)* is a hefty book describing what you'll find along every road in Alaska (it also includes ads for lodges, outfitters, and more). *The Milepost* pinpoints locations and offers practical information about road conditions, travel, and activities, and is found in most Alaskans' vehicles.

Classics about Alaska still merit a read, such as John Muir's 1915 *Travels in Alaska.* In 1944 naturalist Adolph Murie wrote *The Wolves of Mount McKinley.* He followed in 1961 with the broader study, *A Naturalist in Alaska.* Margaret Murie penned another classic, *Two in the Far North,* in 1968. Maybe the best-ever book on Alaska travel is John McPhee's 1977 *Coming into the Country.*

*Alaska: The People, Land, and Events of the North Country* (2020), by Harry Ritter, is a good general history, as is *Alaska: An American Colony* (2002), by Stephen Haycox. Many books focus on narrower aspects of Alaska's past, such as Tappan Adney's *The Klondike Stampede* (1994), which captures the adventure of the Klondike gold rush. One notable account of Alaska native history is *The Epic of Qayaq: The Longest Story Ever Told by My People* (1995), by Lela Kiana Oman, which includes traditional stories of the Inupiat.

Native writers have produced fascinating chronicles of contemporary life, and resident authors also have used fiction to examine life in Alaska (see pp. 38–39). Meanwhile, *Alaska: A Visual Tour of America's Great Land* (2014), by Bob Devine, and *Hidden Alaska: Bristol Bay and Beyond* (2011), by Dave Atcheson and Michael Melford, are stellar coffee-table books. *The Nature of Alaska* (2018), by James Kavanaugh, provides a good introduction to the wildlife.

# RESTAURANTS

Alaska's restaurants are generally more expensive than their counterparts in the lower 48. Many restaurants open only for the summer season—generally mid-May to mid-September.

Seattle and Vancouver have vibrant, imaginative urban food scenes. Anchorage is much smaller than either Seattle or Vancouver, but it's still big enough to harbor a fair number of outstanding restaurants. The rest of Alaska's ports range from small cities to small towns, and the food options are proportionately limited, yet you'll find a few sophisticated gems and plenty of places with good food and local flavor. Prices in Alaska tend to be high, but the portions often are huge, balancing the cost. Many establishments are open only during the travel season and not necessarily every day, but they usually make sure they're open when a cruise ship is in port. We list a small selection of eateries located reasonably close to the docks that offer notable food, a compelling personality, or both.

## Credit Cards

If a business accepts major credit cards, those cards are listed using these abbreviations: AE (American Express), D (Discover), MC (MasterCard), or V (Visa). If the business does not take cards, "Cash only" is indicated.

## LISTINGS

Restaurants are organized by chapter, then by price, then in alphabetical order.

Abbreviations:
L = lunch
D = dinner

## ► SEATTLE & VANCOUVER

## SEATTLE

### 🍴 MATT'S IN THE MARKET
$$$–$$$$$
94 PIKE ST. #32
TEL 206-467-7909
mattsinthemarket.com
Matt's takes full advantage of the bounty of Pike Place Market, seeking fresh, local, and organic ingredients; the market stalls provide the cheeses, veggies, fish, meats, and even the flowers that brighten the tables. You can get intricate, pricey, stylishly presented dishes, such as grilled beef tenderloin flavored with black garlic and squid ink, but there's also a counter with diner-style stools where you can down a bowl of gumbo or a catfish sandwich. Check out the chalkboard that lists which oyster varieties are available and the name of the bay or island where they were gathered. Matt's is located on the top floor of the Corner Market building with big half-moon windows looking out onto the landmark clock.
🛏 50 🚭 🕐 Closed Sun.
🃏 All major cards

### 🍴 ELLIOTT'S OYSTER HOUSE
$$–$$$$$
1201 ALASKAN WAY
PIER 56
TEL 206-623-4340
elliottsoysterhouse.com
Perched on a waterfront pier, Elliott's has remained a seafood standout for more than three decades. Elliot's uses wild Alaskan halibut and salmon caught from sustainable runs. Their more than 30 varieties of

## PRICES

### RESTAURANTS

An indication of the cost of a three-course meal without drinks is given by $ signs.

| | |
|---|---|
| $$$$$ | Over $75 |
| $$$$ | $50–$75 |
| $$$ | $35–$50 |
| $$ | $20–$35 |
| $ | Under $20 |

oysters come from certified sustainable operations. The chef favors simple preparations that emphasize the flavor of the fish and shellfish, with sauces such as the chili-lime beurre blanc. If you crave oysters, an extensive list of varieties, updated twice daily, includes everything from Pacific oysters from Skookum Inlet to Kumamotos from south Puget Sound. The menu also runs to seafood linguine, fish 'n' chips, and crispy Pacific rockfish with peppers, shitake mushrooms, cashew, onion, black bean sauce, and jasmine rice cake.
🛏 300 🚭 🕐 Open daily
🃏 AE, MC, V

### 🍴 THE PINK DOOR
$$–$$$$
1919 POST ALLEY
TEL 206-443-3241
thepinkdoor.net
No one comes to this iconic Pike's Place restaurant—tucked, unmarked, behind an unassuming pink door—for gourmet cuisine. But if aerial performers and burlesque drag cabaret are your thing while you dine, then this elegantly bohemian Italian restaurant is the place to be.

Plus, beyond the surprisingly cavernous interior, the rooftop deck affords a magnificent view of Puget Sound while you down a negroni. The kitchen puts out steadfast Italian staples, such as gnocchi with wild mushrooms, a daily risotto special, and a really great spinach lasagna. Plus, this being Seattle, the ahi tuna crudo, garlic clams and mussels, and notably the cioppino in a white wine broth are guaranteed to satisfy.

🪑 120 🅿 🚭 🕐 Closed Mon.–Tue. 💳 All major cards

### 🍴 WILD GINGER

**$$–$$$$**

**1401 THIRD AVE.**

**TEL 206-623-4450**

**wildginger.net**

A local institution that brings a taste of Southeast Asia and China to downtown Seattle, Wild Ginger occupies a lovely bilevel space with a cosmopolitan ambience. This is fine dining with well-presented dishes, attentive service, and a great wine list. Their signature is the crisp-skinned Fragrant Duck, spiced with cinnamon and star anise. Wild Ginger will take you to Hong Kong for black pepper scallops, to Cambodia for sea bass with green mango marinated in a yellow curry sauce, or to Thailand for Panang beef curry. Or belly up to the mahogany satay bar and order some skewered delights.

🪑 400 🚭 🕐 Open daily 💳 All major cards

### 🍴 CAFÉ CAMPAGNE

**$$–$$$**

**PIKE PLACE MARKET**

**1600 POST ALLEY**

**TEL 206-728-2233**

**cafecampagne.com**

For a classic French brasserie, make your way to this unassuming café tucked into the heart of Pike Place Market. This is sophisticated French fare

done in a deceptively simple way. Drawing on the cuisines of Provence and the south of France, the café serves such well-realized favorites as cassoulet (white bean stew with lamb, pork, duck confit, and garlic sausage) and *calamars a la Provençal* (squid sautéed with olive oil, garlic, parsley, capers, and lemon). Enjoy the cozy interior or the patio seating along Post Alley, where you can watch the swirl of the market.

🪑 70 🚭 🕐 Open daily 💳 All major cards

### 🍴 COMMUNION

**$$–$$$**

**2350 E. UNION ST.**

**TEL 206-391-8140**

**communionseattle.com**

Opened to rave reviews during the Covid pandemic, this superb newcomer to the Central District is well worth the 30-minute walk from the waterfront. Chef Kristi Brown's unique inspired "Seattle Soul" cuisine is rooted in African tradition and her mom's Arkansas cooking, melded with a cross-pollination of globe-spanning infusions. For starters who can resist salmon-roasted corn chowder, or black-eyed pea hummus with a zingy Ethiopian blend of spices, or spiced deep-fried root veggies served with cilantro aioli? Mains span spiced butter-drenched BBQ shrimp and grits to rich beef bone broth with rice noodles and stir-fried Chinese broccoli and eggplant. There's even a fried catfish sushi roll! Leave room for the divine peach cobbler or original banana pudding. The airy contemporary setting with a chic industrial feel is no less inviting.

🪑 60 🚭 🕐 Closed L Wed.– Sat. & all Mon.–Tue. 💳 All major cards

### 🍴 SALUMI

**$–$$**

**404 OCCIDENTAL AVE. S.**

**TEL 206-621-8772**

**salumicuredmeats.com**

Armandino Batali was a master salumist and three generations of his family fashioned cured meats since opening Seattle's first Italian food import store more than a century ago. Although Gina Batali retains a stake in the business, since 2018 Salumi has been owned and run with the same loving care by partners Clara Veniard and Martinique Grigg out of their new restaurant and charcuterie near Pioneer Square. This intimate space has indoor and patio dining but most people get takeout or buy cured meats by the pound. You can also get homemade pastas and soups, but most come for sandwiches stacked with smoked paprika *salame, da vino* (red wine) *salame,* lamb "prosciutto," or *culatello,* which is the heart of a heritage breed ham meticulously dried for a year. Some of the meats are seasonal (Salumi sends out tweets when oxtail is available). And just because the restaurant fosters meat-curing traditions that date back centuries doesn't mean they don't also innovate; try the *mole salame,* which smacks of chocolate, cinnamon, chipotle, and ancho peppers. These exquisite sandwiches cost only $8–$12.

🪑 40 🚭 🕐 Closed Sun.–Tue. 💳 MC, V

## VANCOUVER

### 🍴 CHAMBAR

**$$$–$$$$$**

**568 BEATTY ST.**

**TEL 604-879-7119**

**chambar.com**

As the owners playfully put it, "an unpretentious fling with

---

🍴 Restaurant 🪑 No. of Seats 🅿 Parking 🚭 Nonsmoking 🕐 Hours 💳 Credit Cards fine dining." The bilevel dining room and bar feature soaring ceilings, rough redbrick walls, and carnivalesque globe lights of assorted bright colors dangling like mobiles. The chef starts from his Belgian roots and goes well beyond on forays to Asia, Latin America, and Africa. Perhaps a small plate of pomegranate-marinated yellowfin tuna with coconut jalapeño rémoulade? Or an entrée of braised lamb shank with honey, figs, cinnamon, and cilantro? Then again, you could just sit at the bar with a Belgian beer and an order of poutine, that quintessential Canadian bowl of French fries, brown gravy, and cheese curds—though Chambar does dress it up by using Roquefort and a green peppercorn jus.

🍴 280 🅿 🚭 🕐 Closed Mon.–Tue. 💳 AE, MC, V

## SOMETHING SPECIAL

### 🍴 HAWKSWORTH RESTAURANT

$$$–$$$$$

ROSEWOOD HOTEL GEORGIA
801 W. GEORGIA ST.
TEL 604-673-7000
hawksworthrestaurant.com

Hawksworth was judged the second-best restaurant in all of Canada in 2015. Its gleaming, stylish space is both light and dark, and each ambitious dish is a work of visual art. Try the *wagyu* beef carpaccio with charred scallion vinaigrette, celeriac bark, and edamame; or butter-poached lobster with Gruyère toast, bacon-wrapped endive, and lobster hollandaise—just a few examples from a single night's offerings. These inventive chefs create new dishes all the time. Splurge on the six-course tasting menu. You needn't dress up too much; some patrons come in jacket and tie, others in jeans.

🍴 80 🅿 🚭 🕐 Open daily
💳 AE, MC, V

### 🍴 RAWBAR AT THE LOBBY LOUNGE

$$$–$$$$$

FAIRMONT PACIFIC RIM HOTEL
1038 CANADA PLACE
TEL 604-695-5300
lobbyloungerawbar.com

The RawBar opened in the stylish and cavernous lobby-lounge of the luxurious Fairmont Pacific Rim Hotel in 2013. By 2014 it had become the first 100 percent Oceanwise sushi eatery in Vancouver, a town chockablock with fine sushi spots. (Oceanwise is the Vancouver Aquarium's certification program for sustainable seafood.) You can sit at the gleaming counter and watch the chef concoct exquisite *uni* (West Coast sea urchin), *nigiri*, *bintoro* (albacore tuna), sashimi, or dozens of other raw seafood delights. You also can get small plates, *maki* rolls, or put yourself in the chef's imaginative hands by going with sushi *nori* tacos.

🍴 140 🅿 🚭 🕐 Open daily
💳 All major cards

## SOMETHING SPECIAL

### 🍴 WILDEBEEST

$$–$$$$$

120 W. HASTINGS ST.
TEL 604-687-6880
wildebeest.ca

Formerly known for being all about meat, and all of it, from head to hoof, the Wildebeest has dialed back the cuts of horse and other red-meat rarities in favor of more seafood dishes and health-conscious vegetarian fare. However, the ever-changing menu always includes such gamey species as elk, conjured into sublime dishes with a fusion flair. You might try whole-roasted duck with butter-braised kohlrabi, orange zest, and toasted juniper, or the lamb tartare with a sorrel emulsion, compressed cucumber, and toasted pecans. All this meat is raised naturally, locally,

and ethically. The refined food is served in a laid-back space with wooden tables without tablecloths and staff clad in casual-Friday garb every day.

🍴 91 🚭 🕐 Open daily
💳 All major cards

### 🍴 BAO BEI

$$–$$$

163 KEEFER ST.
TEL 604-688-0876
bao-bei.ca

Bao Bei (it means "precious") has transformed a former tofu factory in the heart of Chinatown into a hip yet homey restaurant that turns out innovative food with traditional roots, all at affordable prices. The kitchen produces creative, constantly changing dishes; it makes almost everything in-house, even the little things like the steamed buns; and it sources sustainable seafood, local and organic meats, and free-range eggs. Bao Bei serves small plates, encouraging sampling. Chinese staples that get the Bao Bei makeover include Kick Ass House Fried Rice, with marinated pork loin, clams, salted halibut, Chinese leeks, preserved cabbage, and chili bamboo. Precious indeed.

🍴 65 🅿 🚭 🕐 Closed Mon.–Tue. 💳 MC, V

### 🍴 FORAGE

$$–$$$

1300 ROBSON ST.
TEL 604-661-1400
foragevancouver.com

Forage is an exemplary farm-to-table establishment that uses local, sustainable sources when possible. It strives for zero waste, uses power from rooftop solar panels, and complies with the green guidelines of the Oceanwise program for its seafood. Unsurprisingly, Forage offers creative vegetarian dishes, such as root vegetable biryani (an Indian rice dish) brimming with spelt, quinoa, lentils, sunchoke *raitha*, and pickled mustard seeds. It also has diverse meat entrées, such as bison rib eye and elk tartare. The dining room is stylish in a casual way.

🍴 80 🅿 ⓢ 🕐 Closed. Mon.–Tue. ⓒ All major cards

### 🍴 MEAT & BREAD
$
370 CAMBIE ST., GASTOWN
TEL 604-566-9003
meatandbread.ca

You walk into this small, spare, Gastown sandwich restaurant and join the line shuffling along the carving station, which is covered with fresh-roasted meats and custom-baked ciabatta buns. You have four choices of sandwich: *porchetta*, meatball, grilled cheese, and a daily special. There is one choice for soup, one for salad, and one for dessert. Quickly you reach the end of the carving station and are handed a paper-lined cutting board with an imposing sandwich on it, and you sit at the long communal table and eat one of the best sandwiches you've ever tasted.

🍴 40 ⓢ 🕐 Closed Sat.–Sun. ⓒ All major cards

## ▶ SOUTHEAST ALASKA

## KETCHIKAN

### 🍴 ANNABELLE'S FAMOUS KEG & CHOWDER HOUSE
$$$–$$$$
326 FRONT ST.
TEL 907-225-6009
annabellesketchikan.com

Located in the historic Gilmore Hotel, Annabelle's has been on Ketchikan's waterfront since 1927. Annabelle herself is no longer with us, but her casual Victorian restaurant continues

to provide several kinds of chowder and beer, plus fresh seafood, steaks, prime rib, and other staples. Consider the crab mac and cheese. Annabelle's is split between the down-home lounge and the somewhat fancier parlor.

🍴 130 🅿 ⓢ 🕐 Open daily ⓒ All major cards

### 🍴 HEEN KAHIDI
$$$–$$$$
CAPE FOX LODGE
800 VENETIA WAY
TEL 907-225-8001
OR 866-225-8001
capefoxlodge.com

You can take the funicular railway from Creek Street up the hill to Heen Kahidi for grand views from this restaurant's windows. Heen Kahidi is likewise spacious and elegant, with a sizeable menu ranging from expected but welcome standards like salmon and halibut to more venturesome fare, such as crab and jalapeño wontons and ahi tuna drizzled in honey lingonberry sauce and served on a cedar plank. Stroll around the lodge and admire the large collection of Tlingit and Haida art in this Alaska native–owned building, including a totem mural by master carver Nathan Jackson on the mezzanine and several fine totem poles outside.

🍴 112 🅿 ⓢ 🕐 Open daily ⓒ All major cards

### 🍴 BAR HARBORALE HOUSE
$$–$$$
2813 TONGASS AVE.
TEL 907-225-2813
bhalehouse.com

Set right on the harbor, this is a great little place to sit and eat while watching the fishing boats come and go. Try the pleasant deck on those days when it isn't raining—and, contrary to rumor, Ketchikan

does get some sunny days. Or brighten your day with a chimichurri prawns pasta with an Argentinian cilantro pesto, or the seared ahi tuna livened with a wasabi dressing. You'll also find clam chowder, steaks, tacos, calamari, and plenty of other fine choices to wash down with any of more than 80 varieties of artisanal beers.

🍴 120 🅿 ⓢ 🕐 Closed Mon.–Tue. ⓒ All major cards

## WRANGELL

### 🍴 THE STIK RESTAURANT
$$–$$$
107 STIKINE AVE.
TEL 907-874-3388
stikineinn.com

The Stikine Inn's restaurant serves well-made, high-quality basic dishes, like halibut fish and chips, steaks, all sorts of burgers, and razor clams. And the portions are big enough to satisfy a deckhand just coming off a long commercial fishing trip. This restaurant does make one radical move, given its coastal Alaskan location; it doesn't always have salmon on the menu.

🍴 130 ⓢ 🕐 Closed in winter ⓒ All major cards

## PETERSBURG

### 🍴 COASTAL COLD STORAGE
$
306 N. NORDIC DR.
TEL 907-772-4177

Petersburg is a fishing town, and Coastal Cold Storage gives visitors a chance to enjoy the fruits of that industry. Primarily a place for anglers to bring their catch for processing, this company also runs a retail shop that offers a lot of take-out and has a few tables inside and a few outside on the sidewalk. You can pick up some fresh halibut beer bits, fish chowder, scallops, crab, and other prime Alaskan seafood including shrimp sushi, or smoked salmon and prawn loaf with roasted red potato side.

🛏 25 🅿 🚭 🕑 Closed in winter 💳 All major cards

## 🍴 INGA'S GALLEY
$

104 N. NORDIC AVE.
TEL 907-772-2090

A modest place with no indoor seating, Inga's is a local favorite that dishes out all sorts of fresh seafood, from simple fish and chips to marinated grilled black cod collars. They also serve food that wasn't caught by a hook or net, such as Korean beef and barbecued burgers. Inga's does have some tables outside and some under a roof in a heated space.

🛏 70 🚭 🕑 Closed in winter 💳 D, MC, V

## SITKA

## 🍴 LUDVIG'S BISTRO
$$$–$$$$$

256 KATLIAN ST.
TEL 907-966-3663
ludvigsbistro.com

Ludvig's is hands-down the best restaurant in Sitka and one of the best in Alaska. Though intimate and informal, it turns out superb, imaginative meals, often using local seafood and organic ingredients. How about some Alaska paella *mixta*, an enticing blend of saffron rice, prawns, scallops, clams, calamari, chicken, and chorizo sausage mixed with vegetables and spices? Though the chef was once a commercial salmon fisher, she also produces such notable land-based food as grilled duck with a pomegranate glaze and lamb chops sprinkled with a cherry wine reduction. Ludvig's added a

wine bar and gallery upstairs, in an airy space with fine views of the art on the walls and Sitka Sound outside. You can sit on the flower-laden deck, munching tapas and sipping wine or microbrews and watch the fishing boats come in. For a simple but savory lunch in summer, try Ludvig's chowder cart, which parks in the historic Mill Building next to the Sitka Sound Science Center.

🛏 80 🚭 🕑 Closed in winter & L 💳 D, MC, V

## 🍴 BACK DOOR CAFÉ
$

104 BARRACKS ST.
TEL 907-747-8856
sitkabackdoor.com

Its official address is Barracks Street, but you actually have to slip down an alley to the Back Door's main entrance. A favorite local take-out joint and hangout, especially with the literary and artistic set, this loud and lively café offers make-your-own bagel sandwiches, breakfast burritos, quinoa lasagna, coffee drinks, and exceptional baked goods. Try the strawberry pecan bread.

🛏 25 🚭 🕑 Closed in winter & D Sat.–Sun. 💳 All major cards

## JUNEAU

## 🍴 GOLD CREEK SALMON BAKE
$$$$

1061 SALMON LN.
TEL 907-789-0052
alaskatraveladventures.com/day-tours/juneau

Set in the rain forest a couple of miles (3.2 km) north of the central city, this establishment caters to cruise ship passengers, but independent travelers can also catch one of the shuttle buses that run hungry travelers out to Gold Creek from downtown (reservations advised).

Sit on benches at outdoor tables covered by translucent roofs and gorge on succulent salmon baked over an alder fire. After your meal you can walk through the forest to a waterfall, watch for spawning salmon, check out the old Wagner mine, or try panning for gold.

🛏 300 🅿 🚭 🕑 Closed in winter 💳 All major cards

## 🍴 HANGAR ON THE WHARF
$$–$$$$

2 MARINE WAY
TEL 907-586-5018
hangaronthewharf.com

In a renovated hangar where Alaska Airlines got its start, the Hangar still roars on occasion as floatplanes take off from Gastineau Channel, whose waters lie maybe 50 feet (15 m) from the front door. An energetic crowd often jams this place—perhaps because more than 100 types of beer are on offer. But they're just as likely attracted by the food; the lengthy menu includes fine renderings of basics like jambalaya and broiled salmon, and more elaborate dishes like halibut macadamia and coconut prawns. On a sunny day the patio overlooking the water and the nearby cruise ships is a pleasure.

🛏 180 🅿 🚭 🕑 Open daily 💳 All major cards

---

🍴 Restaurant 🛏 No. of Seats 🅿 Parking 🚭 Nonsmoking 🕑 Hours 💳 Credit Cards

## SALT

$$–$$$$

200 SEWARD ST.

TEL 907-780-2221

saltalaska.com

Just two blocks from the State Capitol, this upscale surf-n-turf restaurant gives a modern, artistic flair to Alaskan seafood and steaks, using local ingredients fresh from the sea, pasture, and garden. Daily specials include freshly caught salmon or halibut, but you'll also find fresh homemade pastas and sea scallop carbonara, as well as such unexpected treats as roasted chestnut soup with prawns.

🛏 40 🚭 🕐 Open daily 💳 All major cards

## TWISTED FISH COMPANY

$$–$$$$

550 S. FRANKLIN ST.

TEL 907-463-5033

twistedfishcompany.com

The Twisted Fish is located right on the water, down by the cruise ship docks. This lively restaurant with a view specializes in fresh seafood—their motto is "A wild place for wild fish." You can get all the usual seafood dinners, like a pound of Alaska king crab legs or a saucy slab of salmon. But the marine theme permeates pretty much every section of the menu: Consider the wild berry halibut burger or the halibut taco pizza. If you're fished out, you can order steak, ribs, chicken, and such from the "landlubbers" section.

🛏 90 🚭 🕐 Open daily 💳 All major cards

## THE ROOKERY CAFE

$–$$

111 SEWARD ST.

TEL 907-463-3013

therookerycafe.com

This cozy open-all-day café in the heart of Juneau has evolved to be a local institution for its live music and excellent all-American fare. It bakes its own bread, cures its own salmon, and delivers such surefire winning staples as eggs benedict and ham scramble, plus such intriguing dishes as coconut-poached Alaskan scallops, cedar roasted salmon with beet greens, and a BBQ pork potato bowl with spiced Yukon gold potatoes, coffee BBQ pulled pork, two eggs, plus cheddar cheese and green onions.

🛏 48 🅿 🚭 🕐 Closed Sun.–Mon. 💳 MC, V

## SANDPIPER CAFÉ

$–$$

429 W. WILLOUGHBY AVE.

TEL 907-586-3150

sandpiper.cafe

The Sandpiper serves nice lunches, ranging from the exotic, like an elk burger, to the ordinary, like a patty melt, but it is their breakfasts that pack this place. You'll find all sorts of creative surprises, but if you just want some steak and eggs or biscuits and gravy, you'll find that, too. Plan on leftovers; the portions are huge.

🛏 52 🚭 🕐 Closed Tue.–Wed. 💳 All major cards

## TRACY'S KING CRAB SHACK

$–$$

432 S. FRANKLIN

TEL 907-20-2722

kingcrabshack.com

This establishment is a shack in the best possible sense. Sitting right on the dock where the cruise ships come in, Tracy's is a tiny wooden building about the size of a food cart. There's no indoor seating, but the crowds that pack this place find plenty of places to set down and enjoy their crab on the stools at the shack's counter and at the benches and tables (most of them sheltered by a roof) beside the shack. You can taste scallops or shrimp, but most folks come for "the best legs in town" (Tracy's motto): those Alaskan king crab legs, which can be as long as your arm and ordered by the bucket. Also available are crab cakes and crab bisque.

🛏 150 🚭 🕐 Open daily 💳 MC, V

## PEL'MENI

$

2 MARINE WAY

TEL 907-586-0177

The menu at this hole-in-the-wall ranges from meat dumplings to potato dumplings. Well, okay, they do offer a few drinks and some good, stolid, Soviet-style brown bread to go with the dumplings ("pel'meni" is the Russian word for these hearty items), but the set choice of entrées truly runs from A to B. This offbeat establishment appeals to the 20-something crowd, which often throngs the place, especially in the wee hours. Customers can play vinyl records from Pel'Meni's odd collection on a turntable.

🛏 15 🚭 🕐 Open daily 💳 Cash only

# ICY STRAIT POINT

Icy Strait Point is not a naturally evolved community. Opened for business in 2004, it is a cruise ship destination developed in an old seafood cannery complex by an Alaska native corporation. However, in the context of dining, think of it as a very small town with several eateries that share the same contact information. Icy Strait Point also presents a meal option called In Alaska's Wildest Kitchen, which combines great eating with a cultural experience. Led by an expert Alaskan chef and commercial fisher, participants gather around a horseshoe-shaped counter to learn how to prepare and cook seafood the Alaskan way. You'll learn much about local fishing and sample a tasting menu of such culinary delights as grilled halibut, Dungeness crab, wild berries, and seasonal herbs and vegetables. For a finale, you'll fillet your own catch of the day, grill it over an alder-wood fire, and savor all the flavor of Alaska.

### 🍽 COOKHOUSE RESTAURANT
$$–$$$
TEL 907-789-8600
icystraitpoint.com
The food isn't fancy but the quality is high, as evidenced by the right-off-the-boat halibut and the caribou sliders. You might try the Hoonah fish taco, a local staple that uses native fry bread to wrap up fresh cod and all the fixings. If the weather is even halfway decent, eat on the spacious deck and relish the scenery—while also keeping an eye out for whales.
🛏 200 🚭 🕐 Closed in winter
🃏 AE, MC, V

### 🍽 DUCK POINT SMOKEHOUSE RESTAURANT
$$–$$$
TEL 907-789-8600
icystraitpoint.com
The Duck Point Smokehouse is situated at the bottom of one of the most heart-stopping zip-line rides in the world (see sidebar p. 92). As you dine, you can watch live-stream video monitors showing people screaming down the mile-long (1.6 km) ZipRider at freeway speeds. But don't get so distracted that you overlook the salmon dip, seafood stew, grilled halibut teriyaki sandwich, or specialty brick-oven pizzas.
🛏 282 🚭 🕐 Closed in winter
🃏 AE, MC, V

### 🍽 CRAB HOUSE
$$
TEL 907-789-8600
icystraitpoint.com
Set on one of the docks, the Crab House abides by its name; it serves only crab. During Dungeness season, you can watch the staff take crabs out of the water, clean them, and prep them for the meal you can be eating soon thereafter at the outdoor tables scattered around the docks.
🛏 60 🚭 🕐 Closed in winter
🃏 AE, MC, V

## HAINES

### 🍽 COMMANDER'S ROOM
$$–$$$
HOTEL HÄLSINGLAND
FORT WILLIAM H. SEWARD
13 FORT SEWARD DR.
TEL 907-766-2000
OR 800-542-6363
hotelhalsingland.com
This elegant hotel restaurant is named for its location in the building that once served as the commanding officer's quarters at Fort William H. Seward, the historic military facility that houses the Hotel Hälsingland. The chef leans on the seafood caught in nearby waters and produce grown in the cook's garden outside the restaurant. Entrées tend toward the inno-vative, such as house-made rabbit sausage and sockeye salmon with a maple-citrus glaze, but the accompaniments are yet more creative, including dishes like butternut squash-edamame-corn succotash, black beluga lentils, and parmesan-leek rice-noodle flan.
🛏 66 🅿 🚭 🕐 Open daily
🃏 All major cards

### 🍽 FIREWEED RESTAURANT
$–$$$
FORT WILLIAM H. SEWARD
HISTORIC BUILDING #37
BLACKSMITH RD.
TEL 907-766-3838
The owners made a pretty little bistro out of a historic building at Fort William H. Seward. The sizeable menu encompasses plenty of regulars, such as calzones, bison burgers, pastas, semiexotic pizzas, and entrée salads, but check out the chalk-board for the ever changing spe-cials, which often include dishes made with whatever fresh fish is available, such as halibut *puttan-esca* or grilled king salmon.
🛏 50 🅿 🚭 🕐 Closed in winter & Sun.–Mon. 🃏 MC, V

## SKAGWAY

### 🍽 OLIVIA'S RESTAURANT
$$$–$$$$
SKAGWAY INN
655 BROADWAY ST.
TEL 907-983-2289
skagwayinn.com
Built in 1897 as a brothel, the historic Skagway Inn is now a beautifully restored Victorian, a fitting home for a white-table-cloth restaurant like Olivia's. They offer excellent seafood, sure, but also serve tapas and a variety of Alaskan game meats. Most surprising, they are known for their produce, much of which comes from a serious organic kitchen garden beside the restaurant.
🛏 50 🚭 🕐 Closed Sun.
🃏 All major cards

### 🍽 SKAGWAY FISH CO.
$$–$$$
210 CONGRESS WAY
TEL 907-983-3474
At this local favorite, customers rave about the fish and chips: crispy, light, moist, not greasy, big portions, and anchored by fresh Alaskan halibut. On the other hand, diners applaud the king crab legs as well. This family-owned Skagway institu-tion also serves grilled salmon, halibut tacos, and crab bisque. The restaurant sits right on the harbor.
🛏 120 🅿 🚭 🕐 Open daily
🃏 All major cards

## 🍴 STARFIRE

**$$–$$$**

**4TH & SPRING ST.**

**TEL 907-983-3663**

**starfirealaska.com**

Okay, Starfire does serve salmon. And they even offer burritos. But this is a true Thai restaurant that cooks authentic, often spicy Thai food. The chef/co-owner grows as many key herbs as possible in the garden behind the restaurant, and he spends considerable time and money acquiring the aromatics that he can't grow. The authenticity comes through in something as simple as the coconut lemongrass soup or as complex as one of the specialties, Chu Chi (fried catfish with mushrooms, onions, green and red bell peppers, tomatoes, cabbage, basil, and cilantro). Locals and travelers alike find such fare a delicious alternative, so Starfire is usually packed.

🛏 75 🚭 🕐 Closed Sat. 💳 All major cards

## ▶ SOUTH-CENTRAL COAST

## CORDOVA

## 🍴 RELUCTANT FISHERMAN INN

**$$–$$$**

**407 RAILROAD AVE.**

**TEL 907-424-3272**

**reluctantfisherman.com**

Attached to a motel on the bluff overlooking the harbor, the Reluctant Fisherman restaurant has great views of the fishing boats and Orca Inlet. As you'd expect, this menu emphasizes seafood: king crab legs, oysters, halibut fish and chips, mussels, and other bounty from the ocean.

🛏 110 🅿 🚭 🕐 Closed in winter 💳 All major cards

## 🍴 BAJA TACO

**$**

**NICHOLOFF ST. AT THE HARBOR**

**TEL 907-424-5599**

**bajatacoak.com**

For years this quirky café's original owners came north from Mexico in the summer to run a popular food stand out of a small converted school bus. Success led to a larger converted bus and eventually to an actual wooden building. But they built the pleasant café and deck around the second bus, which still houses the kitchen. Baja serves breakfast all day (try the breakfast burrito with salmon or reindeer sausage) and good Tex-Mex fare for lunch, plus their specialty: Copper River salmon or Alaskan halibut tacos.

🛏 55 🅿 🚭 🕐 Closed Oct.– March 💳 MC, V

## 🍴 NAT SHACK

**$**

**239 N. HARBOR DR.**

**natshack.com**

Permanently moored by the harborfront, Nat Shack is a large food truck with outdoor seating. The three owners take great pride to serve delicious artisanal tacos and Cal-Mex fare using the freshest local ingredients and homemade salsas and hot sauces. The menu includes their signature huge burritos and halibut tacos, plus crunch-wraps with seasoned beef, and spicy black beans.

🛏 12 🅿 🕐 Open daily 💳 MC, V

## VALDEZ

## 🍴 POWDER HOUSE BAR & GRILL

**$$–$$$**

**1.5 MILE COPPER RIVER HWY.**

**TEL 907-424-3529**

The killer views over Eyak Lake and Mount Eccles are reason enough to visit, but this laid-back restaurant also delivers the goods. Choose from salads and sandwiches, razor clams, fish tacos, burgers, or even ribeye steaks, and don't miss Sushi Friday and, especially, the hot brownie sundaes!

🛏 70 🕐 Open daily 💳 MC, V

## 🍴 THE WHEELHOUSE RESTAURANT

**$$–$$$$**

**VALDEZ HARBOR INN**

**100 N. HARBOR DR.**

**TEL 907-835-8114**

**valdezharborinn.com/dining**

Much about The Wheelhouse is unexpected, starting with the fact that this fine restaurant lurks inside a motel. Locals consider it perhaps the best restaurant in town, and not simply because dishes come in Alaskan scale portions. The menu offers New York steak and chicken marsala, but the name of the game here is seafood, from parmesan crusted halibut and fish 'n' chips (with a choice of cod, rockfish, or halibut) to cedar-smoked salmon, wrapped in cedar paper and served with baked potato and roasted asparagus. The sunny dining room and excellent harbor views further enhance the experience.

🛏 130 🅿 🚭 🕐 Open daily 💳 AE, MC, V

## 🍴 MACMURRAY'S ALASKA HALIBUT HOUSE

**$–$$**

**208 MEALS AVE.**

**TEL 907-835-2788**

The restaurant's sign features a halibut wearing a chef's hat, and halibut and chips is the house specialty. But this jeans-and-work-boots eatery also offers salmon, clams, shrimp, and other seafood, plus nonseafood choices like burgers and sandwiches.

🛏 50 🅿 🚭 🕐 Closed Sun. 💳 MC, V

## WHITTIER

### 🍴 VARLY'S SWIFTWATER SEAFOOD CAFÉ
$$

TRIANGLE AREA, HARBOR RD.
TEL 907-472-2550

Varly's is a small, down-home, family-owned place that emphasizes seafood caught in Prince William Sound, like shrimp and rockfish. Unless you have a phobia about flatfish, try the halibut and chips; the chips are routine, but the halibut is top-notch. Weather permitting, eat on the little deck and savor the panorama of harbor, sea, and mountains.

🔲 60 🅿 🚭 🕐 Closed in winter 🖒 D, MC, V

## SEWARD

### 🍴 RAY'S WATERFRONT
$$$-$$$$

1316 4TH AVE.
TEL 907-224-5606
rayswaterfrontak.com

Ray's is a local landmark, often filled with anglers fresh off a sportfishing trip. Naturally, it serves lots of seafood, straightforwardly prepared and of the highest quality. Unsurprisingly, Ray's is located on the waterfront and provides superb views of the harbor.

🔲 200 🅿 🚭 🕐 Closed in winter 🖒 All major cards

### 🍴 CHINOOKS BAR & GRILL
$$-$$$$

1404 4TH AVE.
TEL 907-224-2207
chinooksak.com

Seafood rules in this appealing restaurant hugging the smallboat harbor, but it goes several nautical miles beyond fish and chips. Depending on what's fresh, the menu may feature crispy skin black cod or halibut in black garlic aioli. There's even smoked scallop mac and cheese.

If you're feeling terrestrial, try the grilled New York steak in a chimichurri sauce or the pork carnitas sandwich.

🔲 150 🅿 🚭 🕐 Closed Mon.–Tue. 🖒 All major cards

### 🍴 WOODY'S THAI KITCHEN
$$-$$$

804 4TH AVE.
TEL 907-442-0338
woodysthaikitchen.com

When you need a break from grilled salmon and burgers, there's no more worthy spot than this superb restaurant, which fuses traditional Thai recipes with Alaska and Pacific Rim ingredients. Salivate over a menu of fried spring rolls and cream cheese wontons, pad thai, classic curries, and such rice dishes as pad Khing with ginger, garlic, shiitake mushrooms, scallions, oyster sauce, and shrimp.

🔲 34 🅿 🚭 🕐 Closed Sun.–Mon. in winter 🖒 All major cards

### 🍴 LE BARN APPÉTIT
$$

11786 OLD EXIT GLACIER RD.
TEL 907-224-8706
lebarnappetit.com

Le Barn is housed in a fourstory, Belgian-style barn, which doubles as a B&B. Dominating the menu are memorable Belgian crepes, ranging from entrées, like spinach/egg/reindeer sausage crepes, to blueberry apple rhubarb dessert crepes.

🔲 25 🅿 🚭 🕐 Closed Mon. 🖒 All major cards

## HOMER

### 🍴 AJ'S OLDTOWN STEAK-HOUSE & TAVERN
$$-$$$

120 W. BUNNELL AVE.

TEL 907-235-8848
ajsteakhouse.com

First opened in 1941 as a pub, this venerable restaurant is no longer the rowdy venue of yore, but it still has its Old Town false façade and live piano music. Today its wonderfully clubby, wood-paneled atmosphere invites weary fishermen and other patrons to relax and enjoy great seafood, including fresh-caught scallops, King crab, and (inevitably) halibut and salmon dishes. Above all, it's been known from its inception as the best place in Homer for a mouth-watering steak, and it doesn't disappoint carnivores.

🔲 60 🅿 🚭 🖒 All major cards

### 🍴 FAT OLIVES
$$-$$$

276 OHLSON LN.
TEL 907-235-8488
fatoliveshomer.com

Cheerful and informal, Fat Olives is a welcoming Italian bistro with something for everybody: cannelloni, halibut skewers, Kachemak Bay oysters, braised beef short ribs, and lots of sandwiches. A wood oven turns out excellent calzones, strombolis, and a variety of pizzas, many leaning toward the exotic.

🔲 60 🅿 🚭 🕐 Open daily 🖒 All major cards

### 🍴 THE LITTLE MERMAID
$$

162 W. PIONEER AVE.
TEL 907-399-9900
littlemermaidhomer.com

In 2020, this long-time restaurant beloved of locals moved to the former Cups Café building, a colorful space where owners Kathy and Evan Vogl oversee the kitchen with artistic passion. Their globe-spanning menu caters to every taste, from King crab sushi and Sicilian style pizza to a rice bowl with choice of grilled chicken, wild prawns, or rockfish. The decadent desserts

even include homemade ice creams. Plus, you'll find local brews on tap.
🍴 30 🚭 🏧 All major cards

### 🍴 LA BALEINE
**$–$$**
4460 HOMER SPIT RD.
TEL 907-299-6672
labaleinecafe.com
Undoubtedly the best place in town for a great breakfast with a view, this colorful café prides itself on its use of organic and sustainable produce. Everything is freshly foraged or caught. Start your day with a "Musher Meal" of corn tortillas with black beans, brown rice, reindeer sausage, eggs, and trimmings. For lunch, perhaps Alaska crab melt or a bowl of homemade ramen noodles with broth, veggies, and seasonal fish.
🍴 40 🅿 🕓 Mon. & D
🏧 MC, V

## KACHEMAK BAY

### SOMETHING SPECIAL

### 🍴 THE SALTRY RESTAURANT
**$$$–$$$$**
HALIBUT COVE
TEL 907-226-2424
thesaltry.com
The Saltry starts with caught-that-morning seafood, house-baked breads, and greens straight from the mostly organic garden behind the restaurant. The chefs then take these top-of-the-line ingredients and produce top-of-the-line dishes, such as halibut and shrimp ceviche, barley risotto with a rutabaga puree, "salmon three ways" (a plate with seared, cured, and smoked salmon), and Callebaut chocolate cheesecake. All this takes place in a gorgeous setting that includes the isolated cove outside the windows and the art-rich walls of the interior. Unless you're

staying in Halibut Cove or have another way to get there, you'll have to book passage out of Homer on the *Danny J*, whose cruises are timed for lunch and dinner at the Saltry. Reservations for the restaurant and the boat are essential.
🍴 30 🚭 🕓 Closed in winter 🏧 D, MC, V

## ▶ ANCHORAGE & BEYOND

## ANCHORAGE

### SOMETHING SPECIAL

### 🍴 MARX BROS. CAFÉ
**$$$$**
627 W. 3RD AVE.
TEL 907-278-2133
marxcafe.com
The owners describe their renowned restaurant as serving "innovative contemporary cuisine," but such a vague description hardly captures the zest of rack of lamb on a bed of lentils with *tzatziki* or grilled scallops with a lobster-saffron sauce. Always extending the frontiers of fine cuisine, the chefs offer different dishes every night. The remarkable quality stems in part from an intimate focus—no lunch and only a few dozen dinners a night are served in this charming 1916 wood-frame house with views of Cook Inlet.
🍴 34 🅿 🚭 🕓 Closed Sun.–Mon. 🏧 All major cards

### 🍴 CROW'S NEST RESTAURANT
**$$$–$$$$$**
HOTEL CAPTAIN COOK
939 W. 5TH AVE.
TEL 907-276-6000
captaincook.com
The Crow's Nest perches atop one of the Hotel Captain Cook's towers, commanding grand vistas of Anchorage and thousands of square miles of

the wilderness that surrounds the city. Inside, patrons dine on elegant cuisine, a blend of French and New American. Some dishes are simple, such as crab cakes or oysters for starters, and some are complex, such as a starter of roasted bone marrow with a shallot and black cherry jam. You can get king crab legs or a New York steak, or order the duck breast with a crab-apple and fennel chutney. The Crow's Nest is also noted for its 10,000-bottle wine cellar.
🍴 140 🚭 🕓 Open daily 🏧 All major cards

### 🍴 GINGER
**$$–$$$$**
425 W. 5TH AVE.
TEL 907-929-3680
gingeralaska.com
Ginger delivers artfully arrayed Asian food amid the rich, polished woods of its handsome dining room. The Pacific Rim influence begins with starters, such as the tamarind-cashew Alaskan prawns or crispy fried hoisin Duroc pork belly with a wasabi vinaigrette. The contemporary Asian theme carries through the entrées, too, with items like Szechuan coconut-crushed Wagyu beef.
🍴 110 🚭 🕓 Closed Mon. 🏧 All major cards

### SOMETHING SPECIAL

### 🍴 KINCAID GRILL & WINE BAR
**$$–$$$$**
6700 JEWEL LAKE RD.
TEL 907-243-0507
kincaidgrill.com
Acknowledged as one of Alaska's top restaurants since opening in 2001, this off-the-beaten-path culinary mecca serves up quintessential Alaska fare with artistic aplomb. Chefs Christopher "Drew" Johnson and Al Levinsohn oversee an menu that offers a fusion of

each season's freshest flavors with Cajun and Pacific Rim twists. Your fresh Alaskan oyster may come with cucumber-jalapeño mignonette; your miso-glazed black cod with pineapple scallion relish; and your smoked Gouda grits with Cajun shrimp, scallions, Andouille sausage, and wild mushrooms. Plus, you can choose outdoor dining when weather permits.

🛏 44 🅿 🚭 🕐 Closed Sun.–Tues. 💳 All major cards

## 🍴 ORSO

**$$–$$$$**

737 W. 5TH AVE.

TEL 907-222-3232

orsoalaska.com

Pass through the lively downstairs bar and step upstairs into a quiet realm of Oriental rugs and a striking slate-framed fireplace. This Tuscan inn setting foreshadows the traditional Italian items on the shifting menu, but Orso (Italian for "bear") stretches its culinary muscles far beyond Italian, serving dishes such as Alaskan sockeye salmon Niçoise with parsley and lime aioli and slow-braised lamb shank. Orso has many intriguing small plates, too, including the king crab corn dogs and seafood deviled eggs packed with smoked sockeye and king crabs.

🛏 200 🚭 🕐 Open daily 💳 All major cards

## 🍴 CRUSH WINE BISTRO AND CELLAR

**$–$$$**

343 W. 6TH AVE.

TEL 907-865-9198

crushak.com

The exterior is odd and uninviting, but the interior is the very opposite: a casual, friendly place full of animated conversation. The fact that Crush sells dozens of wines by the glass and lots of microbrews from all over Alaska, the U.S., and

Europe no doubt enhances the buoyant atmosphere. At reasonable prices you can get adventurous small plates, like a sweet pea and pistachio gazpacho or dates stuffed with sheep feta and wrapped in house-made prosciutto, or full meals, like the elk-and-pork meatloaf. The allied bottle shop occupies the loft above the bistro.

🛏 80 🚭 🕐 Closed Sun.– Tue. 💳 All major cards

## 🍴 SNOW CITY CAFE

**$**

1034 W. 4TH AVE..

TEL 907-272-2489

snowcitycafe.com

This cheery downtown favorite offers fine lunches, like chicken reindeer gumbo or cowboy meatloaf, but breakfast is king. Repeatedly voted best breakfast in Anchorage, Snow City does regular fare irregularly well: blueberry pancakes, eggs Florentine, biscuits and gravy. But the menu also brims with appealing Alaskan twists, such as a reindeer sausage scramble, sockeye salmon cakes, and the Kodiak eggs benedict, which features king crab. Perhaps most amazingly they manage to do all this at low prices.

🛏 120 🚭 🕐 Open daily 💳 All major cards

## DENALI NATIONAL PARK & PRESERVE

## 🍴 THE PERCH

**$$–$$$$**

MILE 224 PARKS HWY.

TEL 907-683-2523

OR 888-322-2523

denaliperchresort.com

The Perch sits on a hill (actually, a glacial moraine) amid the treetops about 13 miles (21 km)
south of the entrance to Denali National Park. Eat on the spacious deck and imbibe

the expansive views of the Alaska Range as you dine on some first-rate local, organic food. The changing menu may include crab and sweet corn soup in a duck broth, roasted garlic polenta, apple ginger glazed salmon, and juniper-encrusted caribou medallions.

🛏 42 🅿 🚭 🕐 Closed in winter 💳 MC, V

## SOMETHING SPECIAL

## 🍴 229 PARKS RESTAURANT & TAVERN

**$$–$$$**

MILE 229 PARKS HWY.

TEL 907-683-2567

229parks.com

You'll find the lovely log building housing 229 Parks tucked away amid forest and flowers eight miles (13 km) south of so-called "Glitter Gulch" (the crowded strip development along the highway around the park entrance). Its largely local, organic, seasonal, and ethically raised food also sets it apart. Ingredients such as heirloom tomatoes, locally picked, low-bush cranberries, Alaskan salmon, and organic greens crop up in many dishes. The skilled chef/owner fashions memorable meals, like the Alaskan razor clams in a tomato-herbed white wine broth or the king salmon in a sweet mustard glaze. Delectable vegetarian choices broaden the menu. Rotating displays of Alaskan art, much of it for sale, grace the walls.

🛏 60 🅿 🚭 🕐 Closed Mon. & in winter 💳 MC, V

## 🍴 CREEKSIDE CAFÉ & BAKERY

**$–$$**

MILE 224 GEORGE PARKS HWY.

TEL 907-683-2277

or 888-533-6254

mckinleycabins.com

This casual family dining spot

on Carlo Creek, looking up at the Alaska Range, is known for its varied and enormous breakfasts. Try the huge skillet dishes. Lunch and dinner range from chili to salmon, soups to sandwiches, burgers to salads, plus the signature baked Alaskan halibut topped with a creamy blend of spinach, artichokes, and parmesan. Later, try the strawberry-rhubarb coffee cake from the café's highly regarded bakery.

🪑 40 🅿 🚭 🕐 Closed in winter 💳 All major cards

## KODIAK

### SOMETHING SPECIAL

#### 🍴 GALLEY GOURMET DINNER CRUISE
$$$$$
1223 W. KOUSKOV
TEL 907-486-5079
kodiak-wildlife-viewing-dinner-cruises.com
Some of the finest food in Kodiak comes out of Marion Owen's galley aboard the *Sea Breeze*, a 42-foot (13 m) yacht captained by Marion's husband, Marty, who also works as Kodiak's harbormaster. Every evening during the summer, they weigh anchor at 6 p.m. and head out on a dinner cruise with six lucky passengers. After some wildlife-viewing (sea otters, eagles, sea lions, and sometimes whales inhabit these waters), dinner begins on white tablecloths in the teak-paneled salon. A master gardener and expert baker, Marion provides organic greens, homemade bread, and delectable desserts. The dinner often involves fresh seafood, like halibut with couscous and an orange balsamic vinaigrette. After a fine repast, Marty steers the *Sea Breeze* back to St. Paul harbor by 9:30 p.m.

🪑 6 🅿 🚭 🕐 Closed in winter
💳 MC, V

#### 🍴 HENRY'S GREAT ALASKAN RESTAURANT
$$–$$$$
512 W. MARINE WAY
TEL 907-486-8844
henrysgreatalaskan.com
Henry's has been a local hangout since 1957. Situated a block from the harbor in this fishing town, Henry's naturally favors seafood. Much is straightforward but high-quality fare, such as a seafood combo and smoked-salmon fettuccine, but you'll encounter a few surprises, too, like the crawfish pie.

🪑 150 🅿 🚭 🕐 Closed in winter 💳 AE, MC, V

#### 🍴 KODIAK HANA RESTAURANT
$$–$$$$
516 E. MARINE WAY
TEL 907-481-1088
kodiakhana.com
Located in a historic powerhouse on the shore, this restaurant boasts outstanding views of Near Island, and the channel fishing boats pass through as they leave the harbor. Often you can spot marine wildlife, sometimes even orcas, from the deck or through the big picture windows. The menu has lots of seafood, often with a Japanese twist; they specialize in sushi.

🪑 170 🅿 🚭 🕐 Closed in winter 💳 D, MC, V

## UNALASKA

#### 🍴 CHART ROOM
$$–$$$$
GRAND ALEUTIAN HOTEL
498 SALMON WAY
TEL 907-581-7120
grandaleutian.com
If you're looking for fine dining in Unalaska, the Chart Room is it. Like the executive-style hotel that houses it, the Chart Room seems out of place way out here in the back of beyond,

but that's part of what draws people, especially Aleutian residents who crave a dining experience that involves white tablecloths. Much of the menu reflects a restaurant that overlooks some of the world's best fishing grounds: salmon, king crab, halibut, and other seafood. The chefs also cook up several other hearty, meat-centered standards. Locals and travelers alike flock to the Wednesday night seafood buffet and the Sunday brunch. Plus, the Grand Aleutian Hotel has a sushi restaurant, a bar and grill, and two cafés.

🅿 🚭 🕐 Open daily
💳 All major cards

#### 🍴 NORWEGIAN RAT SALOON
$–$$
1906 AIRPORT BEACH RD.
TEL 907-581-4143
A local (and loud) favorite of fishers, Norwegian Rat Saloon serves standard breakfast fare, plus burgers, sandwiches, and pizza. It draws a crowd for its Sunday afternoon crab boil. Plus, it has a pool table and great harbor views.

🪑 40 🅿 🚭 💳 MC, V

# SHOPPING

Seattle, Vancouver, and, to a lesser extent, Anchorage exhibit the full range of shopping choices you'd expect in major cities. This section lists just a few of the standouts, the local, independent businesses that sell distinctive products. In other, much smaller Alaska ports, the focus is on art, crafts, foods, and locally made goods that reflect the land and culture of the state.

## ■ SEATTLE & VANCOUVER

### Seattle

#### Arts, Crafts, & Gifts

**Foster/White Gallery,** 220 3rd Ave. S., tel 206-622-2833, fosterwhite.com. This high-end gallery shows many well-known Northwest artists in its vast space. It's also a dealer for world-famous glass artist Dale Chihuly and other stalwarts of contemporary glass art from the Pilchuck School.

**G. Gibson Gallery,** tel 206-587-4033, ggibsonprojects.com, by appointment only. This leading dealer is renowned for its fine photography, presenting works by celebrated photographers of the past as well as the images of contemporary photographers.

**Greg Kucera Gallery,** 212 3rd Ave. S., tel 206-624-0770, gregkucera.com. One of Seattle's foremost galleries, this nationally recognized dealer displays editioned work by major figures as well as pieces by rising regional and national artists. Known for its willingness to tackle controversial subjects, sometimes its shows explore politics, religion, or other sensitive themes. Don't miss the outdoor sculpture deck.

**Stonington Gallery,** 125 S. Jackson St., tel 206-405-4040, stoningtongallery.com. This stylish, three-level space displays sophisticated Northwest Coast and Alaska native arts and crafts. Though most of the pieces have a contemporary sensibility, you can usually see the traditional roots.

### Clothing

**Diva Dollz,** 624 1st Ave., tel 206-652-2299, divadollz.com. If vintage-inspired clothing, lingerie, shoes, and accessories are your bag, you'll find many different lines plus exclusive designs.

**Freeman,** 713 Broadway E., tel 206-3279932, freemanseattle. com. You'd expect a city that knows rain to make great rainwear, and Freeman's made-in-Seattle, top-quality, flannel-lined rain jackets and cozy basics—from socks to sweatshirts—are just the ticket for when the weather turns south. Closed Sun.–Tues.

**Thowbacks Northwest,** 1507 11th Ave., tel 206-402-4855, thowbacksnw.com. A family-owned business that sells authentic replicas of pro sports clothing, particularly baseball apparel from obscure teams.

**Utilikilts,** 1802 15th Ave. W., tel 206-282-4226, utilikilts.com. Even if you don't have a drop of Scottish blood in your veins, you may still need a utility kilt, like the Workman model, with its capacious cargo pockets.

### Food

**DeLaurenti Specialty Food & Wine,** 1435 1st Ave. (Pike Place Market), tel 206-622-0141, delaurenti.com. An anchor of Pike Place Market for years, DeLaurenti's carries a wide array of artisanal foods, many with an Italian accent. You'll find large selections of prosciutto, olive oils, pastas, capers, and cheese.

**Fran's Chocolates,** 1325 1st Ave., tel 206-682-0168, franschocolates.com. A beloved Seattle shop tucked into the posh Four Seasons Hotel, Fran's offers chocolate-dipped delights.

**Salumi Artisan Cured Meats,** 404 Occidental Ave. S., tel 206-621-8772, salumicuredmeats. com. Well worth a visit is the shop of this master salumist, who meticulously produces some of the finest cured meats this side of Italy, including smoked paprika *salame* and *culatello*.

## Vancouver

### Arts, Crafts, & Gifts

**Circle Craft Co-operative,** 1666 Johnston St., Net Loft (Granville Island), tel 604-669-8021, circlecraft.net. This venerable co-op sells objects made by more than 180 British Columbia craftspeople, fashioned from clay, glass, fiber, wood, and metal.

**Craft Council of BC,** 1386 Cartwright St., tel 604-687-7270, craftcouncilbc.ca. The Craft Council's flagship shop and gallery sells an eclectic range of outstanding arts and crafts—much of it of museum quality—by more than 1,000 native artists, representing every tribe and nation and spanning jewelry to home décor. Closed Mon.

**Silk Weaving Studio,** 1531 Johnston St. (Granville Island), tel 604-687-7455, silkweavingstudio .com. Tucked away on a pretty walkway, this studio offers hand-dyed silk scarves, shawls, and clothing made by a number of resident weavers, often working at the on-site looms.

### Clothing

**The Block,** 350 W. Cordova St., tel

604-685-8885, theblock.ca. Stylish women's and men's clothing, shoes, and accessories from a diverse selection of local, Canadian, and international indie lines. The labels include well-known and up-and-coming designers.

**Dutil,** 303 W. Cordova St., tel 604-688-8892, dutildenim.com. Need some Naked & Famous Weird Guy Indigo Raw Selvedge jeans? Head for Dutil, which carries an extensive variety of men's and women's denim clothing from scores of designers.

**John Fluevog,** 65 Water St., tel 604-688-6228, fluevog.com. For decades Vancouver native John Fluevog has been considered one of the world's most innovative shoe designers. This ultrastylish Gastown store is his headquarters and design studio, where you'll find ever surprising men's and women's shoes and accessories.

## Food

**Artisan Sakemaker,** 1339 Railspur Alley (Granville Island), tel 604-685-7253, artisansakemaker.com. Step into sake master Masa Shiroki's tasting room for sake made from rice grown sustainably in British Columbia—some of the northernmost rice fields in the world. Typical of his creations is his Fraser Valley Junmai Nogori, described as having the fruity aromas of such tropical fruits as lychee, pineapple, and papaya.

**Fresh Street Market,** 1423 Continental St., tel 604-265-1311, freshstmarket.com. Vancouver's smaller equivalent of Seattle's Pike Place Market is no less eclectic, from its bakery, cheese shop, coffee roasters, and deli to bulk foods ready to scoop into a bag.

## ■ SOUTHEAST ALASKA

## Arts, Crafts, & Gifts

**Alaska Indian Arts,** Historic Fort William H. Seward, Haines, tel 907-766-2160, alaskaindianarts .com. This nonprofit carries carved totems, prints, and other traditional Northwest Coast native items. Sometimes visitors can watch artists at work.

**Annie Kaill's,** 124 Seward, Juneau, tel 907-586-2880, anniekaills.com. Fine arts and crafts by Alaska artists. The diverse offerings include art glass, paintings, stoneware, jewelry, pottery, prints, and even artful wooden benches.

**Corrington's Alaskan Ivory,** 535 Broadway, Skagway, tel 907-983-3939, alaskabestshopping. com. This gift shop sells some fine scrimshaw; amazing what Alaska native artists can do with a walrus tusk. A small but excellent museum of ivory-carving is embedded in the store.

**Juneau Artists Gallery,** Senate Mall Building, 175 S. Franklin St., Juneau, tel 907-586-9891, juneau artistsgallery.org. Two dozen local artists operate, staff, and sell their works in this cooperative gallery. Items span a wide range of media, including watercolors, fused art glass, ceramics, photography, and bead art.

**Main Street Gallery,** 330 Main St., Ketchikan, tel 907-225-2211, ketchikanarts.org. Devoted to the development of local talent and run by the Ketchikan Area Arts and Humanities Council, this gallery shows local and national artists in their bright and open space.

**Russian American Co.,** 134 Lincoln St., Sitka, tel 907-747-6228 or 800-742-6228, russianamerican company.com. If you've always wanted nested Russian dolls, this is the place to buy them, along with that samovar or Bogorodsk wooden toy you've always wanted.

**Sea Wolf/Whale Rider Galleries,** Historic Fort William H. Seward, Haines, tel 907-766-2540, tresham.com. The gallery and studio of local artist Tresham Gregg, whose diverse works explore animism and shamanism. His range of media includes carved totems, bronzes, wall sculptures, jewelry, and even puppets.

**Sitka Rose Gallery,** 419 Lincoln St., Sitka, tel 907-747-3030, sitkarosegallery.com. Inside the lovely 19th-century Victorian that houses Sitka Rose you'll find the works of more than 100 Alaska artists, including many Alaska natives. Items include carved whalebone figures, cedarbark baskets, watercolors, alder masks, and lots of carved walrus ivory.

**The Soho Coho,** 5 Creek St., Ketchikan, tel 907-225-5954, trollart.com. Along with other local artists, this gallery features the idiosyncratic works of internationally renowned artist and oddball Ray Troll, known for creating fantastical and funny art combining his love of fish and science. Items range from fine drawings to goofy T-shirts.

**Wild Iris Gallery,** (Shields Art Co.), 22 Tower Rd., Haines, tel 907-766-2300. A pretty gallery framed by charming gardens, the Wild Iris specializes in jewelry, such as unusual pieces made from amber and gold from Alaska gold rush days.

**Wm. Spear Design,** 230 Seward, Juneau, Suite 201, tel 907-586-2209, wmspear.com. This specialty store sells a daunting variety of elaborate enamel pins depicting traditional Alaskan subjects, like bears and puffins, as well as surprising designs, like a martini glass and an *Allosaurus* skull.

## Books & Maps

**Old Harbor Books,** 201 Lincoln St., Sitka, tel 907-747-8808, oldharborbooks.net. A welcoming independent bookstore staffed by knowledgeable book lovers.

**Parnassus Books,** 105 Stedman St., Ketchikan, tel 907-225-7690. Located in the historic Creek Street district, this beloved local, independent store offers plenty of reading, including a wide range of works about Alaska.

**Sing Lee Alley Books,** 11 Sing Lee Alley, Petersburg, tel 907-772-4440. You'll find plenty more than books, including field guides, at this charming store selling Alaskan native art and crafts, such as beautiful belts, bags, and purses.

### Food

**Forget-Me-Not Chocolates,** 221 Main St., Ketchikan, tel 907-617-5800, forgetmenotchocolates.com. Artisanal Belgian chocolates handmade in Ketchikan. It sells a huge range of yummy treats, from chocolate-covered Nutter Butter cookies to polar bear mint barks.

**Taku Smokeries,** 550 S. Franklin St., Juneau, tel 907-463-3474 or 800-582-5122, takustore.com. Taku smokes salmon. Yes, they throw in some halibut and spot prawns, plus products like salmon caviar and salmon jerky, but mainly they procure top-quality Alaska salmon and turn it into savory hot- or cold-smoked treats.

## ■ SOUTH-CENTRAL COAST

### Arts, Crafts, & Gifts

**Bunnell Street Arts Center,** W. Bunnell St., Ste. A, Homer, tel 907-235-2662, bunnellarts.org. You'll find this nonprofit arts center in Homer's oldest commercial building, the **Inlet Trading Post,** yet the center specializes in cutting-edge contemporary art with an ever changing monthly exhibit and a back room where you can browse the works of scores of Alaska artists.

**Resurrect Art Coffee House Gallery,** 320 3rd Ave., Seward, tel 907-224-7161, resurrectart.com. Set in a former church, this favorite local hangout serves up a healthy helping of local art, ranging from simple crafts to pricey paintings.

## Clothing

**Nomar,** 104 E. Pioneer Ave., Homer, tel 907-235-8363 or 800-478-8364, nomaralaska.com. Alaska-tough apparel abounds in this no-nonsense store filled with rugged outdoor clothing. And if you need a set net brailer for your commercial fishing operation, you can get that here, too.

## ■ ANCHORAGE & BEYOND

### Arts, Crafts, & Gifts

**Alaska Native Heritage Center,** 8800 Heritage Center Dr., Anchorage, tel 907-330-8000 or 800-330-8085, alaskanative.net. The state's premier institution devoted to the art and culture of Alaska natives, its gift shop offers all sorts of authentic items.

**Alaska Native Medical Center,** 4315 Diplomacy Dr., Anchorage, tel 907-729-1122, anmc.org. Unknown to most travelers, this medical center's gift shop is one of the best places in the state to buy first-rate and reasonably priced Alaska native arts and crafts.

**Alutiiq Museum & Archaeological Repository,** 215 Mission Rd., Kodiak, tel 844-425-8844, alutiiqmuseum.org. In keeping with the museum's mission to preserve Alutiiq culture, the gift shop sells consignment items—dolls, baskets, ivory carvings, masks—made by native artists and craftspeople.

**Anchorage Museum,** 625 C St., Anchorage, tel 907-929-9262, anchoragemuseum.org. This superb museum has a gift shop to match. You can buy Eskimo yo-yos, scenic posters, and other souvenirs, or fine art such as intricate baleen baskets and carved whalebone sculptures.

**Kodiak History Museum,** 101 E. Marine Way, Kodiak, tel 907-486-5920, kodiakhistorymuseum.org. Hewing to the museum's theme, the gift shop carries classic Russian pieces, including icons, samovars,

painted Easter eggs, nesting dolls, and lacquerware. This is one of Alaska's best galleries, featuring more than a hundred Alaska artists.

### Clothing

**Octopus Ink Gallery,** 410 G. St., Anchorage, tel 907-333-4657, octopusinkclothing.com. Arty, hand-painted women's, men's, and kid's clothing, much with an octopus or other sea creature–inspired motif. Sustainable creations from an owner/designer with a passion for marine life.

**Oomingmak,** 604 H St., Anchorage, tel 907-272-9225 or 888-360-9665, qiviut.com. Some 250 Alaska native women belong to this intriguing co-operative. They hand-knit ultrawarm qiviut (musk ox hair) into marvelous hats, scarves, and tunics.

**Laura Wright Alaskan Parkys,** 411 W. 4th Ave., tel 907-274-4215. Want to look like a true-blue Inuit (Eskimo)? Then check out the custom designs inspired by Alaskan heritage at this store selling singular pieces, from colorful lightweight summer *kuspuks* to thick velvet winter parkys (parkas) with wolf-fur-trimmed hoods.

### Food

**Alaska Max Gourmet,** 737 W. 5th Ave., Anchorage, tel 907-274-0238. In the Glacier Brewhouse Building, Alaska Max Gourmet sells fireweed honey, birch syrup, reindeer sausage, and other Alaskan food and drink.

**Alaska Wild Berry Products,** 5225 Juneau St., tel 907-562-8858, akwildberry.com. Alaska animal candies and chocolates. Klondike toffee crunch. Smoked salmon fillets. Mustards, sauces, and syrups. Heck, why not simply opt for the Homesteader's Basket with two dozen different delicious Alaskan food items.

# ACTIVITIES

Given Alaska's rich cultural legacy and millions of acres of great outdoors, it's not surprising there are hundreds of tour guides to show you around. This section is but a tiny sampler of the opportunities available, and is not meant to recommend any listed activities and companies above others. With cruise ship timetables in mind, it sticks to tours ranging from less than an hour to a day in length.

## ■ SOUTHEAST ALASKA: SOUTHERN PANHANDLE

### Boat Tours

**Alaska Kayak Company,** 2417 Tongass Ave., tel 907-204-0402, alaskakayakcompany.com. Possessing both boat and kayaks, this adventure tour company run by two dedicated nature lovers specializes in getting you close to the shore on coastal kayak adventures by boat. Its 3-hour tour includes a stop by Creek Street to visit the totem park and watch salmon jumping in the Tongass Narrows. However, the main focus is on spotting eagles, whales, and other marine mammals, plus wildlife ashore, as you transfer to stable and easy-to-handle expedition-style tandem kayaks for a coastal paddling foray. A 5-hour tour also includes hiking in the Tongass National Forest, with a focus on old growth rain forest ecology. Plus, you'll get to enjoy a smoked salmon picnic on the beach.

**Alaska Passages,** Petersburg, tel 907-772-3967, alaskapassages.com. It's a 23-mile (37 km) journey from Petersburg to LeConte Glacier, but it's worth it to see this muscular tidewater glacier calving hunks of ice into the sea. Besides, this 4- to 5-hour trip crosses beautiful Frederick Sound, slips up LeConte Bay, and slaloms through a host of glowing blue icebergs on its way to the glacier. A longer day trip also lands at the boat captain's cabin on an island in LeConte Bay, where passengers can walk up to icebergs stranded on the tidal flats.

**Breakaway Adventures,** City Dock, Wrangell, tel 907-874-2488 or 888-385-2488, breakawayadventures.com. For more than 20 years, Breakaway has been taking small groups up the mighty Stikine River, showing them moose, migrating salmon, and bears, and stopping at a hot spring along the way. Both the 3.5- to 4-hour trip and the 6- to 7-hour trip reach Chief Shakes Glacier, where you get to motor slowly amid the icebergs while admiring waterfalls and looking for mountain goats; an 8-hour trip offers a similar experience to LeConte Glacier.

**Sitka Wild Adventures,** 215 Shotgun Alley, Sitka, tel 907-747-6481, sitkawildlifeadventures.com. Carrying a maximum of six passengers, the *Esther G II*'s marine wildlife tours represent the kind of personal, customized tours smart travelers can sometimes find in Alaska. On these 3- or 4-hour trips around picturesque Sitka Sound, passengers are likely to spot some combination of sea otters, puffins, harbor seals, porpoises, auklets, Steller sea lions, and several species of whales, including humpbacks, orcas, and grays. The 4-hour tour usually goes out the mouth of the sound to the rugged volcanic towers of Saint Lazaria Island National Wildlife Refuge, populated by birds of prey, intertidal critters, and hundreds of thousands of seabirds. In addition to enjoying the scenery and wildlife, the lucky few aboard the *Esther G II* have ample opportunity to talk with

and learn from Captain Davey Lubin, a biologist, botanist, educator, and former commercial fisher.

### Cultural Tours

**Saxman Village Native Tours,** Ketchikan, tel 907-225-8001 or 907-225-4421, capefoxtours.com. This tour, operated by Cape Fox Lodge, provides a glimpse of Tlingit life past and present. Tour groups arrive at Saxman Village, just outside Ketchikan, and watch a short introductory video before entering the handsome Beaver Clan House to enjoy a traditional song and dance presentation by the Cape Fox dance group. From there a guide takes you outside to Saxman Totem Park to see one of the world's largest collections of standing totem poles and to learn the stories behind the carvings. Next you get to converse with a carver working on a totem pole at the Village Carving Center. These tours are arranged through cruise ships; independent travelers should contact Cape Fox Lodge to find out how to join in.

### Flightseeing

**Southeast Aviation,** 1249 Tongass Ave., Ketchikan, tel 907-225-2900 or 888-359-6478, southeastaviation.com. These veteran aviators specialize in aerial tours of nearby Misty Fjords National Monument. Carrying up to six passengers, each with a window seat in trusty floatplanes, the tours provide an eagle's-eye view of the monument's fjords, glaciers, waterfalls, and mountains. Often you'll spot bears, mountain goats, humpback whales, and other wildlife. The basic tour lasts

90 minutes and includes a landing on a fjord deep in the wilds.

## Wildlife-Viewing Tours

**Whale Song,** Petersburg, tel 907-772-9393, whalesongcruises .com. During summer, hundreds of humpback whales migrate to Alaska, including a large contingent that feasts in Frederick Sound, near Petersburg. Whale Song takes up to 14 passengers on half-day and full-day trips to watch these leviathans. As you cruise the picturesque sound, you may also spot orcas, sea lions, bears, seabirds, porpoises, and seals.

## ■ SOUTHEAST ALASKA: NORTHERN PANHANDLE

### Boat Tours

**Glacier Bay Lodge & Tours,** Bartlett Cove (Glacier Bay), tel 888-229-8687, visitglacierbay.com. This venerable lodge offers a full-day cruise of Glacier Bay by high-speed catamaran, taking you close to the glaciers. The 8-hour tour is narrated by a National Park Service ranger, who provides insight into local geology and ecology as the ecosystem changes from fully developed rain forest surrounding the lodge to lichen-encrusted moraines at the glaciers' edge. Arriving at the 245-foot-tall (75 m) Margerie and Grand Pacific Glaciers, you can watch 200-year-old ice breaking off.

### Hiking Tours

**Above & Beyond Alaska,** Auke Bay (Juneau), tel 907-364-2333, beyondak.com. Try their strenuous but rewarding full-day hike to and on Mendenhall Glacier, led by a naturalist guide. After a brief van ride, instruction, and setup with glacier-trekking gear, the hike starts in the forest and rises into the high country, yielding tremendous views of rock and ice. At the glacier you get about an hour to explore ice caves (if conditions are safe), check

out meltwater streams, and even try a little ice climbing.

**Chilkat Guides,** Haines (this trip is near Skagway), tel 907-313-4420, chilkatguides.com. Starting just outside Skagway, Chilkat's Chilkoot Trail Hike and Float begins with a moderate hike with a naturalist guide up the first 2 miles (3.2 km) of the historic Chilkoot Trail, the path to the goldfields that felt the boots of thousands of stampeders during the Klondike gold rush. You then board rafts and float down the gentle Taiya River to the ghost town of Dyea, a boomtown in the late 1890s.

### Historical Tours

**Klondike Gold Rush National Historical Park,** Visitor Center Skagway, 2nd Ave. & Broadway, tel 907-983-9200, nps.gov/klgo. A well-preserved gold rush boomtown, Skagway is one of the most historic sites in Alaska, and Klondike Gold Rush National Historical Park sits right in the middle of its downtown. Five to seven times a day, park rangers lead one-hour tours of the park and downtown, visiting some of the original buildings and telling participants about the wild gold rush era. Tours are free, but you must get tickets at the visitor center—no reservations.

### Wildlife-Viewing Tours

**Allen Marine Tours,** Juneau, tel 907-789-0081, allenmarinetours .com. The Whale Watching & Wildlife Quest tour lives up to its name. Cruising the protected waters of scenic Stephens Passage aboard catamarans custom-made for wildlife-viewing, passengers on this 4-hour tour likely will spot Steller sea lions, harbor seals, Dall's porpoises, and seabirds, and are guaranteed to see whales, mostly humpbacks and sometimes orcas. If you don't see whales, you'll get a $100 refund, but in the last 10 years, no refunds have been given. This company also offers its Eve-

ning Whale Quest, which comes with appetizers and desserts.

## ■ SOUTH-CENTRAL COAST

### Boat Tours

**Center for Alaskan Coastal Studies,** 708 Smoky Bay Way, Homer, tel 907-235-6667, akcoastalstudies.org. This nonprofit offers 5-, 8-, and 10-hour tours of Kachemak Bay; the 10-hour tour includes a couple hours of sea kayaking on the bay. Passengers on these small-group tours visit the seabird rookery at Gull Island; the center's field station across the bay from Homer; the forest behind the field station, a transition zone between temperate rain forest and boreal forest; and China Poot Bay, a rich tide pooling site.

**Kenai Fjords Tours,** Seward, tel 888-478-3346, kenaifjords. com. First you get to sail through scenic Resurrection Bay, bounded by mountains and flecked with islands. You'll probably spot some sea otters, harbor seals, humpback whales, and maybe an orca prowling for salmon, or a black bear rambling along the nearby shore. But soon the main event begins, as you cruise alongside the rugged coast of Kenai Fjords National Park and then curl northwest into one of its deep fjords to visit the glaciers and watch them calving. On 4-, 5-, 6-, 7-, and 8.5-hour voyages aboard vessels that carry as many as 150 passengers, you can venture deep into this primordial park.

**Phillips Cruises,** Cliffside Marine, W. Camp Rd., Whittier, tel 907-276-8023, phillipscruises.com. If you're in Whittier and really want to see glaciers, take the 26 Glacier Cruise aboard the *Klondike Express.* Covering 160 miles (257 Km) in 5.5 hours, it traverses the Esther Passage and College Fjord of northwest Prince William Sound, permitting you to see all 26 glaciers during the passage.

Keep your binoculars and camera ready to spot humpback whales, orcas, Stellar's sea lions, and sea otters, plus bears and mountain goats ashore.

**Stan Stephens Glacier & Wildlife Cruises,** 112 N. Harbor Dr., Valdez, tel 866-867-1297, stephenscruises.com. A family-run business since 1971, Stephens is notable for its signature 6-hour trip to Columbia Glacier. Aboard a specially designed boat that holds up to 149 passengers, you weigh anchor in Valdez and head out the long, narrow bay lined with mountainsides streaked by waterfalls. These waters are alive with sea otters, humpback whales, puffins, porpoises, and other wildlife. After about 20 miles (32 km), the boat hooks north into Columbia Bay, where you'll encounter flotillas of sparkling blue icebergs that were shed by the Columbia Glacier, one of the largest and most active in Alaska. Sometimes the icebergs are so thick that you have to stop and watch the glacier from several miles away, but usually you can approach within a mile (1.6 km) or even a half mile (0.8 km).

## Flightseeing

**Rust's Flying Service,** 4525 Enstrom Circle, Lake Hood Seaplane Base, Anchorage, tel 907-243-1595 or 800-544-2299, flyrusts.com. Taking off from the world's largest and busiest seaplane base, the planes of this decades-old company offer an aerial view of south-central Alaska. Try the 3-hour Discover Denali National Park tour. Watch for beluga whales as the floatplane flies north from Lake Hood across Cook Inlet. Soon it reaches the snowy spine of the mighty Alaska Range and soars among the mountains until it comes to the granddaddy of them all, Mount Denali. Watch for moose, bears, wolves, and other wildlife as you look down on alpine tundra, sheer rock walls, and burly

glaciers, including 40-mile-long (64 km) Ruth Glacier as it flows through the Great Gorge. You may even land on a remote lake or perhaps in the quirky town of Talkeetna. These hardy floatplanes feature big windows and two-way headsets that allow you to converse with your bush pilot and other passengers.

## Tours & Excursions

**Denali National Park bus tours,** Aramark, tel 866-761-6629, reservedenali.com. The only way to travel in a motor vehicle into Denali National Park's backcountry is aboard an officially sanctioned bus operated by Aramark. In addition to shuttles, they run tour buses that have driver-interpreters providing narration, plus lunch and water. The gold-standard tour is the Kantishna Experience, which takes 11–12 hours and goes all the way to the end of Park Road and back. (Aramark offers shorter tours of the road, too.) This mostly unpaved 92-mile (148 km) spur cuts through the wild heart of the park and provides excellent opportunities to spot grizzlies, moose, golden eagles, wolves, caribou, and the rest of the Denali menagerie. You'll also see broad braided rivers, husky glaciers, tundra wildflowers, and, if the clouds permit, the Great One— Mount Denali, the highest point on the continent. At Wonder Lake, near the far end of the road, you'll get a tour from a park ranger.

## ◼ ANCHORAGE & BEYOND

## Tours & Excursions

**Downtown Bicycle Rental,** 333 W. 4th Ave., Anchorage, tel 907-279-5293, alaska-bike-rentals.com. Anchorage is not a great city for bike riding, with the exception of its greenbelt trails, the finest of which is the Tony Knowles Coastal Trail. Starting just 5 blocks from Down-

town Bicycle Rental, this 11-mile (18 km, one-way) paved path meanders along the waters of Knik Arm and Cook Inlet, ending at Kincaid Park on the western edge of the city. You're likely to see moose and occasionally beluga whales offshore and bears in the woods. Choose from road bikes and mountain bikes to E-bikes and fat bikes.

## Wildlife-Viewing

**Aleutian Birding & Natural History,** Unalaska, tel 907-581-1359 or 907-391-2345, sgolodoff@ gmail.com. Expert birder, naturalist, and writer Suzi Golodoff conducts personalized tours of Unalaska's coast and upland tundra with some cultural history thrown in. Birds often occupy center stage on her tours, such as puffins, kittiwakes, cormorants, and other seabird species; Golodoff will likely locate some other nesting birds, too, and understands that the hard-core birders come primarily to find rarities, species not seen elsewhere in North America—like the Eurasian Siskin that Golodoff spotted in 2014, a "mega-rarity" blown in from Asia that set off rare-bird alerts all over the continent.

**Island Air Service,** 1420 Airport Way, Kodiak, tel 907-487-4596 or 907-487-5000, flyadq.com. Kodiak bears are the stuff of legend. A subspecies of brown or grizzly bear unique to the Kodiak archipelago, they are the largest, reaching heights of 9 feet (2.7 m) and weights of 1,500 pounds (680 kg). The Kodiak National Wildlife Refuge was largely established to protect these great bears, and that is where Island Air Service flies its floatplanes on many of its 4- to 5-hour summer bear-watching trips. Passengers enjoy a scenic flight over the wilds of Kodiak Island and land in a remote lake. A short hike takes them to an overlook from which they can watch numerous Kodiak bears hunting for salmon.

# CRUISE LINES & LODGES

About 20 companies offer a wide variety of cruises to Alaska, so passengers stand a good chance of finding a trip that will take them where they want to go. In addition to the itinerary, look for the atmosphere you desire. Do you want a floating Las Vegas or a quiet ship more focused on educating you about Alaska's nature and culture? You also need to decide if you want small, medium, or large—small is fewer than 100 passengers, medium is 100 to 800, large is 800 and above, often more than 2,000. (See pp. 10–11 for more information about ship choices.). For those with more time, a stay at a lodge offers opportunities to more fully experience the landscapes of Alaska.

## Cruise Lines

### Alaskan Dream Cruises
With small ships operated by Alaskans of Tlingit heritage, this company's cruises have a casual, family-friendly feel. Because of their size, the ships not only visit the major ports but also smaller ports like Petersburg and Wrangell, and even very small ports like Thorne Bay and Kasaan. The itinerary sticks to southeast Alaska. *alaskandreamcruises.com*

### Carnival
Carnival's large, action-packed ships offer plenty of activities and roaring casinos. The atmosphere is casual, noisy, and aglow with neon, and their Alaska itineraries hit the major ports in the Inside Passage. *carnival.com*

### Celebrity Cruises
Celebrity has large ships that are not luxury liners but are known for near-luxury food, service, and art. Even so, the atmosphere on board is fairly casual. Most itineraries stay in southeast Alaska, but some reach Seward, on the Kenai Peninsula. *celebritycruises.com*

### Crystal Cruises
Crystal has large ships and is known for its luxury cruises with relatively formal dress codes, highly regarded food and service, and ample but not boisterous entertainment. Most of their Alaska itineraries are Inside Passage journeys from Vancouver to the Hubbard Glacier, or even as far as Anchorage. *crystalcruises.com*

### Discovery Voyages
With a small boat (12 passengers), these 3- to 12-day cruises of Prince William Sound are casual and family-friendly. They offer shore excursions to out-of-the-way places, exploring with a relaxed, flexible itinerary. *discoveryvoyages.com*

### Disney Cruise Line
Not surprisingly, Disney cruises take place on large ships with a very family-friendly vibe and offer wholesome entertainment by the bushel (no casinos here). The cuisine is mostly casual American, appealing to picky eaters and their parents, too. Their 7-day trips stick to the Inside Passage, stopping at all the major ports. *disneycruise.disney.go.com*

### Dolphin Charters
This company uses the 8-passenger *Delphinus* during its nature-focused cruises of the Inside Passage, with a focus on whales, bears, and glaciers. Most voyages are led by marine-biologist Ronn Patterson, and many trips have a photography focus. It also offers day cruises for up to 32 passengers. *dolphincharters.com*

### Holland America Line
Holland America cruises take place on large ships where the feel is relatively relaxed, with less partying and more of a family-friendly vibe. They are famed for their onboard art and antiques displays. Itineraries cover mainly southeast Alaska, with some extending on to Seward or Whittier with an excursion inland to Denali National Park. *hollandamerica.com*

### National Geographic–Lindblad Expeditions
Seven ships from the National Geographic–Lindblad fleet cruise southeast Alaska and the Inside Passage, and as far afield as the Aleutian Islands and the Arctic, on 8- to 22-day voyages, offering access to smaller ports and less traveled areas. With accommodations from 62 to 126 passengers and an onboard atmosphere that is informal and friendly, these ships are staffed by an expedition team that includes a marine expert, naturalists, a photography instructor, and often a National Geographic researcher or photographer.

The focus of each voyage is on expedition-style exploration, and each ship is equipped with motorized landing crafts and kayaks to allow guests to get to seldom-visited places on daily excursions ashore or into shoreline nooks and crannies.

Shipboard entertainment is also nature-focused: The crew use underwater cameras and hydrophones to relay the sights and sounds of the ocean to the ships' lounges, and naturalists and local field scientists give presentations in the evenings. There are special departures designated for families or photographers. Some of the Alaska voyages can also be linked up with National Geographic's inland expeditions to Denali and Kenai Fjords. *nationalgeographicexpeditions.com*

### Noble Caledonia

These small to medium ships (80–300 passengers) have a mostly British clientele and a very high-end feel, with onboard naturalists, historians, and ecologists instead. It's all about Alaska, not shipboard entertainment. Expect visits to the wilds and some of the obscure ports of southeast Alaska; in some years itineraries roam even farther north, all the way to the Aleutians. Typically only one or two departures are offered each year. *noble-caledonia.co.uk*

### Norwegian Cruise Line

With large ships and a very casual, family-friendly vibe, Norwegian cruises are famed for their high-octane onboard entertainment and plethora of activities. While most itineraries stick to the main ports of the Inside Passage, some reach Seward and Anchorage, with excursions to Denali National Park. *ncl.com*

### Oceania Cruises

This company's cruises take place on medium-size ships (about 700 passengers) and are known for their upscale tenor and luxury dining for reasonable prices. The atmosphere is adult-oriented, offering a relatively restrained ambience without any noisy partying. Oceania also boasts lots of lectures, art classes, and other presentations, and plenty of time in ports. The itineraries emphasize southeast Alaska including major ports as well as some minor ports that

large ships don't visit. *oceaniacruises.com*

### Ponant

These midsize (about 250 passengers) luxury ships offer spas, superb food, and ample onboard activities but not a party atmosphere. Their infrequent itineraries focus on cultural heritage and wild places, from the Inside Passage to the Aleutians to the Pribilof Islands, often with a special theme in association with National Geographic or similar learned institution. *en.ponant.com*

### Princess Cruises

With large ships that are very family-friendly, Princess balances lively entertainment with more demure pastimes, such as wine-tasting seminars. They offer itineraries covering the Inside Passage, plus longer trips through beautiful Prince William Sound to tiny Whittier and on to Anchorage and Denali National Park. *princess.com*

### Regent Cruises

Medium ships (about 500 to 700 passengers) with luxurious decor, service, and dining make these cruises primarily adult-oriented, but with some offerings for families. The atmosphere is somewhat formal, with strong enrichment programs featuring naturalists, historians, and other lecturers as well as sophisticated entertainment. Mostly 7-day cruises to southeast Alaska, although some go north to Seward. *regentcruises.com*

### Royal Caribbean International

Royal Caribbean offers very large ships that are family-friendly; the focus is on the hundreds of shipboard activities. Itineraries cover the Inside Passage and Seward, with extensions to Anchorage

and Denali National Park. *royalcaribbean.com*

### Silversea

Offering medium-size ships (120 to 382 passengers) and luxury accommodations, service, food, and decor, these cruises are adult-oriented and relatively formal, with refined entertainment. Most trips are one-way from Vancouver via the Inside Passage to Seward or the reverse. The 21-day "Vancouver to Osaka" voyage ranges the length of the Alaskan coastline, including the Aleutians. *silversea.com*

### Un-Cruise Adventures

These small ships include some luxurious yacht-style vessels, that are comfortable but less fancy. Trips are focused on the educational and adventure experience, including lectures. Un-Cruise offers 8-, 13-, and 15-day itineraries in southeast Alaska and spend much of their time in places large cruise ships don't usually go. *un-cruise.com*

## Lodges

### Tutka Bay Lodge

A secluded cove at the tip of Alaska's Kenai Peninsula harbors Tutka Bay Lodge, a wilderness retreat with a culinary twist. In addition to land- and water-based activities, Tutka offers guests the chance to participate in the food-gathering and preparation processes of chef Kirsten Dixon's award-winning sea-to-table cuisine. *withinthewild.com*

### Winterlake Lodge

Perched at the edge of a lake along the historic Iditarod Trail, the wood cabins of Winterlake Lodge offer a beautiful base for exploring Alaska's backcountry. Visit in the summer for fly-fishing, hiking, and rafting. Or stay during the colder months to witness the Northern Lights and try your hand at dogsledding. *withinthewild.com*

# INDEX

# ILLUSTRATIONS CREDITS

All photos by Michael Melford unless otherwise noted.

21, Ken Schulze/Shutterstock; 27, davidhoffmann photography/Shutterstock; 29, Grisha Bruev/Shutterstock.com; 30, Library of Congress Prints and Photographs Division, #3a38169; 38, Lebrecht Music and Arts Photo Library/Alamy; 40, Phil Augustavo/iStockphoto; 41, gregobagel/iStockphoto; 44, Svieta Imnadze/Shutterstock.com; 46, Joseph Sohm/Shutterstock.com; 50, Albert Pego/Shutterstock.com; 54, Volodymyr Kyrylyuk/Shutterstock.com; 57, Verena Matthew/Dreamstime.com; 60, fdastudillo/iStockphoto; 62, Maxvis/iStockphoto; 64, NPS/T. Rains; 81, Design Pics Inc/National Geographic Creative; 84, Todamo/Shutterstock; 91, Lawrence Weslowski Jr./Dreamstime; 98, roclwyr/iStockphoto; 102, Deborah Maxemow/iStockphoto; 104, George Bailey/Dreamstime.com; 105, Robson Abbott/Shutterstock; 112, John Elk/Getty Images; 117, MaxFX/Shutterstock; 121, NPS/Kaitlin Thoresen; 124, John Elk/Getty Images; 127, Larry Maurer/Shutterstock; 130-1, Artwork by Maltings Partnership, Derby, England; 132, OST/iStockphoto; 133, Wildnerdpix/iStockphoto; 136, Design Pics Inc/National Geographic Creative; 138 Chuck Choi/Anchorage Museum; 154, K.C. Goshert/Shutterstock; 160, Steve Byland/Shutterstock; 162, Dai Mar Tamarack/Shutterstock.

National Geographic

**TRAVELER**

# Coastal Alaska:
# Ports of Call & Beyond

SECOND EDITION

Since 1888, the National Geographic Society has funded more than 14,000 research, exploration, and preservation projects around the world. National Geographic Partners distributes a portion of the funds it receives from your purchase to National Geographic Society to support programs including the conservation of animals and their habitats.

National Geographic Partners, LLC
1145 17th Street NW
Washington, DC 20036-4688 USA

Get closer to National Geographic explorers and photographers, and connect with our global community. Join us today at nationalgeographic.org/joinus

For rights or permissions inquiries, please contact National Geographic Books Subsidiary Rights: bookrights@natgeo.com

Second edition edited by White Star s.r.l.
Licensee of National Geographic Partners, LLC.
Update by Christopher P. Baker

Map illustrations drawn by Chris Orr Associates, Southampton, England.
Cutaway illustrations drawn by Maltings Partnership, Derby, England.

The information in this book has been carefully checked and to the best of our knowledge is accurate. However, details are subject to change, and the publisher cannot be responsible for such changes, or for errors or omissions. Assessments of sites, hotels, and restaurants are based on the author's subjective opinions, which do not necessarily reflect the publisher's opinion.

ISBN: 978-88-544-1801-1

Printed in Poland

MIX
Paper from
responsible sources
FSC® C019238

# NATIONAL GEOGRAPHIC TRAVELER
## THE BEST GUIDES BY YOUR SIDE

### More than 80 destinations around the globe

 ARIZONA
 AUSTRALIA
 CALIFORNIA
 COASTAL ALASKA
 COSTA RICA

 CUBA
 HAWAII
 IRELAND
 ITALY
 JAPAN

LONDON
NEW YORK
PERU
PORTUGAL
 PUGLIA

 ROME
 SCOTLAND
 VIETNAM
 WASHINGTON, D.C.